Food Science and Technology

Other books by Magnus Pyke

Nothing Like Science (Murray)
Slaves Unaware? (Murray)
The Science Myth (Murray)
Food & Society (Murray)
Synthetic Food (Murray)
Technological Eating (Murray)
Catering Science and Technology (Murray)
Success in Nutrition (Murray)
Butter Side Up! (Murray)
There and Back (Murray)
Food for all the Family (Murray)
The Manual of Nutrition (HMSO)
Industrial Nutrition (Macdonald & Evans)
Nutrition (EUP)
The Boundaries of Science (Harrap)
Man and Food (Weidenfeld & Nicolson)
Our Future (Hamlyn)
Long Life: Expectations for Old Age (Dent)

FOOD SCIENCE & TECHNOLOGY

MAGNUS PYKE
OBE, BSc, PhD, FIBiol, C Chem, FRSC, FIFST, FRSE

FOURTH EDITION

Revised and Enlarged by Dr Lelio Parducci

With a Foreword by Professor John Hawthorn

JOHN MURRAY · LONDON

To Sir J. C. Drummond
for his inspiration

First published 1964
Second edition 1968
Third edition 1970
Fourth edition 1981
by John Murray (Publishers) Ltd
50 Albemarle Street, London WIX 4BD

Printed in Hong Kong by Dah Hua Printing Press Co., Ltd.

British Library Cataloguing in Publication Data

Pyke, Magnus
Food science and technology. – 4th ed.
1. Food 2. Nutrition 3. Food industry and trade
I. Title
641.1 TX 355
ISBN 0–7195–3850–5

Foreword to the Fourth Edition

In the seventeen years since it was first published Pyke's *Food Science and Technology* has earned the claim of being the most widely read first text in this subject in the English-speaking world.

Its merits are clear. It conveys essentials in plain words. It eschews unnecessary technical phraseology. Its illustrations both illuminate and decorate. Above all, it remains simple but avoids the hazards of oversimplification.

But during this time food science and technology have moved on. New knowledge and new techniques have been developed and the range of foodstuffs in the household shopping basket has increased. A new edition must include the more significant of these changes. For this purpose a co-author with first-hand knowledge of the contemporary situation within the food industry was essential, and, in Dr Lelio Parducci, Dr Pyke has made an astute choice. In consequence the new edition is as up-to-date as this year's apples.

JOHN HAWTHORN, BSc, PhD, ARCST, FRIC, FRSE
Professor of Food Science, University of Strathclyde

Preface to the Fourth Edition

A number of modifications and additions have been made to the text and illustrations since the First Edition was published in 1964. These revisions have been made to keep up with the developments which have occurred in science and technology. In order to keep abreast of the most modern advances, the collaboration of Dr Lelio Parducci, New Product & Process Development Manager of H. J. Heinz Co. Ltd, has been enlisted to ensure that no important current innovation has been omitted.

As I pointed out in previous editions, this book has always aimed to review the principles of science upon which the practice of food technology is based. It should be remembered that in such practice a large number of complex details have to be covered, many of which may be of great practical importance. In writing a book such as this, the main difficulty is to select from among these details those which illustrate general principles. Readers should never forget that foods are complex substances and their successful handling requires detailed knowledge as well as general understanding.

M. P.

Contents

Part 1: Scientific Principles Applied to Food

Part 2: Practical Technology

Plates

Figures in Text

Tables

Acknowledgements

The author gratefully acknowledges the help of Mr John Mackay in preparing the diagrams and the following for supplying photographs and allowing them to be reproduced: Plates 1-6, 72-3, Dr Peter Cardew (St Mary's Hospital, Paddington, Photographic Dept); 7-8, Ranks Hovis McDougall Ltd; 9, Vienna Bakery, Adam Fleck Ltd; 10, from *Bread* by Horder, Moran and Dodds (Constable & Co Ltd); 11, Wallace & Tiernan Ltd; 12, Haven Foods Ltd; 13-21, Fatstock Marketing Corp. Ltd; 22-5, Cavaghan & Gray Ltd; 26-8, 33, 78, 86-90, 95, Findus Ltd; 29-31, Ross Foods Ltd; 32, Kenneth I. Oldroyd; 34-7, Buxted Poultry Ltd; 38, 46, 57-8, United Dairies Ltd; 39, Bowater Liquid Packaging Ltd; 40, 51, 56, De Melkindustrie Veghel; 41-4, Milk Marketing Board; 45, British Egg Information Service; 47-50, Croda Colloids Ltd; 52-5, 64, J. Bibby Edible Oils Ltd; 59, *The Times*; 60, 62, 65, 103, Van den Berghs & Jurgens Ltd; 61, 80, Unilever Research Laboratories; 63, Unilever Ltd; 66-71, 91, Tate & Lyle Ltd; 74, Anne Bolt; 75-6, Fyffes Group Ltd; 77, Cranberry Inst. of America; 79, 94, 96-7, Bird's Eye Foods Ltd; 81, Batchelors Foods Ltd; 82-5, Golden Wonder Ltd; 92-3, Metal Box Ltd; 98-9, Rheon Automatic Machinery GmbH; 100-2, Protecon UK Ltd; 104, Gardner & Gulland Ltd; 105-7, Wenger International Inc.

Fig. 13 is after Hammond: *Growth and the Development of Mutton Qualities in the Sheep* (Oliver & Boyd Ltd, 1932). The table in Appendix 1 is reproduced by permission of the Controller of Her Majesty's Stationery Office.

PART 1

SCIENTIFIC PRINCIPLES APPLIED TO FOOD

1

Modern conceptions of chemistry, physics, biology

It is very important for all those who deal with food to understand the scientific basis of modern methods of food processing. Underlying every technique of food handling, whether it is a traditional operation such as bacon-curing or cheese-making or an entirely new technique such as the manufacture of dried egg or the preparation of quick-frozen peas, there are certain scientific principles. The purpose of this book is to describe in simple terms what these principles are and how they may be applied in the various methods of food manufacture and preservation that are now used. Many people—administrators, businessmen, manufacturers, social workers in various fields, economists, or food producers, or simply responsible citizens and students who wish to understand the reasons underlying what may appear to be incomprehensible or inexplicable procedures that they see foodstuffs undergoing—may possess no formal qualifications in science. For this reason, the first chapter of this book contains a brief summary of the main tenets of chemistry and a description of how they apply to food processing. This is followed by an outline of the present understanding of some of the ways in which chemical principles are linked to biology and consequently how the chemical components of foods—the carbohydrates, proteins and fats, the vitamins and minerals—operate as nutritional substances upon which the living body depends for health.

The rest of the book, as the title implies, deals successively with the main food commodities: cereals, meat and fish, eggs and milk, vegetables and fruit, and the principal processes of food technology applied to each. In a single short volume it is not possible to describe in detail how every operation is done and no attempt is made to provide working instructions for the man who wishes to open a factory for the manufacture of, let us say, potato crisps. The purpose of the work is to outline the way in which the knowledge of the chemical composition of different food commodities, or of the biological characteristics of certain types of micro-organisms has been applied to achieve a certain result.

Science may be applied to develop technological processes designed to produce sophisticated foods to titillate the palates of already well-fed consumers. Serious scientific research may sometimes be done to produce an article with some unnecessarily elaborate quality. Frozen 'television dinners' and other articles to be found in the luxurious supermarkets of the West may appear to represent an extravagant waste of scientific knowledge and technological skill. But on the other hand, the developments of food science and technology that enable foods to be preserved by canning, dehydration and freezing so that they can be produced and processed in those parts of the world best suited to their culture, transported safely half round the world and be made available to distant markets at any season of the year—these developments are clearly valuable and useful. Food technology also comprises those processes by which the edible parts of basic foodstuffs are separated, for example, as flour, and often presented in digestible form, for example, when flour is converted into bread.

A number of interrelated factors have led to a continuing increase in the world's population so that by the end of the century there will be more people on earth than ever before. This presents science with a serious challenge. On the one hand, its methods are applied to agriculture to increase and improve the supply of food. And on the other, science and technology can contribute towards solving the world's food problem by developing methods for preserving and processing foods and for improving the quality of such processed foods to keep pace with the rising standards which applied science can bring in other aspects of modern life.

1. Food and chemistry

Chemistry is the science that studies the composition of the earth and in its modern form it has been built up mainly from observation and experiment over the last 250 years. One can readily see that the world around us contains different materials—rocks differ in colour, structure and hardness, for instance—and many centuries ago it was recognized that substances with common names such as gold, silver, lead, tin, were special kinds of stuff, different from each other. It was found that they could not be broken up into simpler components although they could combine together and produce more complicated ones. These basic materials were named *elements* and as well as their common names they were given for chemical purposes symbolic letters to distinguish them—Oxygen (O), Carbon (C), Hydrogen (H) and so on. So far, ninety-two have been found to exist naturally.

No one could observe directly the structure of these elements, but from their behaviour a general theory was produced. An element is thought to consist of a vast number of minute—and for all practical purposes indivisible—particles or *atoms.* Although indivisible the atoms' behaviour could only be explained by the supposition that each one had an identical internal structure: a central *nucleus*, from which the element's particular characteristics are derived, and round it a system of rapidly revolving *electrons*. It is thought that by means of this outer electron belt individual atoms of different elements cohere to form the infinite range of substances, or *chemical compounds* which go to make up the earth and all that is in it or on it. To take an example, limestone was found not to be an elemental material but to be composed of calcium and a so-called carbonate 'radical', itself made up of the elements carbon and oxygen. In simplified chemical terminology, limestone can be written down as $CaCO_3$, that is to say, one atom of calcium (Ca), combined with one carbonate radical (CO_3), itself composed of one carbon atom (C) and three atoms of oxygen (O). Or again, salt is not an elemental substance but is, in fact, made up of a combination of sodium (Na) and chlorine (Cl).

The science of chemistry is divided into two parts: *inorganic chemistry*, which deals with inert materials, rocks and the metals derived from them, with sulphur and chlorine, with chemical reactions by which mineral acids and alkalis are formed and much else. In fact, all the ninety-two elements can play parts in the various interactions that make up inorganic chemistry. *Organic chemistry*, on the other hand, differs from inorganic chemistry in dealing solely with chemical compounds whose basic components are combinations of the element carbon. All living tissues, whether they are derived from animals or plants, are basically composed of an intricate variety of carbon compounds. Many other elements—nitrogen, oxygen, hydrogen, sulphur, a variety of mineral elements, calcium, iron, copper, magnesium, phosphorus—may be combined as parts of organic molecules, but, in general, organic chemistry can be defined as the chemistry of carbon compounds.

(*a*) INORGANIC CHEMISTRY

Elements follow basic rules of behaviour when they combine or when they separate from more complex compounds. For example, metallic copper and iron are made to separate from the other elements with which they are combined as ores in nature, or salt is used as a source of the element, sodium, for the manufacture of soda. These rules were eventually found to form a logical system, sometimes described as the Laws of Chemistry.

The Laws of Chemistry, that is, the principles by which the chemical elements combine and recombine with each other, apply no matter what the material is in which a particular element may occur. For example, if the element, phosphorus, occurs in a living muscle—or in meat—or in bone or, for that matter, in rock it always obeys the Laws of Chemistry and behaves chemically in the same way. It is, in fact, the same stuff. Chemistry is the science that covers the composition of all matter. It is sometimes argued that some particular substance, baking soda, perhaps, or vitamin C made by synthetic means, ought not to be put into foods because it is a 'chemical'. This argument is meaningless because it is now quite clearly understood that every substance, whether it is an inorganic material such as rock, sea salt or wood ash, or an organic substance such as mutton-fat, dried fish or cane sugar, has a specific chemical composition. In many instances, furthermore, this composition is well known. It follows also from this that the identical food component can sometimes be produced equally well by a plant in the field or by a chemist in the laboratory. While this is true, however, it is also important to remember that a natural foodstuff may be composed of a very large number of different components.

(*b*) ORGANIC CHEMISTRY

Although the different types of material to be found on earth are composed of ninety-two different elements, covering such substances as gold and iron, which occasionally occur alone as pure elements, as well as chemical combinations such as chalk or limestone, water (hydrogen-hydroxide) or Epsom salts (magnesium sulphate heptahydrate), the numerous different types of stuff that go to make up living creatures and the substances they use as food, while like inorganic compounds being governed by the same Laws of Chemistry, are peculiar in being, for the most part, primarily constructed from the one element, carbon.

The special chemical peculiarity of the element, carbon, is that the carbon atom possesses four points of attachment, each of which is capable of linking *with other carbon atoms* as well as with an atom of hydrogen or oxygen or some other element. This is a peculiar and special attribute not possessed by most other elements. For example, calcium and magnesium or sulphur and nitrogen do not link together in chains whereas carbon atoms can form straight chains, branched chains, cross-linked series of chains like knitting, or folded and crinkled filaments. Carbon can, furthermore, join as 4-, 5-, 6-, 7- or more membered circles, which in turn may be single rings or merged together like pieces of honeycomb of two, three, four or more rings sharing parts of their circumferences with each other.

It is important to appreciate that in organic chemistry it is not only necessary to know how many atoms of carbon, hydrogen, oxygen and nitrogen, and whatever other elements there may be, are present in a particular compound—say, starch or vitamin B_1 or coconut oil—but also what is the *molecular structure* of the compound. The conception of molecular structure is an essential part of modern chemical science. It is now well established that the separate atoms of which a compound is composed are arranged in a particular relationship to one another in space. It is, therefore, not enough to know that a molecule of the sugar, glucose, is composed of six carbon, six oxygen and twelve hydrogen atoms, and that its 'formula' is consequently $C_6H_{12}O_6$. In order to understand the reason why certain things occur when foodstuffs of which glucose forms a part are treated in a certain way, it is also necessary to be aware that the molecular structure of glucose has roughly the following form:

```
            CH2OH
              |
    H       /C——O\        H
    |     /  |     \      |
    C        H        \   C
    | \    OH    H      / |
   OH  \   |     |    /  OH
         C———C
         |     |
         H    OH
```

One of the main reasons why chemists and technologists are able to exercise such a remarkable degree of control over material as complex as foodstuffs is because of the comparatively new understanding of the nature and properties of the very large chemical molecules of which biological materials in particular are made up. Most of these very large molecules are *polymers*; that is to say, they are the same class of compounds as the artificial polymers that we commonly call 'plastics'. These not only include the structural materials such as Bakelite, Perspex and polyethylene, and the 'plastic' sheetings such as Cellophane and PVC but they must also be taken to cover the fibres of nylon and terylene and all the rest which revolutionized our ideas about textiles in a single generation.

(c) POLYMERS AS FOOD COMPONENTS

A polymer is a very large chemical molecule made up of a repeating series of one or more simpler molecular units. For example, the purely artificial polymer, polyethylene—often called by one of its trade names 'Polythene'—is a useful material out of which plastic bottles or bowls or, indeed, objects of all sorts can be made. Polyethylene, which is a tough, durable, resilient solid, is produced by linking together, under the appropriate conditions for making the chemical reaction take place, a long series of simple molecules of the gas *ethylene*. The ethylene molecule is, in fact, nothing more than C_2H_4, and has a molecular structure that can be represented like this:

$$\begin{array}{ccccc} H & & & & H \\ & \diagdown & & \diagup & \\ & & C{=}C & & \\ & \diagup & & \diagdown & \\ H & & & & H \end{array}$$

In just the same way, starch, which is the main component of cereal foods, wheat flour, barley, rice and maize, and also of roots such as potatoes and manioc, which are used in the diets of people almost all over the world, is a polymer too. The chemical unit of which starch is composed is the simple sugar, glucose.

It is worth while considering in some detail the chemical composition of starch because it throws general light on an important aspect of the basic chemistry of a number of foods. Sugars, of which glucose is one, are formed in the green leaves of plants under the action of sunlight. Certain plants retain the sugar as sugar in their tissues. Notable among these are sugar-cane and sugar-beet. Other plants, however, link the sugar units together chemically to form the polymer, starch, which is stored in special parts of the plant such as the grain in cereals or the tuber in potatoes. But plants also combine glucose units together in a different way so that, while using the same chemical component, they produce another polymer with very different properties. This different polymer is *cellulose*, which is one of the principal ingredients in the structural framework of plant cells and is a major constituent of wood. The significance of what might be thought to be comparatively slight differences in chemical configuration on the properties of the actual substance produced is shown up clearly in the diagram below. First, is the diagram of a portion of a molecule of starch, a food component; below is the structure of cellulose, which is valueless as human food unless it is broken down in a chemical factory by a quite rigorous industrial process. At best it serves as indigestible 'roughage'.

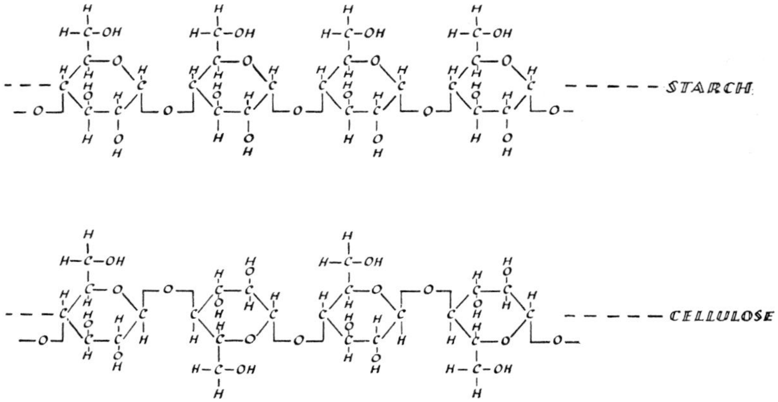

Fig. 1. The chemical configuration of starch can be broken down by digestive enzymes; the chemical configuration of cellulose, in which the glucose units are coupled in alternate planes, cannot be utilized.

The lesson to be gained from the above diagrams is that the way in which a chemical molecule is put together has almost as much significance as the chemical components that go into it. The starch molecule in which all the glucose units are arranged the same way up is an important food whereas the same accumulation of glucose units linked alternately upwards and downwards is unavailable to the human body. It will be seen later on that the diagram is a simplified one, since the polymer chain is not necessarily straight but may be wound and twisted and entangled with neighbouring chains in the substance as it occurs in nature.

2. The main components of foods

Food is composed of three main groups of constituents: carbohydrates, fats and proteins. In addition, there is a group of inorganic mineral components and a group of organic substances present in comparatively small proportions: these are the vitamins.

(a) CARBOHYDRATES

To this class of compounds the sugars belong. *Sugars* are soluble substances of which the best known is the common sweet substance 'sugar', a compound molecule technically known as *sucrose* and composed of *glucose* and *fructose*. *Maltose*, a compound molecule composed of two glucose units, is formed when grains germinate; and *lactose*, another compound molecule, occurs in milk. *Starches* are also carbohydrates. As has already been mentioned, they have very much larger compound molecules and are the form in which plants store food for themselves in their seeds and other storage organs. Although the starches from diverse grains and from potatoes and other plants are basically the same, the structure and conformation of the polymer chains of which they are composed differ in detail. These differences become apparent in practice when they are processed.

Starch is a major component of cereals and of roots and tubers. There is another form of starch that occurs in animals, *glycogen*. Like the starch in seeds, it functions as a fuel-storage material in the living animal. Liver contains comparatively large amounts of glycogen, as do horse-meat and oysters—two muscular tissues which in life are capable of prolonged exertion.

Sugars are soluble in water and readily form syrups; starches are not, as a general rule, soluble at all. There are, however, compounds midway in molecular size between the one- or two-glucose length of simple sugars and the very large, polymer structure of starches. These compounds are *dextrins*. They occur in nature—in malt, for example—but they are more commonly recognized when produced during food processing: the brown substances that arise when bread is turned into toast are dextrins. The gum on postage stamps is usually dextrin.

(*b*) PROTEINS

Carbohydrates are basically fuels—first, for the living plants in which they are formed and, later on, for animals and men. While the structure of starch grains is more complex than the comparatively simple chemical molecules of sugars, nevertheless it is less intricate by far than the elastic substance of animal muscle or even than the gluten fibres of wheat, the rubbery casein of cheese or the gelatinous substance of egg-white. These are all *proteins*.

Consider meat as an example. It is mainly muscular tissue, strong, contractile yet destructible if wrongly handled. Like the artificial 'plastics' that have now been invented to be like it, it is a polymer, but a very much more complex one than starch or cellulose.

(i) *Structure*

The polymer chains of starch are made up of links, each of which is the same. They are, as I have said above, each one a glucose unit. Proteins, however, which are more versatile structures, are polymer chains made up with a varied collection of more than twenty different substances, called *amino acids*, as links. These units, although they are all different, are similar in general design and all possess the peculiarity of containing one or more nitrogen atoms. The separate links of an amino-acid chain out of which the protein molecule is formed are connected by way of the nitrogen atom. Some of the amino acids also contain a sulphur atom and this allows protein chains to become attached to one another, side by side, in much the same way as the separate strands of a rope that are twisted together can also have cross fibres tangled across from one to another. The diagram on p. 12 shows in a simplified way how the molecular structure of protein from different food sources may vary.

This very brief and superficial description of the composition of proteins is sufficient to show that their chemical structure is exceedingly complex. This is one of the underlying reasons why protein foods, which may possess similar analytical composition in terms of carbon and nitrogen and sulphur, can at the same time differ in texture and in their characteristic qualities as foodstuffs. Furthermore, the complex and subtle chemical configuration of protein molecules can readily be changed, not only by chemical agents, but also by physical means.

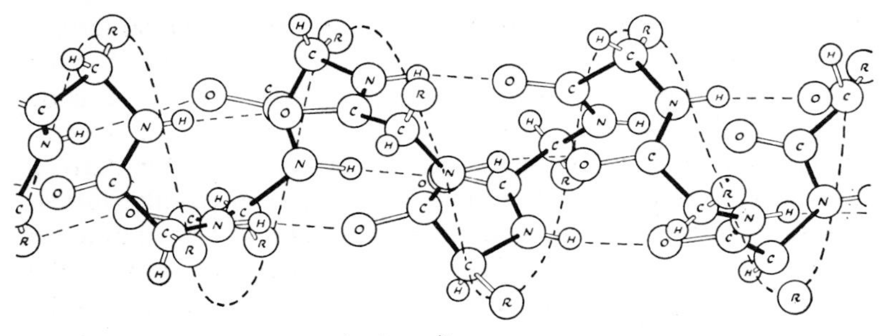

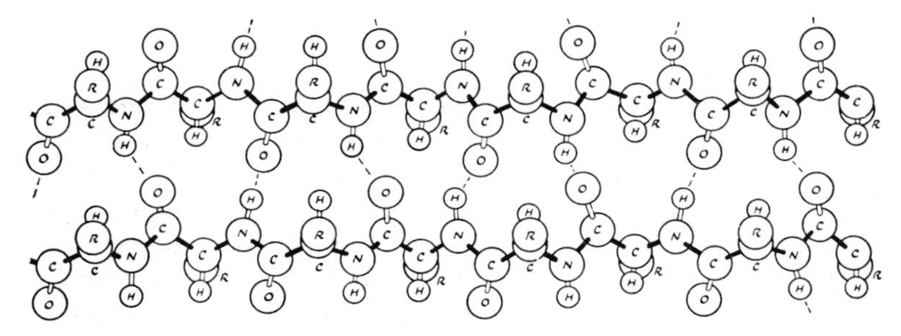

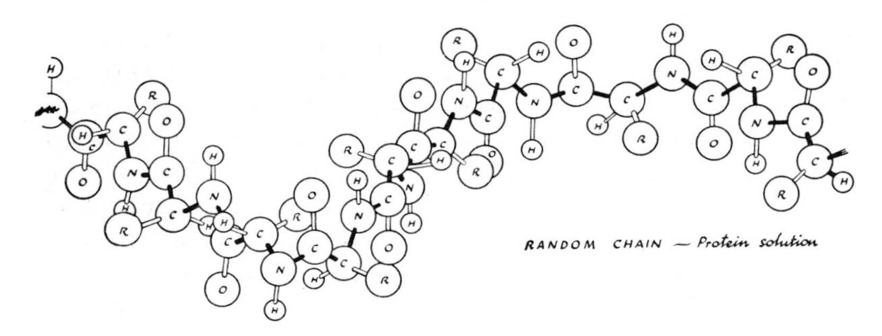

Fig. 2. Varying chemical configurations of different types of protein molecules.

(ii) *Effect of physical handling*

The polymer, nylon, is made artificially by purely chemical means in a chemical factory. But before it becomes a marketable fibre suitable for weaving into stockings or shirts the fibres of nylon have to be 'cold drawn'—that is to say they are stretched in a particular way. This *physical* operation causes a rearrangement to occur in the *chemical* configuration of the nylon molecules. In just the same way, the long complex molecules of protein in foodstuffs may be changed by physical treatment. A skilled cheese-maker makes a good cheese, whereas an incompetent one will produce a tough, unsatisfactory cheese simply by the way he handles the curd. Similarly, a good cook will make a good omelette and light pastry when a bad cook using the same ingredients will not. The food technologist must always remember that the *chemical* structure of protein, the most complex of the components of foodstuffs, can be affected by physical stresses which include mechanical work as well as heat and cold.

(iii) *Effect of heat*

The influence of heat on protein is easily recognized in practice. When an egg is boiled, the albumen, which is the protein of egg-white, is converted from a viscous fluid into the firm solid of hard-boiled egg. When bread is baked, the soft elastic protein of dough, the gluten, becomes stiffened and thus contributes to the firm, springy consistency of breadcrumb. In technical terms, heat can be said to change the chemical configuration of the protein molecule. This may disrupt the even coils of the helical twist in which the atoms are wound.

Although the food technologist is mainly concerned with the effect of heat and cold and the other physical processes he uses on the food quality of the substances he handles, there are certain more fundamental aspects of chemistry which are also of importance to him. For instance, it is interesting to understand the complex polymer structure of muscle protein and its significance in determining the quality of meat. It is well understood from everyday experience that heat changes the structure of wool and causes it to shrink; wool is a protein. Muscle protein does the same; a steak shrinks when it is cooked.

But proteins have a higher biological significance than to act as food. The constituents of protein, the amino acids, are important as nutrients when protein is eaten. The complex structure of protein in its unaltered form, however, is essential for biological life. The immense complexity of the protein molecules, shown in a simplified diagrammatic form opposite, not only affects the texture and character of the living tissues from which they are derived but is also an integral part of the process of life. Firstly, muscular tissue possesses the function of movement and, secondly, protein molecules function in the chemical mechanism by which life operates. It is for these reasons that it is useful for food technologists to appreciate something about protein structure. A comparatively moderate degree of heat—for example, only enough to warm milk a little above blood heat—may so disrupt the chemical configuration of a complex protein molecule—for example, the *enzyme*, rennet—that it will no longer carry out its biological function—that is, to coagulate the milk protein and thus convert the milk to 'junket'.

(c) FATS

The food technologist can usually recognize fats when he sees them because they are quite different both in their physical properties and in their chemical composition from the other two main food constituents, carbohydrate and protein. Unlike the starch grains, which form the main carbohydrate fraction, and even more unlike the muscle fibres of meat or even the gluten strands in bread, two examples of protein that have already been mentioned, fats possess no structural form. Fat is, indeed, primarily a fuel source, either for the animal or plant in which it originally occurs, or for the man who eats the food in which it subsequently forms a part. A slice of bread possesses an obvious and characteristic structure, the butter smeared on it does not.*

We recognize fat when we see it as a smooth, greasy substance. There are a number of different fats which differ primarily from each other in the temperature at which they melt. A fat that is liquid at the normal climatic temperature at which one happens to live is by convention called an oil, but the chemical compositions of fats and oils are similar and the same fat in Europe may be an oil in Africa just as an oil in Europe may be a fat in Alaska.

(i) *Visible and invisible fats*

It is sometimes convenient for a food technologist to classify fats as visible when they are handled by themselves as, for example, cooking fat, margarine or frying oil; and as invisible when they form integral parts of such items as nuts, cheese or packeted potato crisps.

* The firmness of such commodities as butter and margarine is partly due to the crystal structure of the fat but this is quite different from the visible crumb structure of bread or the fibres in meat.

(ii) *Trace substances associated*

Fats often contain dissolved in them certain pigments that give them their characteristic colour or contribute to their smell. There are also present in some fats small amounts of so-called 'fat-soluble vitamins'; the more important of these are vitamins A and D. Fats also sometimes contain in them traces of chemical components which delay the onset of rancidity; these are *anti-oxidants*.

(iii) *Chemical nature*

In plants and animals, fat may occur combined with protein and other cellular components, but for the most part the chemical molecule of fat is composed of three molecules of *fatty acid* combined together by being attached to a single molecule of *glycerol*. The nature of this combination is shown diagrammatically below:

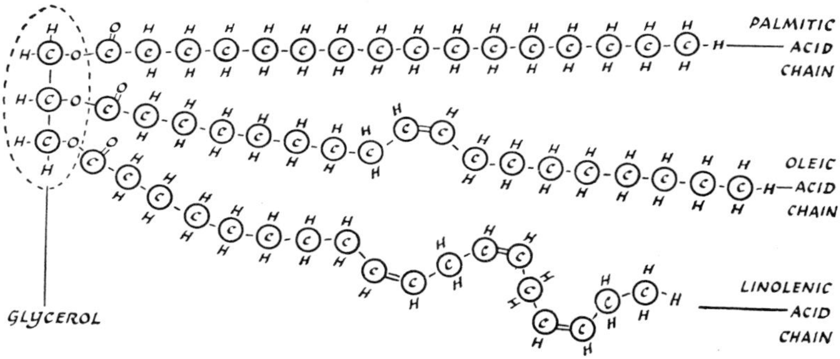

Fig. 3. The structure of a fat molecule.

There are two points to be noted about the chemical nature of fat. So long as the fatty-acid chains remain attached to the glycerol radicle, the integrity of the fat is maintained—for example, it will not mix with water. This integrity is broken, however, during the process of digestion. When this happens, the glycerol is released and the fatty acid chains become *saponified*, that is, they are converted into soap, which *is* soluble in water. It may happen in practice that fats become partly broken down, for example, when they become rancid, and free fatty acids are found in them. Technical refining processes are used to remove these free fatty acids. The topic of rancidity is discussed in detail on p. 159.

The second important feature in the chemical composition of fat is that the nature of the fat—whether it is a hard fat or a liquid oil and whether it has the characteristics of tallow or lard, or of olive oil or sardine oil—depends to a very large degree on which of a number of different fatty-acid chains its molecule contains. In the diagram on p. 15 the first chain shown is composed of sixteen carbon links. This is *palmitic acid*. Butter fat is peculiar in containing a proportion of shorter four-carbon chains of *butyric acid*. Perhaps even more important than the length of the fatty-acid chains, however, is whether or not these chains contain one or more points where two carbon atoms are doubly linked together and are consequently lacking in two hydrogen atoms. Fatty acids thus lacking in hydrogen atoms are called *unsaturated*. The direct effect of unsaturation on fat consistency, is, first, that unsaturated fats tend to be softer and more liquid than saturated fats; second, that they have a greater tendency to become rancid. Food technologists can fairly readily process natural fats so as to obtain whatever degree of saturation they wish, and thus make the fats they handle harder or softer at will. This operation—so called *hydrogenation* or *hardening*—is discussed in more detail in Chapter 6.

(d) VITAMINS

There are present in most foods a number of organic components which may not seem to be of direct interest to the food technologist so far as the apparent quality of the foodstuff is concerned. These substances, however, are of great importance to the nutritional value of the diet as a whole. Although they may be present only at the level of a few parts per million, their absence from the diet would lead to malnutrition, deficiency disease and ultimately death.

Vitamins can be conveniently classified into two groups:

(i) *Water-soluble* vitamins, notably a group of *B-vitamins*, fairly widely distributed in grain products, meat, milk, potatoes and vegetables, and *vitamin C*, which is largely restricted to fruit and vegetables.

(ii) *Fat-soluble* vitamins, including *vitamin A*, present in fish, egg and milk; yellow pigments which possess *vitamin A-activity* found in carrots, yellow maize, green vegetables, palm oil, sweet potatoes and a number of other foods; and *vitamin D*, found in milk, fish oils and in some other fatty substances that have been irradiated either by sunlight or artificially.

(e) MINERAL COMPONENTS OF FOOD

Foods contain in small amounts a comparatively long list of mineral components. These include:

(i) *Calcium* compounds; calcium phosphate is a component of bone and, as might be expected, occurs also in milk. Calcium from milk becomes concentrated in cheese and in dried milk. Fish may also be a significant source of calcium phosphate.

(ii) *Iodine*. An element that is of considerable importance for health and that is also present in sea fish. The absolute amounts of iodine present are exceedingly small, but so is the quantity required in a good diet.

(iii) *Iron* is a further necessary mineral occurring in foods; it is present in meat and in a specially available form in liver. Vegetables also supply significant amounts. Iron is notably lacking in milk.

(iv) *Salt*. The mineral combination present in largest amount in foodstuffs is *salt*. In chemical terms, this is sodium chloride. Although it is present naturally in a number of foods, salt is for the most part added, for example, in cooking and food processing, in making bread and in cheese-making.

3. Biology, biochemistry and nutrition

The food technologist is concerned with two main problems. On the one hand his purpose is to process foodstuffs so that they can be transported and stored and—this is often most important of all—presented to the people who are going to eat them in an attractive and palatable form. It has often been demonstrated in modern history that a perfectly satisfactory foodstuff may be refused by those who could benefit from it if it appears to be in some way unattractive and unfamiliar. His second purpose is to process and handle foods in such a way that their nutritional qualities are unimpaired and that the people eating them may obtain a diet that is in every way nutritionally satisfactory. This being so, it may perhaps be useful to summarize briefly the scientific principles of nutrition as they are at present understood.

(a) DIGESTION

Each of the different chemical components of food—protein, carbohydrate, fat, vitamins and minerals—are required in appropriate amounts for good nutrition. However, before the nutrients are able to do any good to the body, they must be *digested*; that is to say, they must be brought into such a state as to be capable of being *absorbed* into the bloodstream.

(i) *Carbohydrates*. Sugars require little or no digestion and are readily absorbed. The long, polymer molecule of starch must, however, be broken up into its component sugar units before it can be absorbed. This digestion occurs partly in the mouth and partly in the small intestine.

(ii) *Protein*. The large molecule of protein, like that of carbohydrate, must be split up into smaller units before it can be absorbed. This chemical breakdown occurs partly in the stomach and partly in the intestines.

(iii) *Fat*. Fat is mainly absorbed after the splitting off of the fatty-acid units from the glycerol. This breakdown occurs in the intestine.

(iv) *Vitamins and minerals*. These food components are in general readily absorbed.

The chemical breakdown of the food constituents that occurs during digestion is brought about by specific *enzymes*; these are special substances which possess the ability to bring about such breakdown and they are released by the body at various stages during the digestion process.

(b) ABSORPTION

When the large molecules of food are brought into an adequate degree of chemical subdivision by the process of digestion they permeate through the walls of the digestive tract into the bloodstream. The blood then carries them to appropriate storage depots in the body or to the muscles or such other sites where metabolism (the machinery of living) takes place. The indigestible food residues that cannot permeate through the gut wall pass through the intestinal tract and are eventually voided from the body.

(c) BIOCHEMISTRY

Life is a chemical process and it requires energy to keep it going. In this the body is similar to any other kind of engine, whether it be a diesel locomotive or a petrol-driven motor car—it requires fuel. But whereas it may be possible to run a power station on coal or on oil, or even on wood, the biological system can function only under certain restricted conditions. There are certain physiological and biochemical limitations which must be met. One obvious example for human beings is that the temperature of the body must be maintained within quite close limits. Another that the blood must always remain accurately adjusted at a certain fixed degree of slight alkalinity.

I have already touched on the preliminary conditions which food must conform to if it is to be satisfactory: each item must be capable of digestion into a state in which it can be absorbed. When it has passed into the body, part of the food is metabolized and used as fuel. 'Combustion' in the body is, in its end result, closely similar to combustion in the cylinder of a motor-car. The carbon combines with oxygen to form CO_2 and the hydrogen may combine also to form H_2O. These are the basic *chemical* reactions by which energy is released. The fundamental difference between the biochemical reactions in a living body and the chemical reactions in an engine are that in the engine high temperatures are reached and in the body the process of 'combustion' is brought about by an interlocking series of linked reactions which occur, one after the other, at only blood heat. These continuous chemical changes are subtly geared so as to activate appropriate reactions: in muscles the muscle fibres are caused to contract and the body thus enabled to move.

A further respect in which a living organism differs from a machine is that it is self-perpetuating and must obtain the components needed for growth and repair from the foodstuffs it ingests.

(d) NUTRITIONAL REQUIREMENTS

The amount of energy provided by different foods is customarily measured in terms of *Calories.** Fats are the most concentrated sources of Calories; carbohydrates and protein each provide, weight for weight, the same amounts, only four-ninths of the quantity provided by fat.

Water is not a fuel, consequently moist foods supply proportionally less energy than dry foods.

Calories are required by the body for three purposes:

(i) *To maintain the life processes:* the beating of the heart, the

*1 Calorie = 1000 calories. A calorie is a unit of energy which, in terms of heat, is the amount of heat required to raise the temperature of 1 gram of water 1°C. In the international SI units which it is proposed to introduce 1 Calorie can be expressed as 4200 joules (4·2 kilojoules) or 1000 Calories as 48 watts.

movement of the lungs in breathing, the tension of the muscles, and a number of other vital activities. For an 'average' man, this *basal metabolism,* as it is called, requires the expenditure of 70 Calories an hour, or 1680 Calories in the 24 hours of the day. The Calorie requirements are, on average, proportional to the vital mass of the body. It follows, therefore, that men require more Calories than women and big men more Calories than little men.

(ii) *For the performance of muscular work.* Men doing heavy manual labour consume more Calories than those who work sitting down, and they need more to eat.

(iii) *The daily routine of getting dressed, moving about, going out to work and coming back, and sport.* All these must be taken into account. Only *thinking* consumes so little mechanical energy that it can be ignored in assessing the Calories of the diet. When an excess of Calories is absorbed, obesity occurs.

But besides supplying energy, the combination of foods making up the daily diet must provide appropriate amounts of *protein* of the correct composition. Protein is made up of about twenty different types of amino acids of which eight are essential. These eight are not all represented in the right proportion in the protein in every food. It is therefore good nutritional practice to make up the protein of the diet from a number of different sources: for example, to eat a proportion of animal protein with vegetable protein, or to mix leaf protein with cereal protein. Since protein is primarily concerned in the growth of the body tissues, growing children and expectant mothers need proportionally more protein than adults.

The main nutritional function of *carbohydrates,* which comprise starches and sugars, is to supply Calories. *Fat* also supplies Calories but in more than twice as concentrated a form. A good proportion of fat is therefore useful in the diets of heavy workers. Fat also markedly improves the palatability of other foods. A recent conclusion that has been reached is that in prosperous communities where excessive amounts of fat are eaten there appears to be a connection between too much fat and the appearance of certain kinds of heart disease. This is particularly so when the fat is rich in *saturated* fatty acids.

A long list of *mineral* substances plays a part in nutrition. *Calcium* and *phosphorus* are essential for the growth and maintenance of bones and teeth, *iron* is found in red blood cells and an iron-deficient diet may lead to the disease anaemia. A shortage of *iodine* may be the cause of goitre due to an enlargement of the thyroid gland in the neck. And salt—sodium chloride—is required to maintain the necessary uniform composition of the blood and tissue fluids.

The variety of trace substances categorized as *vitamins* are also needed for a number of biochemical reasons. *Vitamin A* is necessary for health although its precise function is still obscure; the group of *B-vitamins* functions in connection with the enzymes which are concerned with the energy-release system by which the fuel for the body is 'combusted'. *Vitamin C* is somehow concerned with the health of the body's tissues and *vitamin D* is needed to integrate dietary calcium into the growing bones.

All this knowledge is brought into focus for the food technologist through the table shown in Appendix 1, on p. 287, in which average values are given for the *amounts* of each of the various nutrients required for health by different types of people engaged in work of differing degrees of activity. So far as the food technologist is concerned, it is his business to ensure that the foods with which he deals, when combined together by the people who eat them as part of their diet, shall jointly provide the necessary sum of each nutrient. Appendix 2, on pp. 288-93, lists the composition of a number of foods in terms of these nutrients.

2

Traditional methods of processing food and their scientific significance

1. Progressive refinement

Traditional methods of processing and storing foods have all been based on certain scientific principles. For instance, the principle underlying the use of cereal grains for food is the separation of concentrated nourishment from bulky and indigestible residues. The plant, whether it is wheat, rice, oats, maize or millet, concentrates starch in its seed, the grain, to serve as food for the embryo when it germinates the following season before its green leaves, on which it will later depend for sustenance, have had time to develop. In preparing grain for human food, the stalk and outer husks must be removed by some process of threshing or winnowing and then, later on, the starchy fraction of the grain itself must be separated from the mainly indigestible bran by some method of milling. Modern scientific technology has taken this process a long way further by developing machines for harvesting and threshing—the modern combine-harvester does both these operations at once—and subsequently milling the separated grain with an elaborate series of rollers and sieves, by means of which very precise control may be exercised over the exact physical structure and the chemical composition of the resulting flour.

The next operations, making dough and baking it, are ancient customs and have been required because, even when flour has been prepared from wheat or rye, the starch granules of which the flour is principally composed cannot be readily digested by the human gut. When the flour is wetted, formed into a more or less porous mass of dough and then subjected to the heat of an oven, an expansion of moisture occurs that bursts the starch granules. The broken-down starch is digestible. With partial drying of the cooked flour, the final product can be kept for some length of time without deteriorating.

The preparation of sugar is another example of quite an ancient piece of food technology, the purpose of which is to concentrate a carbohydrate—this time the sweet and attractive *sucrose* which is found in sugar-cane or beet. Sugar is today a cheap commodity that is available almost anywhere in the world. This cheapness and ample supply are entirely due to the development of efficient technical methods for extracting, concentrating and purifying it.

In the separation of sugar from cane, as in the separation of starch from a sheaf of wheat, first of all the main part of the unwanted plant has to be removed. In the earliest times, this was done by crushing the sugar-cane between heavy stone rollers, when the juice containing the sugar could be collected and the crushed stalks discarded. Nowadays cane-milling machinery—like the flour-milling machinery which is applied to a problem quite different in detail but similar in principle—is complex and elaborate and enormously more efficient than the primitive mechanism from which it was derived.

After the sugar has been separated as juice, it must be concentrated by boiling, until the syrup is sufficiently saturated for crystals of sugar to form when the syrup cools. The first crystals to form are not pure sugar but a mixture of sugar and various dark contaminants called molasses. To the problem of separating these substances great technological ingenuity has been devoted for some hundreds of years.

Pure sucrose was successfully separated from these miscellaneous brown compounds that adhere to its crystals, and white sugar-loaves were manufactured, long before the present refining process was invented. The early system was probably derived from the Arabs. The boiled syrup was allowed to crystallize in conical moulds. A dunce's cap of crystals formed inside the mould and the mother liquor drained away through a hole at the pointed end. A mixture of clay and water was then poured in and allowed to percolate slowly through the sugar. As the clay trickled through, the dark molasses became attached to it, much as a dark ring of soapy dirt becomes attached to the side of a bath, and was thus separated from the sugar. This operation, termed 'claying', was repeated until the crystalline mass eventually became white. A similar method has been used in India up till modern times, with a certain type of leaves in place of clay. Such sugar-loaves were first imported into England in 1319, and appeared at the coronation banquet of King Henry V in 1413.

2. Preservation from decay

The separation of flour as food, which depends on the two successive technical processes of first threshing the grain from the harvested crop and then milling the flour out of the husk of the grain, and the somewhat analogous process of sugar-refining are paralleled by many other processes of food gathering. These all have their own technologies of refining. Very many of the food technologies described in this book are based on a different principle, that of protecting the foods from decay and thus allowing them to be stored.

(a) THE NATURE OF DECAY

Except in a very few extremely inclement places, where it is either very cold or very dry, the world is full of living organisms. We are familiar with the wild and domestic animals we see around us and with the birds, insects and lower creatures which form so characteristic a feature of the earth on which we live. But besides all these there is another community of creatures, as diverse in relative size as the animals we know and equally widespread, who share the same living space. We are not normally aware of these 'little animals' because they are too small to see with the naked eye, but they are easily visible under a microscope. One, called *yeast*, is used in baking and brewing. If we were to imagine a single yeast cell to be the size of an elephant, we should on this scale find that another, a *bacterium* that causes gangrene, would be as big as a horse. Other organisms cause the parrot disease psittacosis—they would be the size of guinea pigs. Yet others, *viruses*, cause influenza, for example; these would relatively be the size of a mouse. Finally, the organism causing foot-and-mouth disease in cattle would be only as big as a gnat.

The major discovery of modern biology is the extraordinary uniformity of all life. Although there are, of course, significant differences between the biochemical mechanisms of some of the more primitive bacteria and that of higher organisms such as ourselves, the underlying similarities are even more striking. Micro-organisms, like higher animals, consume and break down foodstuffs to obtain the energy they need for their life process, and just like ourselves they require appropriate conditions of warmth and moisture in order to do this. This is the reason why moist foods that are left standing about in a warm place 'go bad': the process of decay which is commonly described as 'going bad' is merely the result of the rapid multiplication of micro-organisms. Either these were already present on the surface of the food itself or on objects with which the food has come in contact, or else they came by air.

Micro-organisms, whether they are bacteria, yeasts or moulds, may be thought of as if they were a species of 'vermin'. Just as rats or mice destroy and damage food on a large scale and leave behind their droppings, so on a microscopic scale micro-organisms live off the carbohydrate or protein of the food and leave behind, too, acid (such as when milk 'goes sour') or other partial breakdown products. These may produce 'off' flavours, and sometimes even the actively toxic substances causing food poisoning. But just as micro-organisms behave in many ways like higher animals so can their vital activities be brought to a stop by the same causes. Among these the commonest are heat, cold and deprivation of water.

(b) METHODS OF PREVENTING DECAY

The well-known process of 'bottling' depends on killing by *heat* the micro-organisms that naturally envelop fresh food and then preventing any other micro-organism gaining access to it. When, as not infrequently happens, a housewife finds that one of her bottles of fruit or vegetables has gone bad, this implies that the degree of heat applied was not sufficient to kill all the micro-organisms in her particular preparation or that there was a leak through which new organisms got in.

The purpose of domestic bottling and also of canning under industrial conditions is to kill the bacteria that would cause decay and then to keep the food in a closed container into which other micro-organisms cannot penetrate. *Refrigeration* and *deep-freezing* do not kill bacteria but merely slow down their metabolic activities or bring them virtually to a standstill.

The third method of preventing spoilage by micro-organisms is to arrange for the food to contain *insufficient moisture* for the micro-organism to be able to grow either in it or on the surface. This can be done directly by having the foodstuff dry enough to put it effectively beyond the reach of the micro-organism's metabolic capabilities. Grain, for example, must be stored at a moisture content not exceeding, say, 13%. In many traditional processes meat is dried as 'biltong', fish is also dried, and peas and beans are stored dry so that they may be kept for prolonged periods without deteriorating. As an indirect method of preventing micro-organisms from using food-stuffs one can add a readily soluble substance to the food. Sugar and salt are employed for this purpose. A man dies of thirst in an open boat at sea just as quickly as he does in a waterless desert because the high concentration of dissolved salts in sea water prevents it reaching his tissues. For a similar reason strongly salted herring will not decay, and strawberries preserved in a strong concentration of sugar—as in jam—will keep almost indefinitely.

As I have already said, many of the processes used in food technology are designed to prevent micro-organisms from causing deterioration and decay. These processes include canning, freezing and dehydration. Their effectiveness depends on the use of *(a) heat* sufficient to kill the organisms, *(b) cold* sufficient to slow up their activities or bring them to a stop, and *(c) withdrawal of moisture.* But in addition to these it is sometimes possible to add to food a substance that, while not being significantly toxic to human beings, will poison the micro-organisms. Because it is extremely difficult to destroy or inhibit the invading bacteria or moulds without at the same time affecting—even if to only a very slight degree—the wholesomeness of the foods concerned, the use of 'preservatives' is considered nowadays to have only very restricted application in food technology and is controlled by stringent regulations in most countries.

Besides the use of heat, cold and desiccation, the most effective preliminary operation to minimize or avoid the microbiological spoilage of food is to reduce the unnecessary contamination of food to a minimum by taking rigid precautions at every stage in harvesting, preparing and processing to maintain *cleanliness.*

Although micro-organisms are the main causes of foods decaying, certain kinds of spoilage are due to other causes. Oxygen can cause some food to go brown and enzymes naturally present in plant cells may cause changes in taste. These can be controlled by the use of sulphite or of blanching as described on p. 217.

3. Types of micro-organism capable of causing the deterioration of foods

(a) MOULDS

Moulds, or fungi, may appear in a wide variety of forms. They grow as a unicellular filament which extends from the tip and may form a complex, branched network called *mycelium.* This net or mat of mould growth may extend until it covers the entire article of food on which it is growing. The mycelium may, here and there, produce a specific structure bearing clusters of dry spores, which are blown by the air as 'seeds' and may carry the mould infection to a distance. These *spores* are of particular importance to the food technologist because owing to their strongly knit structure they are very resistant to heat.

Moulds tend to grow on the surface of moist foods. Their rate of growth increases with a rise in temperature: at 10°C growth is slow, at 30°C very rapid; at still higher temperatures the rate of growth diminishes again, and at about 36°C it stops entirely. In order to destroy mould it is necessary either to sterilize foodstuffs under pressure to ensure the destruction of the spores, or to heat to, say, 75°C on two or three successive days so that spores not killed by the first heatings may germinate and be destroyed in their vegetative form in subsequent treatments. Moulds grow most readily at a pH* of 4 to 6 and are inhibited or greatly restricted at very acid pH values of 1 to 2 or very alkaline pH values of 8 to 9, although there are certain fungi that can grow at extreme ranges of acidity or alkalinity. A number of common moulds require oxygen for their growth and it is for this reason that they are commonly found on the surface of infected foodstuffs.

(*b*) BACTERIA

Bacteria are very small. They multiply by fission, that is to say, one organism divides into two and so on. This division may be very rapid and, in circumstances favourable to them, bacteria may divide every 20 minutes, so that within a single day thousands of millions of bacteria may have arisen from a single parent organism. Although bacteria are so small that 10^{13} weigh only 1 g., by the time a bacterial population has reached 1 to 10 million/g. of foodstuff it will begin to produce chemical changes which are apparent to the senses, and by the time the numbers have increased to somewhere between 100 and 10,000 million (that is 10^8 to 10^{10}), which may easily occur, the food will be reckoned to have 'gone bad'.

* 'pH' is a convenient scale of measurement for recording the degree of effective acidity or alkalinity. *Neutrality* is at pH 7·0. All pH values less than 7·0 indicate increasing degrees of *acidity*. A pH of, say, 6·0 to 6·5 could be considered slightly acid; a pH of 2·0 or 3·0 would be very acid. All pH values exceeding 7·0 are alkaline. The blood has a pH of 7·4 and is slightly alkaline. A pH of, say, 10·0 is very alkaline.

(i) *Bacterial spores*

A number of bacteria are capable of forming spores but, unlike moulds, bacteria do not form their spores in enormous numbers in special fruiting bodies but they are produced inside the normal vegetative bacterial cells. The function of bacterial spores is, like that of mould spores, to survive under unfavourable conditions, so they present a special problem for the food technologist.

(ii) *Distribution*

Under ordinary circumstances, the number of bacteria present in the air and in clean water is small. Foods in the natural state always have bacteria on them; soil always contains a numerous bacterial population; sewage contains immense numbers; and any surface on which there is a trace of nutrient substance upon which bacteria can thrive—dirty dish-cloths, hands, used crockery—will carry its load of bacteria. Very wet conditions favour the growth of bacteria and wet meat kept too long may develop 'bacterial slime'; on somewhat drier surfaces moulds grow more readily than bacteria and it has been observed that by partially drying the surface of hams by light smoking, bacteria are discouraged and instead certain moulds grow which actually contribute to the flavour of the ham. The same effect is also obtained with cheese; if it is stored too moist, bacteria may grow on it and it will be spoiled, but at the right degree of dryness, moulds grow on the surface of the rind and a good flavour develops. Mould is encouraged to grow within the substance of some specialized cheeses to provide a characteristic flavour.

(iii) *Response to acidity*

Bacteria grow most readily at a pH of 7·0, that is to say when a foodstuff is neutral. On the other hand, they are mostly inhibited at a moderate acid pH of, say, 5·0 to 5·5. For this reason it is very much easier to bottle acid fruits like gooseberries or blackcurrants than more neutral foods such as French beans. Similarly, traditional processes of food technology involving pickling may owe their success to the acidity of the vinegar used.

The bacterial populations that are found naturally occurring are almost always made up of a variety of different types of organisms. For this reason it is not possible to know without considerable study exactly what the bacterial population as a whole will do under any particular set of circumstances. For example, although as was stated above, most bacteria grow most prolifically at a neutral pH near 7,

MOULDS. 1: A saprophytic fungus on an uncovered bottle of gooseberries.
2: *Penicillium* growing on an exposed slice of meat loaf.

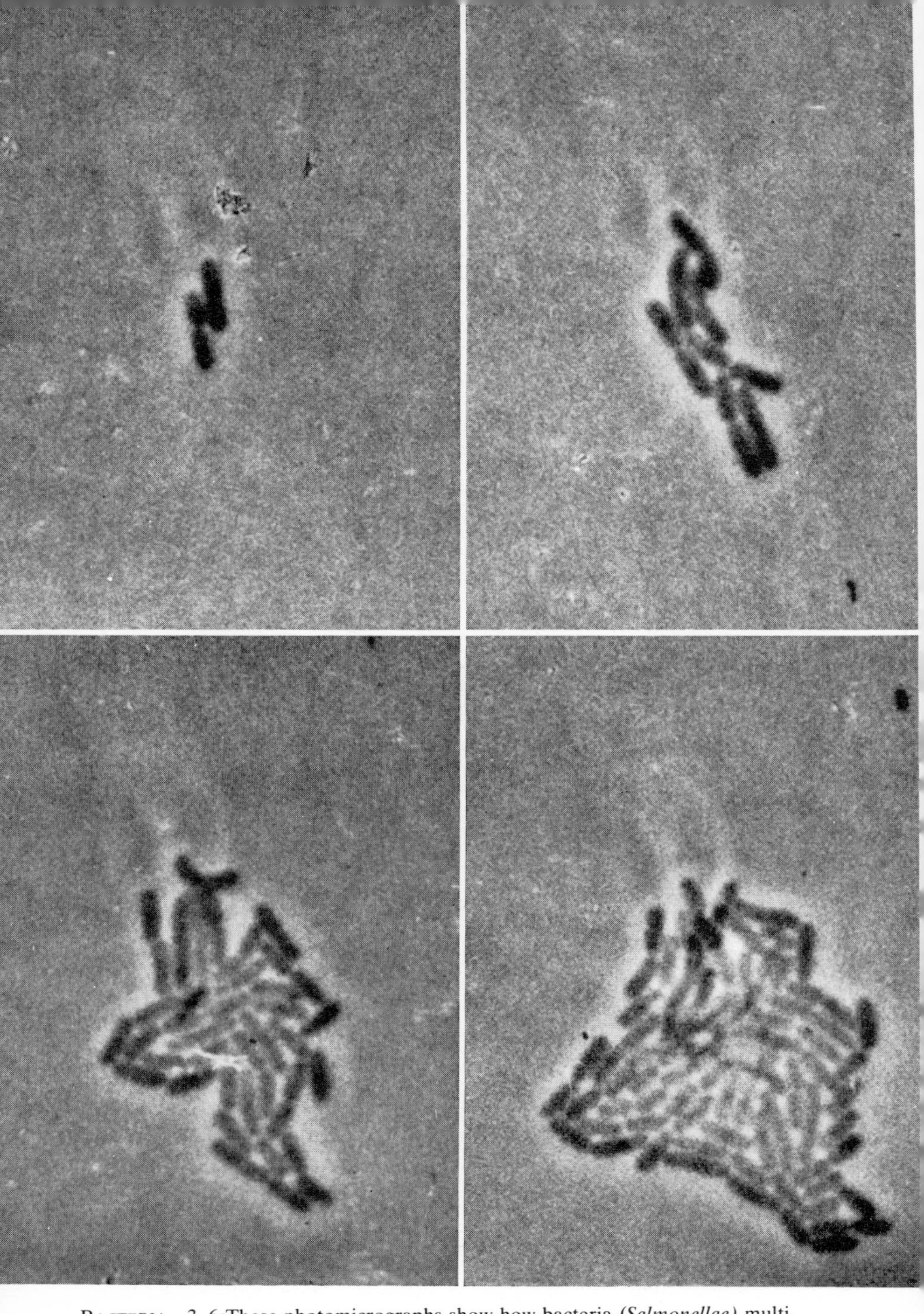

BACTERIA. 3–6: These photomicrographs show how bacteria (*Salmonellae*) multiply in warm meat broth.

there are certain types which produce lactic acid and grow in an acid medium of pH 6 or less. These are milk-souring bacteria; they also play a part in the production of sauerkraut. Again, although as a general rule bacteria are not as dependent on oxygen as moulds, some types find oxygen necessary for their growth, while others again will only grow in the complete absence of oxygen. These differences are reflected in the practical observation that foods which are kept until they decay will deteriorate in different ways. If they are left in the open no smell may develop; if, on the other hand, they are left in a closed vessel, highly disagreeable smells frequently develop due to the growth of bacteria that can thrive without oxygen: these are called *anaerobes*.

(iv) *Response to temperature*

Bacteria show equally diverse characteristics in their response to temperature. It is convenient to distinguish three groups:

(A) *Psychrophilic bacteria.* Bacteria that have their origin in air, water and soil usually grow their fastest at about 20°C, but some of them are capable of developing at quite low temperatures. People who have ever forgotten about foods left in a domestic refrigerator, in which the temperature may be 5-10°C above freezing, will know that food eventually goes bad even under cool conditions. Similar problems confront food technologists handling foods on a larger scale in cool stores for meat, fruit or vegetables. Bacterial contamination will also grow, even if slowly, in refrigerated milk.

(B) *Mesophilic bacteria.* Bacterial species originating in warm-blooded animals but also occurring in soil, often by way of droppings or sewage, thrive best at 37°C, that is, blood heat. These are the commonest spoilage organisms.

(C) *Thermophilic bacteria.* There is a small miscellaneous group of bacteria capable of growing at quite hot temperatures up to 60°C (140°F) or thereabouts. These are particularly troublesome in food canning. Not only may they escape destruction during processing if the penetration of heat into the middle of a food pack is not complete, but they often produce spores which are even more resistant to high temperature. Since these spores can develop and grow at warm temperatures they can escape detection and survive in ostensibly sterile materials to cause trouble later on.

(c) YEASTS

Yeasts are fungi which normally exist, like bacteria, as single cells. Yeasts differ from bacteria, however, by producing offspring as buds which grow and then become detached: bacteria reproduce by simple division. Yeasts are capable of forming spores, but these spores are less resistant to heat than those produced by bacteria and moulds. Yeasts occur in soil and also on the surface of fruit, notably grapes. One of the main reasons why wines from particular geographic localities possess different flavours and bouquets is the difference in the local strains of yeast occurring on the surface of the grapes. Although the principal chemical action of the yeasts is to convert the sugar in the grape juice into alcohol and carbon-dioxide gas, the different races of yeasts each tend to give special minor side reactions. From these, small amounts of *higher alcohols*—which differ from the ethyl-alcohol, commonly called 'alcohol'—are formed, as well as *esters,* which are compounds of alcohols and acids. Although the esters and higher alcohols produced by these reactions are formed in very small amounts, their subtle effect on the character of the wine is important.

Yeasts are able to grow freely at a quite acid pH, and some of them are also able to withstand high concentrations of salt; yet other strains are resistant to very concentrated sugar solutions. Thus yeasts may be troublesome to food technologists who are dealing with salted meat and fish, or fruit syrups.

Yeasts can thrive either with or without air. Without air, they convert sugars into alcohol, a characteristic which is the basis of all wine-making, brewing and potable spirit production. When air is available, the growth of new yeast cells is encouraged and less alcohol is produced.

4. Deliberate use of bacterial agents

(*a*) CHEESE-MAKING AS A PRESERVATIVE PROCESS

Milk is a highly nutritious foodstuff. It is composed of the sugar, lactose, several soluble proteins, fat and a varied group of vitamins and mineral substances. Because it is also a liquid food it is very susceptible to bacterial infection and is consequently perishable. Cheese-making is a traditional process, developed to preserve some of the seasonal flush of milk which was produced on farms when cows were allowed to calve 'naturally' in the spring, just when the first rich grass was coming along in the fields. Without cheese-making, much of this milk would have gone to waste and nothing would have been available during the winter when, until quite recent times, the cows gave no milk.

Cheese keeps because it represents a concentration of the protein and fat and much of the calcium of the milk, most of the watery liquid fraction containing dissolved lactose having been removed as whey. The manufacture of cheese is based primarily on causing the soluble protein molecules to change their structure and coagulate. This is not done by heat—as when egg albumen is made insoluble by boiling—but by the use of acid. This acid is normally formed by milk-souring bacteria which are added as 'starters' in cheese-making. The presence of added salt is also important in this lactic acid fermentation. It is interesting to note that in making milk less perishable—that is to say, more resistant to bacterial attack—appropriate types of bacteria are themselves used.

When the protein coagulates it drags down the milk-fat with it and—in most varieties of cheese, as mentioned above—the calcium as well. In the normal kinds of hard cheese the moisture content is reduced to about 40% of the total weight. This together with the presence of salt and acidity makes them tolerably resistant to harmful microbiological attack. The moulds that commonly grow on the rind exposed to the air and in crevices in the cheese into which air can penetrate do no harm to the nutritive value of the cheese, do not break down much of the cheese components to cause decay, and are often considered to improve the attractiveness of the flavour. In many modern processes the cheese may be covered with a plastic coating or wrapper which prevents the formation of rind.

(b) FISH CURING AS A PRESERVATIVE PROCESS

Fish is a food that, like milk, is also highly perishable. 'Stinking fish' is a phrase of great antiquity in the English language which forcibly points to the readiness with which fish decays and the speed with which the smell and flavour can deteriorate to a point at which a valuable, nutritious food becomes uneatable.

Cheese-making is an example of traditional food technology based on the principle of drying as a means of preventing microbiological attack. Many of the traditional processes of fish curing are also based on the withdrawal of water, but this is sometimes partly brought about indirectly by adding salt. By exposing the fish to smoke, its surface becomes coated with tarry materials—phenols and other compounds—which possess antiseptic activity.

Red herring, for example, is prepared by first soaking the split and eviscerated fish in strong brine, made of a 70-80% saturated salt solution. The salted fish is then hung in warm wood-smoke for a period of days. At the end of the process, the herrings will have taken up 8% or more of the salt which inhibits microbiological growth; it will be substantially dried, and the outer layers of protein previously made soluble by the brine will have been coagulated into a glossy pellicle by the effect of the smoke. On this pellicle will be the deposit of phenols, tars, aldehydes, ketones, alcohols and acids which—like the layer of creosote with which wooden fence-posts are treated and for the same reason—also serve to discourage micro-organisms and thus preserve the fish. This traditional example of food technology has become modified in more modern processes because, although it is effective and is based on sound scientific principles, it produces a foodstuff that is highly salted and possesses a strong characteristic flavour which has progressively become less acceptable to our more sophisticated tastes.

5. Food technology and live foods

We are accustomed to consider an egg as an article of human food but it is, in fact, initially a living system.

So long as a shell egg maintains its integrity as a closed system it is substantially resistant to microbiological infection and decay. An undamaged egg-shell and the two layers of membranes below it allow the passage of air, carbon dioxide and water-vapour through but, like healthy human skin, are resistant to the passage of micro-organisms. If the shell is damaged, or even if it is washed in water, bacteria become able to pass through and if they then penetrate the membranes they will infect the egg inside. It follows, therefore, that a poultryman who allows his hens to dirty their eggs and who has, therefore, to wash them before taking them to the market, is more likely to have some of them become rotten than is his neighbour who does not have to wash his eggs at all. Particularly, if the washing water is cold enough to cool the eggs, micro-organisms will actually be drawn into the interior through the shell.

There were a number of traditional methods of storing eggs. One of the commonest of these was to submerge them in a solution of 'water-glass'. Although this process, in the form in which it was used in domestic households, is only of limited practical interest to the modern food technologist, it does nevertheless exemplify several scientific principles which are of general significance.

The purpose of storing eggs in water-glass, which is a viscous solution of sodium silicate, was not to protect them against infection, but merely to prevent evaporation taking place; that is to avoid their becoming partly dried out.

Apples, like eggs, are also living things and the processes used in handling and transporting them must take this fact into account. Apples, like eggs, contain much moisture but so long as they maintain their integrity, so long as their skins are undamaged and their tissues unharmed by bruising, they are fully capable of resisting infection and decay in just the same way as does the body of a living man. It is true that a stored apple will not live for ever although it remains alive in store very much longer than an egg. Gradually as it becomes older and after the stage of full ripeness is past it will tend to shrivel and it will become increasingly susceptible to infection. This is the reason why a prudent housewife will store apples in a clean place and will wrap each one in paper, so that the first one to die and become infected with mould will not immediately pass on the mould infection to its neighbours.

But recognition of the fact that stored eggs and fruit and potatoes are living organisms has a more fundamental scientific significance to the food technologist. It is sometimes said that these foodstuffs 'breathe' and, in general terms, this is approximately true. For this reason the atmosphere around them is of importance. Significant advances have been made in the successful storage and handling of such articles by the appropriate adjustment of the relative concentrations of oxygen and carbon dioxide in the atmosphere of the store. These points are discussed in more detail in later chapters.

6. Consistency, flavour and colour

Although the fundamental purpose of food technology is to preserve food from deterioration and to present it to the consumer in a digestible and nutritious form, a secondary interest of the food technologist and one to which he devotes a large amount of time, knowledge and effort is that of modifying the quality of foodstuffs so that they may become acceptable and attractive to the people for whom they are intended.

(a) THE TEXTURE OF FOODS

People like the meat they eat to be tender. Although raw meat is as digestible as cooked meat it is not normally considered by civilized people to be a palatable article of diet. Many types of meat become tender when they are cooked, either in a domestic kitchen, or in the large vessels of a food factory where meat products are prepared for consumption as pies or various types of sausage or where, after treatment under pressure, they are canned in one form or another. Certain meats, however, remain tough and difficult to chew even after having been subjected to these processes. This toughness can be modified in several ways, for example:

(i) *Mechanical tenderizing:* The traditional operation of beating a steak with a piece of wood serves the purpose of loosening the structure of the muscle fibres of which the meat is composed.

(ii) *Ageing:* The muscular tissue of game birds and animals tends to be strong and the meat is consequently tough. When such meat is 'hung', a certain amount of decay occurs, partly due to the gradual break-up of the integrity of muscle cells and partly to the action of micro-organisms.

(iii) *Artificial tenderizing:* When protein is eaten it is eventually broken down into its constituent amino acids through the action of digestive *enzymes* in the stomach. It has recently been found possible to make concentrated preparations of appropriate enzymes which can be applied to tough meat to make it tender. This development in food technology is discussed more fully in Chapter 4.

Much of the work of modern cereal chemistry has been aimed at producing a satisfactory loaf of bread, one that will not only keep and be wholesome to eat, but which will also be soft and of agreeable texture. This acceptable consistency is obtained by appropriate kneading of the dough, either by hand or by proper amounts of mechanical work. The operation in scientific terms is the stretching of the long protein molecules of the gluten so that they are rearranged in such a way as to produce the desired result. The modern food technologist working with bread, just like the technologist handling meat, can today also use enzyme preparations which will modify the structure of the flour protein and that of the starch in which it is embedded in order to obtain the desired consistency.

The use of fat and particularly of egg in flour confectionery, quite apart from their nutritional value, has an important effect on the structure of commodities in which they are incorporated. The protein of the egg white, the albumen, produces what is considered to be an attractive structure. By studying this action of the fibres of the egg-protein, the modern food technologist can advance beyond the point reached in traditional food handling. There have been developed egg substitutes prepared from fish and from slaughter-house blood which possess a chemical structure analogous to that of egg-white and which will, in consequence, when incorporated in flour-confectionery produce the softness and consistency desired.

(b) FLAVOUR

The traditional spices and flavouring agents—pepper, ginger, caraway and anise seeds, onions and garlic, mint, borage, mustard and vanilla—do not, so far as is known, contribute any significant food value to the articles to which they are added. Yet they are highly prized as contributing attractive qualities to food. Considerable efforts have been made by scientists to determine the chemical composition of the substances from which these diverse flavours are derived. Yet although the main components of each flavour are known, modern analytical techniques have shown that a natural flavouring agent does not owe its character merely to a single chemical substance but to a large group of compounds, many of which may be of the same chemical class but each with minor variations one from another. The list below gives the identity of a few of the chemical compounds comprising the main flavouring agents of various foods and spices, yet none of these by itself contributes the full subtlety of the natural food.

Table 1

Food	*Principal flavouring ingredient*
Butter	di-acetyl
Pineapple	methyl-β-methyl-thiol-propionate
Pear	propyl acetate
Strawberry	methyl-phenyl-glycidate
Apricot	undecalactone
Onion	ethyl thiocyanate
Garlic	diallyl disulphide
Mustard	allyl thiocarbimide
Coconut	gamma-nonalactone

A major interest of the traditional food technologist and one that is still of importance to the modern scientist concerned with food is the selection of natural commodities of good flavour and aroma. Indeed, 'quality' is often based almost entirely on the taste and smell of a foodstuff. It is insufficient for a consumer to be told—what is, indeed, entirely true in scientific terms—that stale eggs or fish possess nutritional values fully as good as new-laid eggs and fresh fish. The consumer may decide that the smell of the articles stored for an unduly prolonged period is disagreeable and distasteful.

The modern technologist can in some few instances use pure chemical compounds to add flavour. Monosodium glutamate enhances the flavour of meat and saccharine simulates the taste of sugar. Nevertheless, for the most part, technology is more profitably applied to the problem of providing consumers with food in a condition as closely approaching its fresh state as possible.

(c) COLOUR

Colour exerts a remarkable influence on people's attitude towards food and it is essential that food technologists should bear this in mind. Although colour may sometimes be an indication of nutritional value or freshness, more often than not its significance is based solely on strongly held likes and dislikes. The type of food that people eat depends to a very much larger degree than we think on custom rather than nutritional need. And many of the most strongly ingrained food habits and traditions are concerned with colour. For example, the only eggs which can be successfully marketed in the city of Boston, Mass., are brown-shelled eggs, whereas only white-shelled eggs are accepted by dealers in the city of New York. Then there is a long and obscure history of colour prejudice about bread. Before the invention of the modern steel roller, the production of really white flour was an expensive process and the whiteness of flour acquired a prestige value. When the new developments in milling technology made it possible to produce white flour cheaply it was found that white flour made even whiter by artificial bleaching was more popular than the same flour unbleached.

In contrast to flour and bread, where the colour desired by custom and prejudice is whiteness, butter is required to be yellow and in many countries where butter is made on a large scale in industrial creameries the yellowness is enhanced by means of an artificial colouring material added for purely cosmetic reasons.

The desire for some special colour in food is of great antiquity. Saffron, a yellow pigment prepared from the blossoms of the saffron crocus, *Crocus sativus,* was used in cooking in China in early times and today is widely employed in Spain and in Iran as a colouring agent for rice. But although the attractions of colour may seem irrational, they are just as strong today as they were in historical times and the food technologist must act accordingly. And, as is described in Chapter 9, he has today at his disposal new chemical colouring agents as well as the traditional vegetable pigments.

PART 2

PRACTICAL TECHNOLOGY

3

Cereal chemistry and technology

Human civilization has depended upon cereals from the first. It was only when primitive man developed the ability to grow cereal crops that settled communities could become established, and even today cereals still provide a major source of calories in the diets of people throughout the world. Wheat is grown on a larger area of land than any other cereal. Although it is capable of growing in a wide variety of climates, the main wheat-producing areas are in temperate countries with an annual rainfall of between 13 and 35 in. Barley and oats are grown in much the same areas. Rye is also suited to a temperate climate and can be grown successfully on poorer land than wheat and will survive colder winters.

Rice is the principal cereal crop grown in warm, humid areas of the temperate zone and in tropical territories where water is available for irrigation. Maize is an important cereal; it was originally derived from America but is now grown extensively in South Africa, Argentina, Brazil, the USSR and China and on irrigated land in Egypt and in the Danube basin. Sorghum, one of the main types of millet, is an important cereal in Africa, Asia and parts of America where the climate is too hot and dry for maize. Typical figures for the analytical composition of these cereals are shown in Table 2.

Table 2

Typical analyses of the more important cereal grains

(per 100 g.)

	Moisture	*Carbohydrate*	*Protein*	*Fat*	*Calories*	*Indigestible fibre*
	g.	g.	g.	g.		
Wheat	13	69	12	2	340	2
Rice	11	65	8	2	310	9
Maize	13	69	10	4	352	2
Sorghum	12	68	10	4	348	3
Oats	13	58	10	5	317	10
Rye	13	69	11	2	338	2

A. WHEAT

1. Structure and classification

The grain of wheat consists of an outer covering, the *pericarp* and *testa,* which is hard and indigestible; an *aleurone layer,* which contains a higher proportion of protein than flour; an *embryo* attached to a small structure, the *scutellum,* at the lower end of the grain; and, finally, the *endosperm,* comprising 85% of the whole grain from which the flour is derived. This structure is shown diagrammatically opposite.

The composition of wheat varies with the variety of the seed, the nature of the soil, and the climate. Wheats can be classified as:

Table 3

		Protein content %
(i) *Bread wheats:*	hard spring wheat	12–14
	hard winter wheat	9–13
(ii) *Pastry wheats:*	soft winter wheat	10
	white wheat	8–11
(iii) *Macaroni wheat:*	durum wheat	11–14

These wheats and the flours made from them may be blended in order to obtain the desired quality for the manufacture of the types of bread, biscuits, cakes and pastries required for a particular market.

2. Processing of wheat

(a) STORAGE

Grain should have a moisture content less than 20% before it is harvested. If it is stored in a moist condition bacteria and moulds will grow and will cause the temperature of the bulk grain to rise. The quality of the wheat will consequently be damaged. In order to store it successfully it is, therefore, necessary to reduce the moisture content to, say, 13% by a process of drying. This can be done in a simple kiln or in a more complex type of drier but it is important that the temperature of the grain is not allowed to exceed 50°C (122°F). Even drying temperatures little above 40°C will be harmful if the drying is unduly prolonged. The use of excessive temperatures damages the wheat *enzymes* which, as will be described later, are essential in flour during the baking process.

(b) MILLING

The milling process as a whole can be divided into two parts, the preliminary cleaning of the grain and the adjustment of its moisture content to an optimum level and the separation of the husk and the outer layers of the grain from the flour.

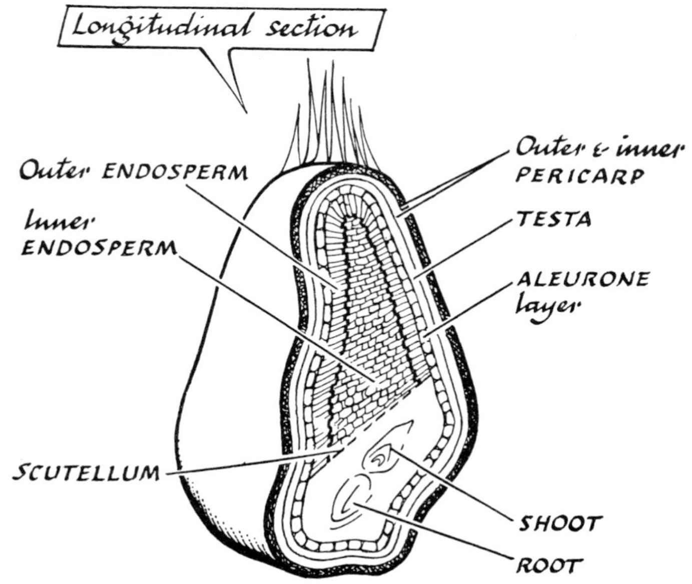

Fig. 4. Diagram of a grain of wheat.

(i) *Cleaning and conditioning (or tempering)*

A. *Rubble separator.* The cleaning and conditioning of wheat before milling in a modern plant is an elaborate process. The grain is passed initially over a set of sieves in a 'rubble separator' in order to free it from gross contamination. This machine is fitted with fans to blow off dust. The first separator may be followed by a second to remove impurities still remaining.

B. *Disc separator.* The grain is then allowed to pass to a 'disc separator'. This machine is fitted with discs containing slots, or indents, designed to pick up and hold the wheat grains while allowing oats, barley and other grains to pass through; other discs with smaller indents separate seeds and broken wheat grains.

C. *Magnetic separators.* The wheat, cleaned so far, is then passed over a magnetic separator to remove any nails or pieces of metal.

The complete removal of iron is very important, not only to avoid damaging the milling machinery but also to prevent any possibility of a nail or a metal washer striking a spark during later stages of the process and thus igniting a dust cloud of flour, *which is highly explosive.*

D. *Washer and whizzer.* The final cleaning operation is carried out by passing the grain through a 'washer and whizzer' or similar device. The wheat is carried into the machine in a stream of water and is rapidly sluiced round at high speed. The wheat, separated from dirt, is conveyed upwards out of the water by means of inclined vanes. Besides cleaning the grain, the machine can be adjusted so as to allow it to take up a desired amount of water for 'conditioning'.

E. *Conditioning.* Conditioning, or tempering, is a complex process which, even now, is not fully understood. It is well known, however, that different wheats behave most satisfactorily during the milling process if their moisture content is adjusted to an exact proportion that may differ for different batches of grain; and it is not enough for the percentage of water to be at a particular figure, this water must have penetrated into the grain structure in an appropriate way. In order to obtain the desired condition, the wheat after having been washed or 'whizzed' is run into a 'conditioner'. This is some sort of holding container in which it is possible to adjust the temperature and provide a controlled amount of air. It is generally considered that most wheats can be best conditioned if they are held at 20°C to 25°C for 48 hours at a moisture content of 15·5%. Conditioning occurs more rapidly at higher temperatures so that at 50°C, the time may be reduced to 24 hours. Very rapid conditioning occupying only a few seconds can be achieved by applying a temperature of 70°C to 75°C. Clearly this temperature must be precisely controlled or the grain will be harmed; the purpose in conditioning is to accelerate the transfer of moisture within the grain.

(ii) *Separation of flour*

Modern flour mills in technologically developed countries contain a complex combination of elaborate equipment. The object of this expensive plant is to obtain the maximum proportion of flour from the wheat and to produce it to a very precise specification of quality. Quality is obtained by a sharp separation of the different parts of the grain structure. The flour is designed to be made up almost solely from endosperm free from any admixture of aleurone structure, of germ, or of the outer husk. This separation is achieved by passing the grist through a series of rollers and sieves.

A. *Break rolls.* First, the grain is passed between horizontal rollers (the 'break rolls'). These rollers are fluted, not smooth, and are not in actual contact with each other. The upper roll, in fact, is made to revolve two and a half times for each one revolution of the lower. Hence, the grain is caught between the fluted serrations of the rolls and is broken or cut by the faster roll as it is held back by the slower. The grist coming from the rolls is sifted through a 'plan-sifter'. This is a sieving machine containing tiers of nests of sieves. Each tier is divided into several groups of sieves of different degrees of fineness designed to separate the fine flour from the coarser particles. Only a small amount of flour is produced by the first break rolls.

In a modern mill, the broken grain from the plansifter associated with the first break roll will be passed to a second break roll where a little more flour will be sifted out. From thence it may be passed to a third and a fourth pair of associated rolls and sieves. The rolls are set progressively closer together and are each more finely fluted than the pair before.

B. *Reduction rolls.* The series of break rolls and sieves eventually converts the grain into *semolina,* which is small granules made up largely of endosperm; the outer husk will have been sifted out and collected as *bran* or *coarse wheatfeed.* The semolina is separated in a special plansifter into three grades—fine, medium and coarse—and these three streams, after being put through a 'purifier' which is an arrangement of sieves coupled to suction fans to draw off branny particles, are each passed through a further series of paired rollers and sieving machines.

This second part of the milling operation is called the 'gradual reduction system'. Here, the rolls are smooth and one rotates only one and a quarter times for each rotation of the other. This arrangement produces a crushing action which powders the granules of semolina into flour. It also flattens out the embryo of the grain and any branny particles that may be present so that they are more readily removed by the sieves. The general arrangement of the machines in a modern flour mill is shown diagrammatically on p. 48.

(c) FLOUR EXTRACTION RATE AND FLOUR COMPOSITION

The so-called 'extraction rate' of flour is the percentage of the original weight of wheat entering the mill that is recovered as flour.

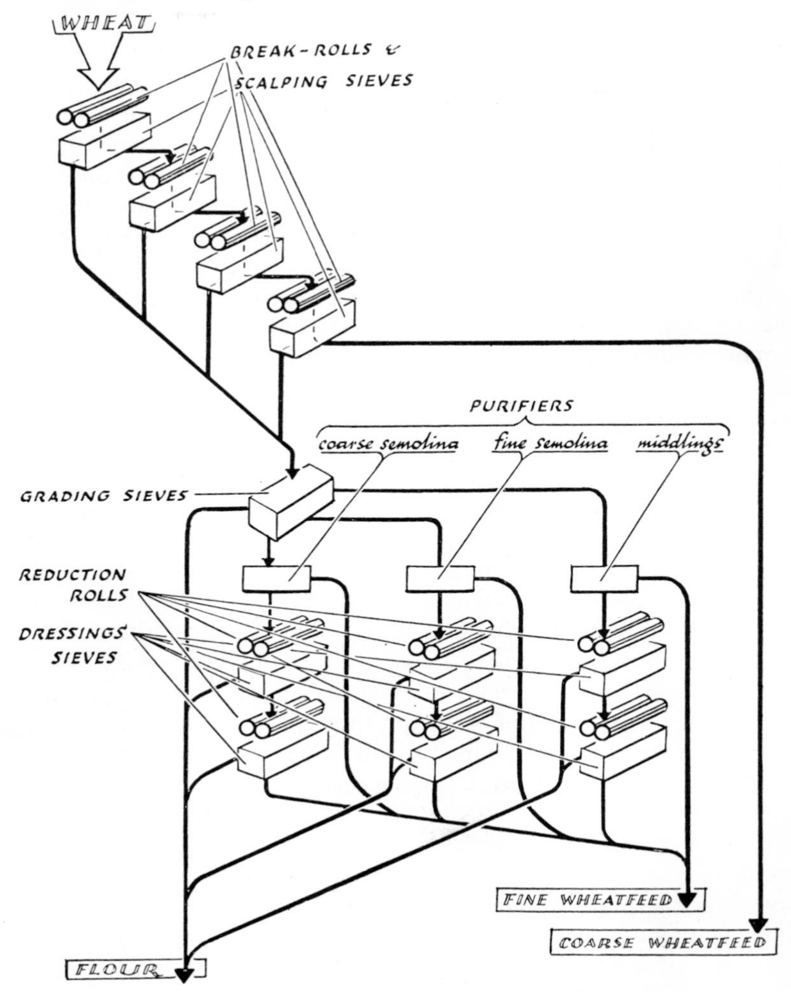

Fig. 5. Simplified flow-diagram of the processes of flour milling.

'Wholemeal' flour, which is usually the fraction leaving the break-rolls with only the coarse bran removed, has an extraction rate of about 95%. By an appropriate adjustment of the sieves in the reduction system, the miller can vary the extraction rate of the flour he recovers and produce a brownish flour of 85% extraction, a creamy flour of 80% extraction or a white flour of 70% extraction or less. White flours are more stable to store and produce bread usually considered to be of superior quality than darker flours. The flours of higher extraction rate, however, possess certain differences in nutritional value; these differences are shown in Table 4.

Two different groups of chemical compounds, designated as 'additives', are commonly incorporated in flour. One group comprises vitamins and mineral substances designed to improve the nutritive value, particularly of low-extraction flour; the other includes bleaching agents and 'improvers' to enhance the technical quality of the subsequent bread. These additives are discussed in Chapter 9.

Table 4

Composition of flours milled to different extraction rates

(per 100 g.)

Percentage extraction	*Calories*	*Protein*	*Fat*	*Fibre*	*Calcium*	*Phytic acid* phosphorus*	*Vitamin B_1*	*Riboflavin*	*Niacin*
		g.	g.	g.	mg.	mg.	mg.	mg.	mg.
100	328	13·6	2·5	2·2	28	242	0·37	0·12	3·5
85	339	13·6	1·7	0·3	19	96	0·29	0·07	2·1
80	341	13·2	1·4	0·1	15	63	0·24	0·06	1·6
70	341	12·8	1·2	trace	13	30	0·08	0·05	1·2

* This is an undesirable component.

The figures shown in the table can only be taken as characteristic of one particular wheat. Values for individual wheats will vary according to:

(i) *The wheat variety* or mixture of varieties.
(ii) *The weather* during the growing season and the *nature of the soil.*
(iii) The precise *conditions of milling.*

It is even possible for flour milled from the same wheat to the same extraction rate at two different mills to possess different analyses. The reason for this might be the different degree to which the *aleurone* layer and particularly the *scutellum* were either incorporated in the flour or excluded from it by being powdered during the milling process and allowed to pass through the sieves by which the flour was separated. The relative content of vitamins in the different structures of which the wheat grain is composed is shown below in Table 5.

Table 5
Vitamin content of different parts of the wheat grain

	Proportion of whole grain	*Vitamin* B_1	*Riboflavin*	*Niacin*
	%	mg./100 g.	mg./100 g.	mg./100 g.
Whole wheat	100	0·36	0·16	5·0
Endosperm flour	85	0·48	0·07	2·2
Bran and aleurone layer	12	0·45	0·50	25·0
Scutellum	1·5	16·55	1·50	6·0
Embryo	1	0·90	1·50	6·0

(d) THE AIR CLASSIFICATION OF FLOUR

During the 1950s an ingenious technical method was developed to enable the miller to separate the components of flour more completely than can be done by other means. Although flour is mainly composed of the endosperm of the wheat grain, this is itself a complex structure in which starch grains of different sizes are contained within a honeycomb structure. The cells of this framework are composed of very thin cellulose within which there is a lining of protein. When the endosperm is broken up into flour, the flour itself consequently comprises separated starch grains, fragments of the protein shell of the honeycomb cells, and larger pieces in which the starch cells and the outer framework are still stuck together. In the so-called 'air classification process', the flour is first passed through an 'impact grinder'. This serves the purpose of knocking the agglomerated lumps to pieces without breaking up the starch grains themselves. One form of machine consists of two parallel discs, fitted with a large number of pins, one of which is rapidly revolving. The flour then goes into a circular chamber in which a fan is creating an air vortex. This sucks the smaller particles towards the middle from whence they are drawn out of the machine, while the larger

Table 6

The component fractions of flour from an English wheat

Proportion of flour	*Size*	*Protein content*	*Types of particles*		
%	μ	%	Starch grains	Separate wedges of protein	Agglomerate material
4	0–13	19	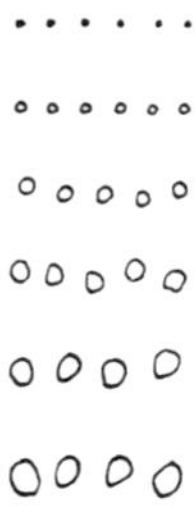		
8	13–17	14			
18	17–22	7			
18	22–28	5			
9	28–95	7			
43	over 35	11·5			

particles tend to be thrown towards the outer circumference of the chamber.

The make-up of a characteristic flour made from English wheat is shown in Table 6.

Table 7

The protein content of fractions separated from two different types of flour by air classification with and without pinned-disc grinding

	Protein content, %	
	Without grinding	With grinding
1. *Flour from soft wheat (8·3% protein)*		
Fine fraction (0–17μ)	15·9	18·8
Medium fraction (17–35μ)	3·9	5·7
Coarse fraction (over 35μ)	9·7	8·9
2. *Flour from hard wheat (11·3% protein)*		
Fine fraction (0–17μ)	17·4	20·6
Medium fraction (17–35μ)	9·8	8·6
Coarse fraction (over 35μ)	11·6	10·0

Air classification enables the miller to produce a fine flour with a very low protein content or alternatively he can obtain flour with significantly increased amounts of protein. Table 7 shows the variation in composition of the fractions which can be separated from a single sample of flour by this means.

(e) 'STRONG' AND 'WEAK' FLOUR

The structure of a baked commodity, whether it is bread, flour confectionery or biscuits, is affected not only by the total amount of protein in the flour but also by the chemical structure of the protein. 'Hard' wheats grown in dry climates, particularly Canada, produce 'strong' flour well suited for bread-making. 'Soft' wheats grown under more humid conditions are used to make cakes and pastry.

The selection of uniform flour of the appropriate 'strength' is important for the successful operation of automatic cake-making and biscuit-making plants. Besides being of a low extraction rate of 70% or less and consequently of low protein content, the particle size of such flour should be very fine.

A number of specialized laboratory instruments have been developed to measure flour 'strength'. The use of chemical agents to 'improve' the protein structure of flours is discussed in Chapter 9.

3. Baking bread

Three technological principles underlie the baking of bread:

(i) *Conversion of starch.* Part of the starch comprising the major component of the flour must be converted into sugar capable of being fermented by yeast. The fermentation involves the conversion of the flour-sugar into alcohol with the simultaneous release of carbon-dioxide gas (CO_2). The CO_2 gas gives the dough the light porous structure which is retained to form the open honeycomb texture of the finished bread.

(ii) *Mechanical stretching.* The gluten fibres of the flour protein are stretched mechanically to obtain a fine, silky structure; this becomes fixed when the protein is *denatured* by the heat of the oven as the bread is baked. The stretching of the gluten is partly achieved by the development of CO_2 bubbles during the fermentation and partly by mechanical mixing.

(iii) *Flavouring.* The alcohol and the numerous other products of yeast fermentation give the bread its flavour, together with the products formed primarily in the crust by the heat of the oven.

(a) NORMAL BAKING TECHNOLOGY

(i) *Dough mixing.* A usual method of converting flour into dough is to mix two 'sacks' (usually 560 lb.) of flour, together with 4 lb. of fat and 10 lb. of salt, with 30 gallons (135 litres) of water, in a small fraction of which 5 to 6 lb. of pressed bakers' yeast has been suspended. The temperature of the water is adjusted so that the dough after 15 minutes' mixing in a mechanical mixer has a temperature of about 24°C (78°F). Mixing the flour with water has two important effects: (A) The flour *enzymes* convert part of the starch into *maltose,* which commonly forms the main nutrient for the yeast. In the United States and in some other countries, sugar is added to the flour-fat-salt mixture; when this is done, the flour becomes largely independent of any maltose to be released by the enzymes. (B) The mechanical work done by the blades of the dough-mixer starts to stretch the fibres of gluten, the protein of the flour.

(ii) *Bulk fermentation.* The dough is maintained at its temperature of 24°C, covered to prevent the evaporation of moisture, and allowed to ferment for, say, two and a half hours. Varying fermentation times are used in different processes. At the end of this period the dough will have risen to the top of the bowl. It is cut up with a knife, remixed mechanically for five minutes and then allowed to ferment for another one and a half hours.

(iii) *Dividing and moulding.* After this four-hour period of fermentation in bulk, the dough is put through a 'divider'. This is a machine that cuts it into accurately weighed pieces, usually of 2 lb. each, out of which the individual loaves will be produced. These pieces are rolled mechanically into balls by a machine called a 'moulder', and dropped by the machine into a series of slowly moving canvas pockets, which travel in a temperature-controlled compartment called a 'first prover'. The time spent in the 'first prover', usually about 10 minutes, allows the gluten fibres, which have been rather roughly stretched by the 'moulder', to recover.

(iv) *Proving.* The relaxed dough pieces are dropped out of the canvas pockets into a second moulding machine which, in its turn, drops the now sausage-shaped pieces of still-fermenting dough into individual baking tins. These travel slowly through another 'prover' for 40 to 50 minutes, where the temperature is maintained between about 95°F and 100°F (35°C to 38°C).

(v) *Baking.* If the physics and biochemistry of the whole operation have gone exactly to plan, that is to say, if the fermentative activity of the yeast has been precisely what was expected and the 'strength' of the flour protein has been the same as that for which the times and temperatures of the process used has been worked out, then the dough will have risen to the appropriate height in the tins—and no higher.

In a modern bakery, the prover is so arranged that the emerging tins can be transferred directly into the oven; if a travelling prover is used, then it will be employed in association with a travelling oven. This is commonly adjusted so that the loaves are exposed to an atmosphere of 480°F to 500°F (250°C to 260°C), injected with steam, for a period of 40 to 50 minutes.

(b) CONTINUOUS DOUGHMAKING

Continuous doughmaking is a modern development in food technology. A powerful mixer pulls out the protein fibres of the gluten in a single rapid operation in place of the slow stretching brought about by the production of gas bubbles in yeast fermentation.

The main differences between the more conventional fermentation process and the process using continuous doughmaking are shown diagrammatically in Figures 6 and 7.

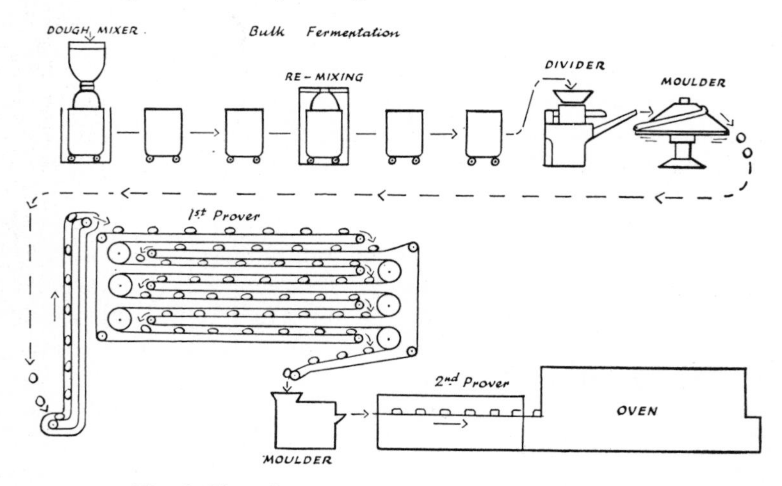

Fig. 6. Flow-diagram of a conventional plant bakery.

The dry flour is metered through a pipe into a pre-mixing tank and at the same time a measured amount of a brew of fermenting sugar is pumped in. This brew is prepared about two hours beforehand and is composed of the groups of ingredients as shown in Table 8 on p. 59.

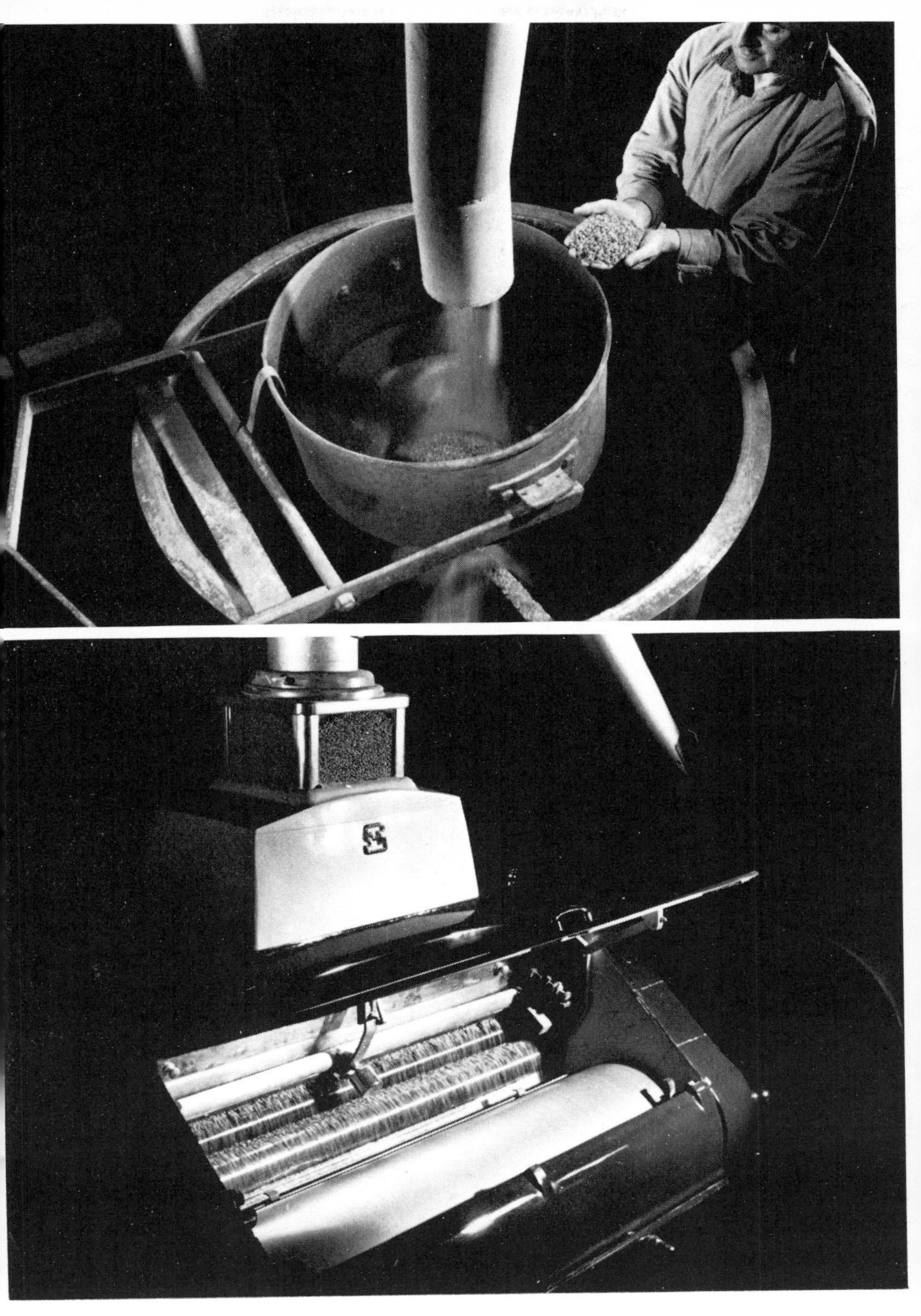

WHEAT. 7: Preliminary sieving of the wheat before milling. 8: Grist passing through one of the sets of break rolls.

BREAD. 9: A long dough moulder, which extrudes dough in 150 cm long loaves, kneading, shaping, rolling and depositing it into proving trays for baking.

BREAD. 10: The effects of 'improver' treatment on bread quality; (*left*) no treatment, (*centre*) normal improver treatment, (*right*) over-treatment. This is discussed in Chapter 9. 11: Different bread textures obtained by appropriate settings of a continuous doughmaking machine.

RICE. 12: A machine for cleaning milled rice and packing it into weighed 1 lb packets.

When the brew and the flour have been put together with the right amount of water for the particular flour in use, they are mixed by means of a powerful arrangement of blades. It has been found that 0·4 to 0·5 horse-power-minutes of work/lb. of dough must be applied by the blades of the mixer to obtain a satisfactory 'development' of the gluten. This work causes the temperature of the dough to rise.

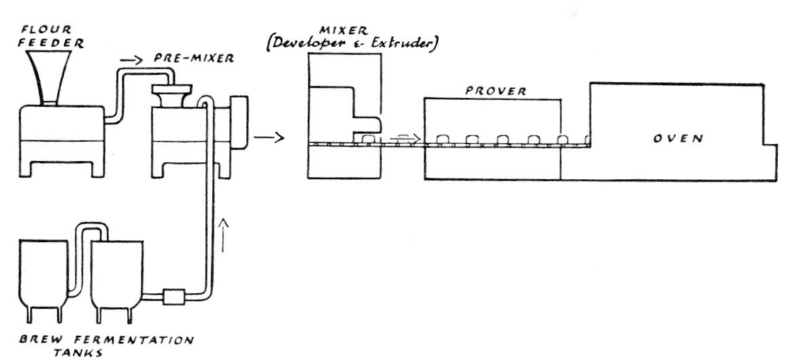

Fig. 7. Flow-diagram of a plant bakery using a pre-mixed brew and a mixer-developer for continuous dough-making.

Table 8

Composition of brew for continuous doughmaking (per 100 lb. flour)

(A) *Fermentable sugar:* usually white sugar (sucrose).	6 to 12 lb.
(B) *Other yeast nutrients:* calcium acid phosphate, chlorides and sometimes small amounts of magnesium and trace substances. Malt is sometimes added as a source of nutrients.	4 to 8 oz.
(C) *A 'buffering' system* to maintain an appropriate acid/alkali balance. The most suitable pH is between 4·0 and 5·4. Substances found to maintain this pH most effectively in the brew are dried milk, soya flour or even a proportion of normal wheat flour.	1½ to 6 lb.
(D) *Yeast.* It is usually found that for continuous doughmaking about three times as much yeast, in proportion to the flour, as the quantity used for the normal batch process is required for good texture and flavour.	2 to 3 lb.

It is necessary, therefore, to arrange matters so that the pieces of dough extruded from the mixer into the baking tins are at a temperature of about 24°C. It is while the tins are travelling from the doughmaking machine to the oven that the sole opportunity for fermentation occurs. In the continuous process, however, the function of fermentation is only to produce a porous structure in the bread and contribute flavour. The attainment of an appropriate gluten structure must be brought about by the mixing operation.

(c) THE DEVELOPMENT OF DOUGH

(i) *Mechanical 'development'.* The purpose of continuous doughmaking is to substitute mechanical working of dough for the working which must otherwise be done by yeast more slowly during bulk fermentation. At the same time, the continuous process aims to do away also with the divider, moulder and first proof of conventional breadmaking. Many bakers have found, however, that better results can be obtained by restricting mechanization simply to doing away with bulk fermentations.

In the CBP process, 5-6 lb. of yeast, 5 lb. of salt, ½ lb. of hardened lard, 2 lb. of soya flour and ascorbic acid and potassium bromate equivalent to 70 p.p.m.* and 25 p.p.m. of the flour are put into an automatic high-speed dough mixer-developer and a sack of 280 lb. of flour automatically weighed in together with approximately 16 gallons of chilled water. A strong lid then closes automatically and vacuum is applied, since it has been found that if air is present when the dough is worked, bread of coarse texture is produced. Specially designed 'impact plates' revolving at about 400 r.p.m. and powered by a 60 h.p. motor then mix the dough, applying approximately 5 watt hours per lb. The exact amount of work is automatically measured and is delivered in 3 to 3½ minutes. This brings the flour protein to the correct degree of 'development'. The vacuum is then relaxed and the dough automatically discharged.

Following this mechanical 'development', the dough, which has a temperature of 88°F, is passed to a divider and a moulder and thence to a first prover as described in paragraphs *(a)* iii and *(a)* iv, p. 53.

(ii) *Chemical 'development'.* Bulk fermentation and mechanical 'development' both serve the purpose of drawing out the gluten fibres of dough to achieve a desirable 'silky' consistency in the final

* Parts per million.

loaf. The same result can be achieved by chemical means in a way similar in principle to the 'permanent waving' of hair. In the so-called 'activated development' process, the dough is mixed in a conventional machine. Before the mixing starts, however, a chemical reducing agent—30-50 p.p.m. of cysteine or 20-30 p.p.m. of sodium metabisulphite—is sprinkled on to part of it and at the same time an oxidizing agent—a mixture of 50 p.p.m. of potassium bromate together with 50 p.p.m. of ascorbic acid—is sprinkled on to another part of it. The whole is then mixed for 7 minutes so that the work consumed is about 1 watt hour per lb. and the final temperature 86-88°F. Dividing, rounding and proving followed by moulding, proving and baking are then done in the usual way.

B. RICE

1. Structure

The structure of a grain of rice is shown in the diagram on p. 62. The grain of rice, like the grain of wheat, consists of an outer *pericarp* and *testa* which make up the husk or hull. Next comes the *aleurone layer* part of which remains on undermilled or brown rice. The *scutellum* divides the *endosperm,* which is the main, starchy portion of the grain, from the *embryo* or *germ.*

2. Classification

Very many different varieties of rice are grown in different parts of the world. They can be classified into two main groups:

(a) Hard-grained rice. Commercial rice is derived from this. It has a hard, starchy consistency and breaks with a vitreous, glass-like fracture.

(b) Soft-grained rice. Rice possessing a soft, dextrinous grain is usually found in local varieties grown for consumption only in the areas in which they are produced.

3. Quality

For the food technologist, the quality of a sample of unmilled rice paddy depends on:

(i) The size and shape of the grain.
(ii) The conditions under which it was grown.
(iii) The degree of ripeness.
(iv) The amount of exposure to the sun.

The degree of ripeness, the moisture content and conditions of storage all affect the behaviour of rice during milling. Over-ripeness and excessive exposure to sun lead to cracks in the grain which cause breakage and it is primarily on the proportion of broken grains that occur during the milling process that the technologist assesses a quality grading.

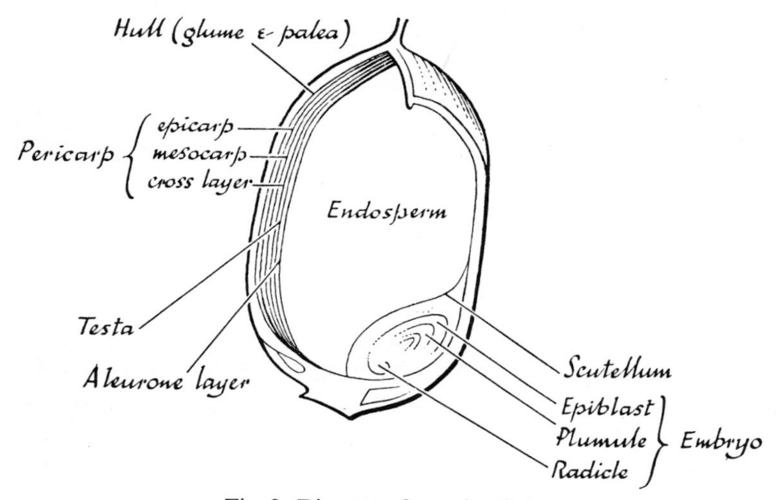

Fig. 8. Diagram of a grain of rice.

The technology of rice is less elaborate than that of wheat because the milled grain is commonly eaten whole and is not converted into flour.

4. Normal milling procedure

The grain is received at the mill in the form of *rough rice*.

(*a*) CLEANING AND SHELLING

The rough rice is first cleaned and then passed through a machine which removes the hulls. The hulls cannot be used as food but are sometimes incorporated as roughage in animal feeds. More often they are used for the manufacture of furfural which is employed as a chemical intermediary. The rice with the hull removed is called *brown rice*.

(b) SCOURING

The brown rice is subjected to a scouring process, which removes the germ and then gradually removes the outer layers of the bran. The combined germ and bran separated from the rice grain is marketed as 'rice bran' and forms a valuable animal feeding-stuff. The rice grain at this stage retains only a small fraction of the inner layers of bran.

(c) POLISHING

The grain is now passed to a polishing machine, often called a 'brush', in which the remaining bran is removed. This last bran fraction is marketed for animal feeding as *rice polishings*. The grain, now fully processed, is called *polished rice*.

5. Rice milling technology

(a) SMALL-SCALE MILLING

Most of the rice that is grown is milled and used in the households of the growers. When rice is milled by hand the paddy placed in a mortar is pounded with pestles which are sometimes worked by hand and sometimes with the feet, and after some time, the rice is sifted from the hulls. The pounding is usually repeated several times. The home-milled rice retains a proportion of the pericarp, testa and aleurone layers and its vitamin content is, therefore, greater than that of rice produced by large-scale machinery. Small-scale machines for hulling rice or for carrying out combined hulling and polishing are also available.

(b) LARGE-SCALE MILLING

(i) *Moisture content*

For satisfactory storage and subsequent milling, the moisture content of paddy must not exceed 15%. Rice grown in tropical countries is not likely to contain more moisture than this, but in America it is sometimes found necessary to dry the grain before processing.

(ii) *Cleaning*

The machines used for cleaning paddy are similar in principle to those used for cleaning wheat. The paddy may first be passed over a screen to remove large particles, straw and string; a second screen with small perforations allows the rice to pass over but removes dust and sand. The rice then flows in a thin layer into a channel where a current of air carries away dead grains and light impurities. Finally, there may be a magnetic separator to remove metal particles.

(iii) *Hulling*

The separation of the hull from the cleaned rice may be done with a number of different types of machines, but the commonest is the disc huller. The paddy is fed from above into the centre of a fixed horizontal disc, below which there is a similar disc rotating. Both discs are covered with emery to make them rough. Adapting the grade of emery to give the right degree of roughness is important, as different types of rice require different treatment.

The mixture of hulled grain, small paddy that has escaped hulling, husk and broken rice is passed over a series of sieves and blowers to separate the hulled rice.

(iv) *Pearling (whitening or scouring)*

The remaining layers of pericarp, testa and aleurone material are removed from the hulled rice by passing it through a series of 'pearling cones'. These are machines in which the rice passes through the narrow annular space left between an inverted cone coated with abrasive revolving in a conical casing made of steel wirecloth. As it passes down and is spun round by the cone the rice is 'milled' and the 'bran' is pushed through the interstices of the wirecloth.

(v) *Polishing (or 'brushing')*

To obtain a really fine white rice, the rice technologist passes it through a further series of 'polishers'. These are machines similar to 'pearling cones' except that the revolving cone, instead of being coated with abrasive material is covered with leather or sheepskin. Sometimes when a particularly sophisticated degree of whiteness and smoothness is required a small amount of talc is added when the rice is going through the last polisher.

The whole process of rice milling is shown diagrammatically in fig. 9:

(c) PARBOILING

The wheat technologist producing wheat flour finds that he can obtain a sharper separation of his various fractions if he 'conditions' or 'tempers' his grain before milling by treating it in water that is sometimes raised momentarily to as high a temperature as 75°C

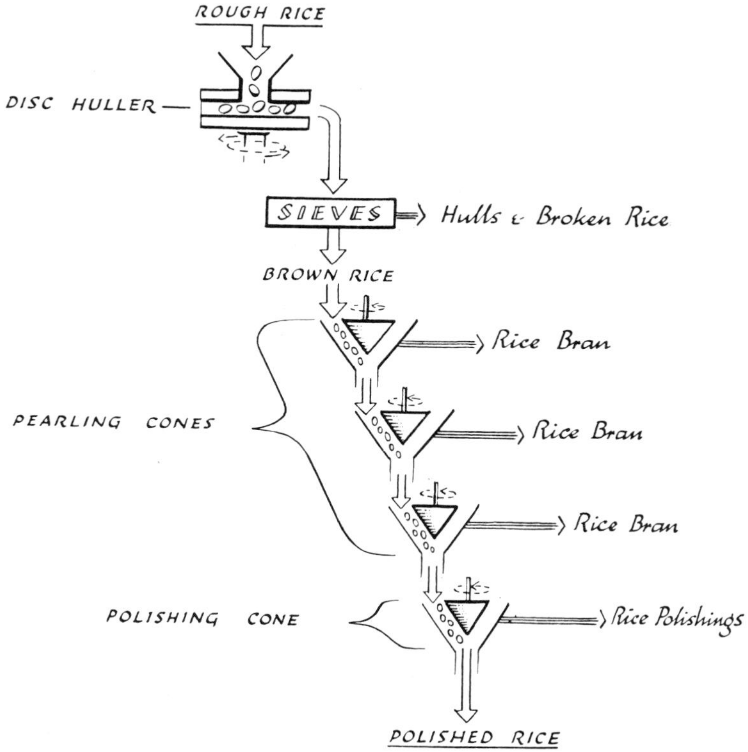

Fig. 9. Simplified flow-diagram of the processes of rice milling.

(167°F). In just the same way the rice miller finds that the proportion of polished rice free from broken grain obtainable from a unit quantity of paddy can be increased—from a figure of 66% up to 70% for normal grades of paddy, or from 50% up to 70% for low-grade paddy—if the paddy is treated with hot water before it is milled. This so-called 'parboiling' process is carried out in the following way. An additional advantage of parboiling is that it causes some of the vitamin B_1 from the outer parts of the grain to migrate into the endosperm and consequently improve the nutritional value of the milled rice. Figures are noted in Table 9.

(i) *Steeping*

The paddy is steeped in water in large brick tanks for from one to three days. The initial temperature of the water is raised to from

Table 9

Composition of rice before and after milling

	Carbo-hydrate %	*Protein* %	*Fat* %	*Mineral content* %	*Fibre* %	*Vitamin* B_1 mg./100 g.
Brown rice	86	8·7–9·9	2·2–2·4	1·2–2·1	0·6–1·1	0·40
Milled rice	90	6·7–8·6	0·3–0·4	0·4–0·9	0·2–0·4	0·07*

* Rice milled after parboiling has a vitamin B_1 content of 0·15–0·20 mg./100 g.

140° to 180°F. The length of the steeping must be judged by experience and depends on the quality of the paddy and the season of the year. Sometimes, instead of steeping for a period of days, the paddy is boiled for 20 minutes.

(ii) *Heating and drying*

After it has been steeped, the paddy is transferred to a steel tank and treated with steam at 15 lb. pressure for 10-20 minutes. It is then spread out and dried in the sun or in a steam-heated drying tower.

It is then milled. Although parboiled paddy yields a higher proportion of whole milled grain than untreated paddy, the parboiled rice is not always considered as acceptable by consumers because it is not so white. This defect is, however, counterbalanced by a very significant improvement in nutritional value.

6. Effect of milling on rice composition

Milling removes the indigestible husk of the rice grain but at the same time it reduces the proportion of fat and protein. The most serious effect, however, is the removal of the major proportion of the vitamin B_1. This is more harmful than the parallel reduction which occurs in wheat milling since in countries where rice is the staple diet it frequently constitutes a large proportion of the total food supply. A deficiency in this single item will, therefore, affect the completeness of the diet as a whole.

Table 9 shows the relative compositions of husked 'brown rice' and the same rice after milling and polishing.

The loss of vitamin B_1 in milling can be readily understood from Table 10 which shows the distribution of the vitamin in the different parts of the rice grain.

7. Artificially enriched rice

Where rice constitutes the major part of the diet the disease, beri-beri, which is due to shortage of vitamin B_1, may be a public health problem. Authorities may prevent it either by insisting on the paddy being parboiled before milling or by artificially enriching it.

One method of enrichment is to impregnate a proportion of polished rice with a water solution of 1 mg. of vitamin B_1 and 13 mg. of niacin per 1 g. of rice. Sodium phosphate is also added to the solution. The impregnated rice is dried and coated with a thin collodion membrane to prevent loss of vitamins when the rice is

Table 10
Vitamin B_1 content of the fractions of the rice grain

		Proportion of the grain %	*Vitamin B_1 content* mg./100 g.
Milled rice	—Inner endosperm	73	0·03
	—Outer endosperm	19	0·13
Rice bran	Pericarp, aleurone	6	0·31
	—Epiblast	0·3	0·78
Embryo	—Plumule	0·3	0·46
	—Radicle	0·2	0·64
Scutellum		1·2	1·89

washed before being cooked. This enriched 'pre-mix' is mixed with untreated rice in the ratio of 1:200. The mixed enriched rice is designed to have a vitamin B_1 content of 0·50 mg. per 100 g. and a niacin content of 6·5 mg. per 100 g., which is approximately the vitamin content of brown rice.

8. Manufacture of puffed rice

For the manufacture of puffed breakfast cereals, the grain may be pearled rice or wheat or other cereal including maize, rye or millet. The process has also been applied to peas and beans or to cooked dough. The grain or other material is put into a strong vessel usually constructed out of steel or bronze to avoid corrosion. This vessel, called a 'puffing gun', is heated and may be revolved in order to obtain uniform conditions for the contents. Steam is injected and the pressure increased until the required temperature is reached. This may be as high as 572°F (300°C). At this point the 'gun' is discharged by the operator suddenly releasing the pressure. This causes the steam inside the structure of the grain to expand and blow up the volume of the grain to about ten times its original size.

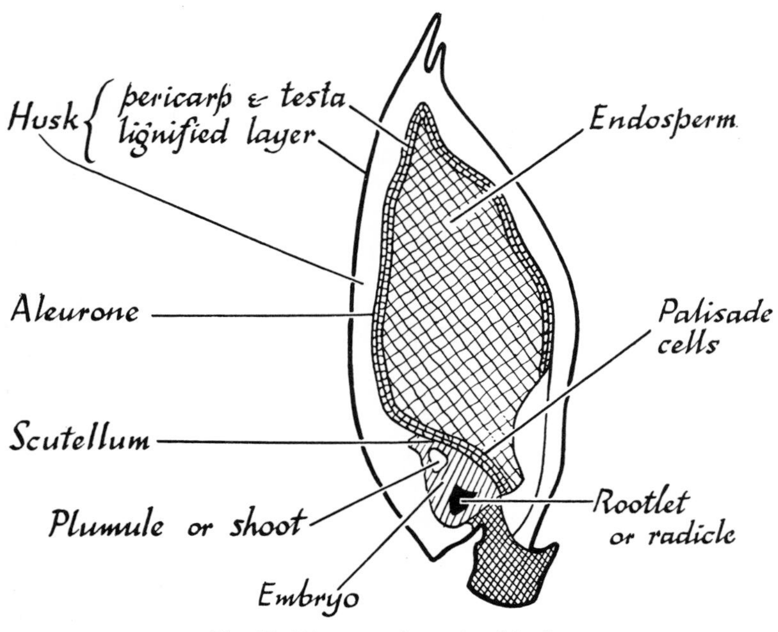

Fig. 10. Diagram of a grain of barley.

When the 'puffing' operation is over, the cereal is dried, often in a 'rotary toaster' and packed in a moisture-proof wrapper or carton.

9. Quick-cooking rice

One of the reasons why rice has not been particularly popular in Western countries is that it takes from 20 to 30 minutes to cook. Suitable treatment by the food technologist can provide quick-cooking rice which can be prepared for the table in from 1 to 5 minutes.

One successful commercial process involves heating the dry rice for 15 minutes at 93°C (200°F). This causes cracks of fissures in the grain. It is then soaked, cooked in hot water or steam, washed to stop the cooking process and dried in hot air to a moisture content of 8-14%. It is the initial fissuring that allows the final product to be so quickly cooked.

C. BARLEY

Barley is used widely for animal feeding. It is also employed extensively for the manufacture of malt used in brewing and distilling. Malting is a specialized procedure which is not included in the scope of this book.

1. Structure

The structure of the barley grain is shown in the diagram on p. 68.

2. Processing

Barley may be processed in a similar manner to rice. The husk can be removed by means of a disc huller and the whole grain then milled and polished, sometimes with the addition of talc, to produce pearl barley.

D. OATS

1. Structure

The structure of the oat grain is shown in the diagram on p. 71.

2. Food value

Oatmeal, made up of the whole grain with the hulls removed, has been employed as a valuable food, particularly in Scotland. In more highly industrialized times, its use tends to be restricted to prepared oat-flakes. The nutritional value of oatmeal or rolled oats prepared from the dehulled kernels is high. As can be seen from the figures in Table 11, it contains more protein and more fat than other cereal products.

3. Processing

The moisture content of oats stored for milling must not be more than 13%. As with other cereals, oats must be cleaned by appropriate sieving and aspiration before milling. To facilitate milling, the grain must be dried to about 6% moisture. If the final stage of drying is carried out at 180°F, the raised temperature makes the hulls more brittle and they are easier removed. Hulling is usually carried out by passing the oats between horizontal circular discs, the upper one of which is revolving. The dehulled oats, now called groats, are separated from the hulls by sieving. They may subsequently be steamed and passed between smooth rollers to produce oat flakes. Broken grains may be ground further to produce oatmeal or oat flour.

Table 11

Average composition of oats and oat products compared with other cereal preparations (%)

	Moisture	*Protein*	*Fat*	*Calories* (per 100 g.)
Oats				
Entire grain	10	12·2	4·3	319
Groats, oatmeal, rolled oats (without hulls)	9	16·0	5·6	380
Wheat				
Entire kernel without hulls	10	12·4	2·2	353
White flour	11	11·0	1·3	360
Rice				
Entire kernel without hulls	12	8·1	1·8	305
Brown rice	12	9·1	2·0	353
Polished rice	11	7·0	0·6	352
Maize				
Entire grain	11	10·0	4·3	366
Degerminated maize meal	11	7·8	1·3	357
Barley				
Entire grain	12	10·5	2·2	350
Pearled barley	11	8·5	1·1	355

The treatment of oats with live steam during the manufacture of rolled oats serves two functions. It raises the moisture content which prevents the formation of small particles and dust while the oats are going through the rollers. But the steam also destroys the enzyme, lipase, which would otherwise break down the fat in the oatflakes and produce a bitter taste.

E. MAIZE

1. Structure

The structure of the maize grain is shown in the diagram on p. 72.

2. Milling

(a) Cleaning. The maize is weighed and conveyed to a 'separator' consisting essentially of two sets of sieves equipped with an air aspirator. Dirt and foreign matter are removed by the sieves and dust blown away.

(b) Conditioning. The cleaned grain is passed into bins and is at the same time dampened by water sprays so that its moisture content shall become 14% to 16%, at which condition it is best suited for milling.

(c) Milling and degerminating. The conditioned maize is passed through a worm conveyor in which it is softened by being exposed to

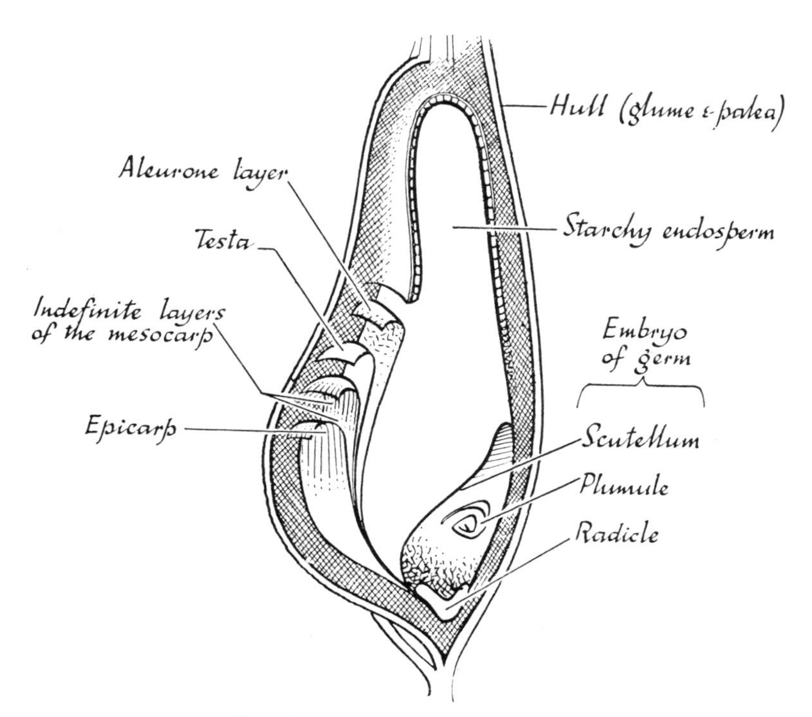

Fig. 11. Diagram of a grain of oats.

live steam. It is then dropped into a degerming machine consisting of a conical rotor revolving inside a conical stator. Both parts are fitted with rounded studs which break up the grain.

(d) Separation of meal. The milled grain is next passed through a rotary drier to reduce its moisture content to about 11%. It is then passed through a cooling worm into two rotating cylindrical sieves which remove the maize meal (corn meal).

(e) Separation of husk, germ and 'grits'. The milled grain from which the finer meal has been removed is passed through a separator. This sieves out the husk and germ, which are sold for animal feed. The remaining broken particles of grain are known as 'grits'.

3. Manufacture of cornflakes

(a) Cooking. Grits of uniform size, preferably derived from white maize, are cooked with live steam for two to two and a half hours, usually in rotary cookers. A flavouring syrup of sugar, malt syrup, salt or other ingredients is added.

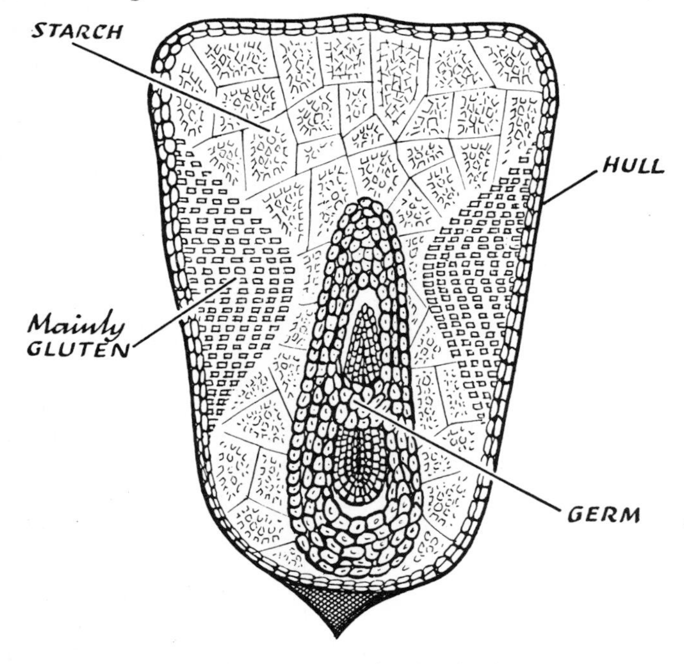

Fig. 12. Diagram of a grain of maize (corn).

(b) Drying. The cooked material is transferred into hot-air driers which are often cylindrical vessels fitted with agitators. The moisture content is reduced to 15% and the maize allowed to stand for six to eight hours so that its moisture is uniform throughout.

(c) Flaking and roasting. Flakes are formed by passing the cooked 'grits' between water-cooled rollers. They are sifted and passed immediately to a rotary oven. Thence they are again sifted, inspected and packed in moisture-proof containers.

4. Corn starch

To obtain the starch from maize, the grain is not milled dry, like wheat rice, but suspended in water as a slurry. The process is carried out in the following stages:

(a) Steeping. The cleaned grain is steeped in warm water, slightly acidified with sulphur dioxide, for 40 hours. (The steep-water is drawn off and, when concentrated by evaporation, can be used as part of the nutrient medium for the production of penicillin.)

(b) Degermination. The steeped grain is run through attrition mills to break it and free the germ. The slurry of ground maize is allowed to stand; the germ is lighter and floats, so it can be skimmed off. It is commonly used for the production of maize oil.

(c) Separation of starch from gluten. The settled grain residue is washed through a series of nylon screens on shakers to remove coarser particles. The remaining mixture of starch and gluten is then allowed to pass through a series of long sloping troughs. The starch settles to the bottom and can be removed and dried. The gluten is also recovered and dried and then mixed with the fibre fraction for use as maize gluten feed for animals.

5. Corn syrup

In order to break down chemically the long glucose chains of which starch is composed, the starch slurry from the mill is acidified with hydrochloric acid and heated under pressure. When the conversion of starch to glucose has gone far enough the acidity of the liquid is neutralized with sodium carbonate; the neutralized liquor is filtered; activated carbon is added to absorb impurities; the liquor is filtered again and then evaporated. This produces glucose syrup.

Modern methods, designed to produce corn syrup rich in fructose for the manufacture of soft drinks, bakery and dairy products, make use of enzyme technology. This is discussed in Chapter 11.

6. Glucose

To obtain crystalline glucose, the conversion with acid is carried out more completely. The subsequent evaporation is done more slowly and with mechanical agitation to encourage crystallization.

4

Meat, fish and poultry

A. MEAT

The food technologist who has to deal with meat must be properly informed about the structure and composition of meat derived from different types of animals; about the different kinds of bacteria and other micro-organisms which may infect it; the appropriate conditions for transport and storage; the factors affecting quality; and the principles of different types of technological processes. As well as all these, he must also possess an adequate understanding of the effect of the growth of an animal upon the character of its meat and the significance of the conditions under which an animal is slaughtered.

1. The effect of animal growth on meat quality

(a) RATES OF ANIMAL GROWTH

Studies of the details of animal growth have now made it possible for the farmer to change the conformation of the animals he produces, and consequently the quality of their meat, by the way he feeds them. For example, the proportion of parts of low meat-value, that is the head, shins and shanks, is greatest in a newborn lamb. As the lamb grows, its body lengthens and thickens and the proportion of head to shanks becomes less. There are two waves of growth; the first starts at the head, which is already advanced in its growth at birth, and moves backwards. The second starts at the feet and tail. These waves of growth eventually meet at the loin, where the meat is considered most valuable.

This rhythm of growth implies that the butcher obtains a smaller proportion of carcass weight from a young lamb (53 lb. for each 100 lb. of animal) than from a ram and the consumer gets less edible meat (31% of meat and 17% of bone); from a full-grown ram the butcher can obtain 67 lb. of meat for each 100 lb. of live weight and the consumer can expect 62% of edible meat and only 4% of bone. Of the meat of the lamb, only 2% is recognizable fat, but there is 30% of fat in the meat from the ram. It follows from this that the composition and quality of meat can be controlled to a very large degree by the way the animal is fed. If the beast is underfed throughout its life, the earlier maturing and dietetically less attractive parts—the legs and tail—grow, and the more desirable structures—particularly the loin—and the fat become less well developed. On the other hand, if the animal is richly fed in the early stages of its development, the age changes are speeded up and a young animal is produced with the desirable proportions and dietetic attributes of an older one. This is important in two respects. Firstly, smaller animals giving joints of meat that are smaller but contain the right proportion of meat and fat are produced. A second factor is that 'improved' breeds can be selected which are more readily affected by a high level of feeding. For example, whereas the growth of an 'unimproved' animal such as a wild boar is not much influenced by levels of diet, a modern meat animal is highly susceptible to this type of controlled husbandry.

(b) FAT

The 'quality' of meat depends to a large degree on the proportion of fat in it. The relative proportion of muscle, tendon and fatty tissue is not the same in all parts of the carcass. For example, in the same mutton carcass there may be 36% of fatty tissue in the loin and 22% in the leg. And different animals may put on fat in different parts of their carcass at different rates: for instance, the loin of South American lamb is usually more highly valued than the leg because it contains the 'right' amount of fat and the leg contains too little. On the other hand, in mutton from South America the leg brings a higher price than the loin because in the older animal the loin now contains too much fat.

Fat laid down under the skin is valuable because it prevents the meat from drying out during storage and cooking. This fat tends to be lacking towards the end of the limbs and it is partly for this reason that breeders select animals with short legs as meat producers. Fat deposited during the later stages of feeding is most desirable, especially in beef, because it tends to be laid down in the muscles as 'marbling' fat, where it breaks up the muscle bundles and makes the meat tender. It can be seen that fat in the right places improves meat

MEAT. The preparation of carcasses. 13: Dressing. 14: Hanging in store. 15: Grading.

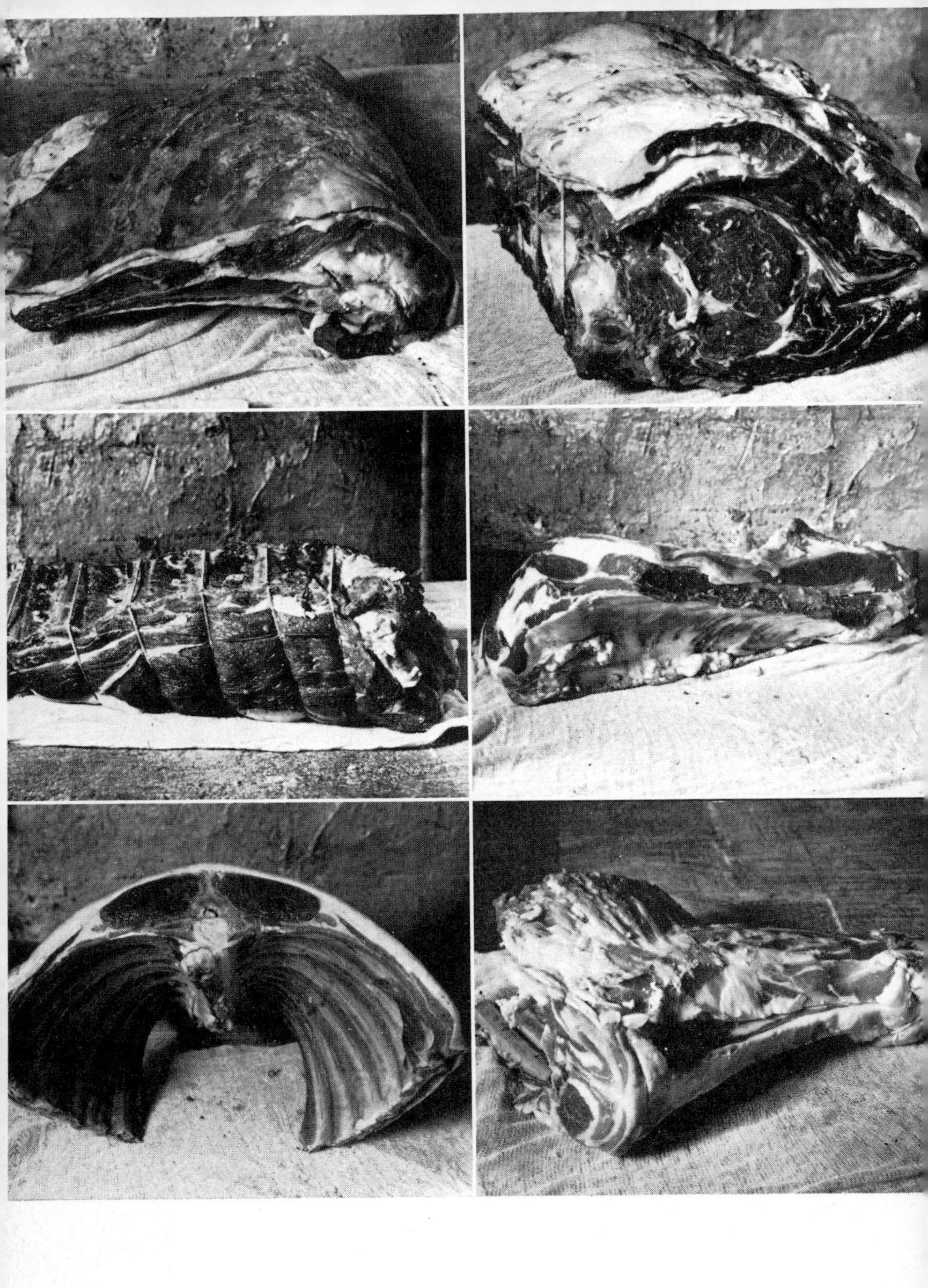

MEAT. Different cuts of beef and lamb. 16: Flank of beef. 17: Back rib of beef. 18: Top rib of beef. 19: Brisket of beef. 20: Best end neck of lamb. 21: Scrag and middle of lamb.

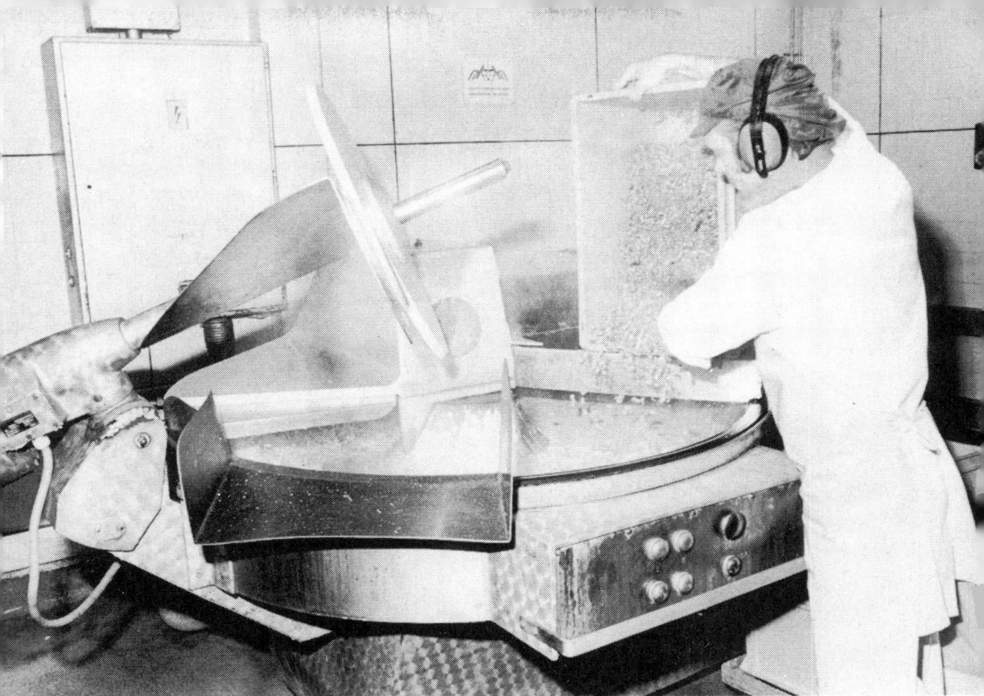

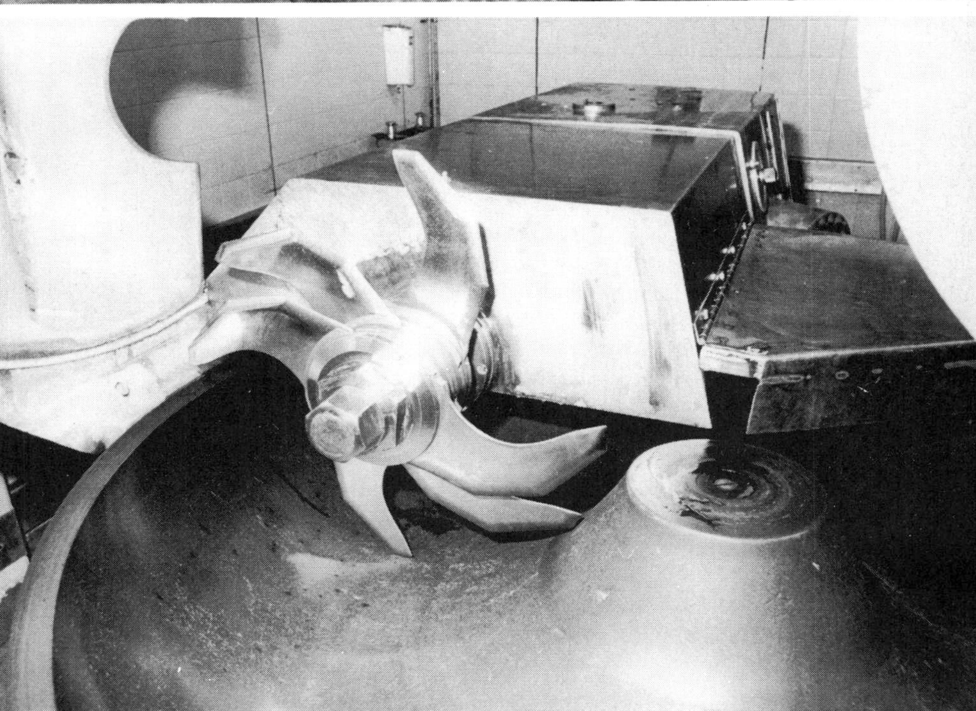

SAUSAGES. 22: A bowlchopper for preparing meat emulsions is seen being loaded with minced meat and other sausage ingredients. 23: The very sharp blades of an open bowlchopper are shown. The chopping blades rotate at high speeds and the product is carried through them by the rotating bowl.

SAUSAGES. 24: Skinless sausages being filled automatically into plastic casings from the bulk-product hopper at top right of picture. 25: When the sausage emulsion is heat set the skins are removed. As the sausages pass through the machine the temporary skins are slit by a fixed blade and blown off by compressed air.

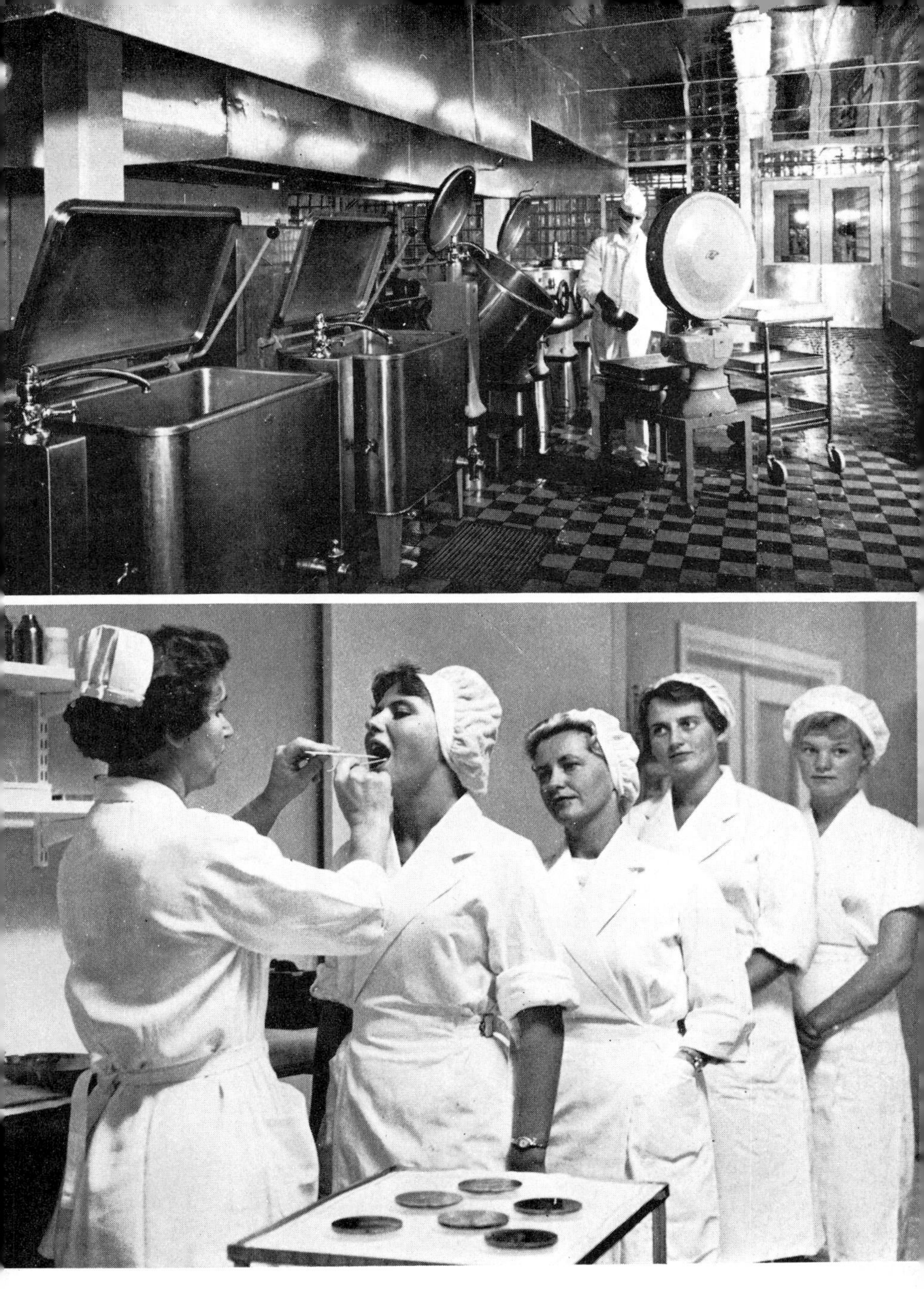

HYGIENE. 26: Sterile plant for the large-scale preparation of meat products. 27: Examination of food handlers to ensure their freedom from throat infection, boils, or infected hands capable of contaminating meat.

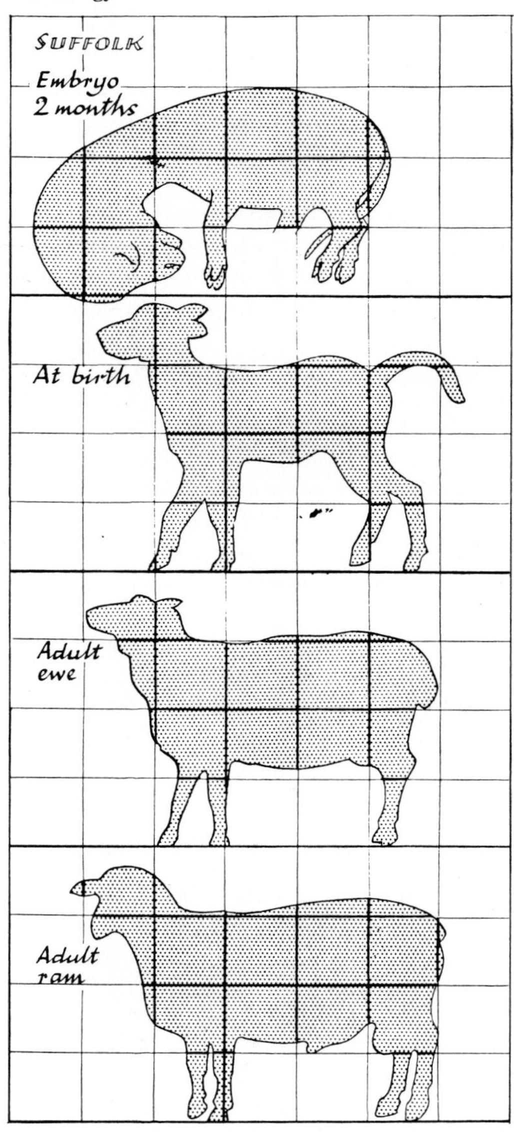

Fig. 13. This diagram shows the change in the relative sizes of the different parts of a lamb as it grows from a foetal embryo to a full sized ram or ewe.

quality; in the wrong place, for example round the kidneys, it makes no contribution to meat quality and is sold separately as suet.

(c) COLOUR

The colour of meat enables the consumer to estimate quality with some accuracy. An orange pigment in grass tends to be taken up gradually by beef animals into their fat. If the animal then goes short of food, fat is withdrawn from the animal's body but the pigment remains. Thus cows and old animals usually have darker fat than younger animals. Apart from fat, the colour of muscle is also an indication of quality. Muscles whose function is to sustain prolonged action are darker and more highly flavoured than those which are less used. Mild-flavoured meat is usually preferred, so it follows that pale-coloured muscle is an index of 'quality'. The muscles of a horse are relatively dark as also are those of an old animal, and neither of these is usually considered to give meat of high quality. The texture of muscle, and so its tenderness or toughness when eaten, depends on the grain or size of the 'bundles' within the muscle. In large animals, such as cattle, these bundles are coarser than in small animals such as sheep. Since the size of the fibres and the amount and strength of the connective tissues in the muscles increase with age, the meat of older, larger animals tends to be coarser, and tougher than that of younger beasts. Colour is, therefore, to some degree a measure of toughness. This is discussed in more detail later on.

2. Slaughter and meat quality

Butchering does not come within the scope of this book, but there is one important aspect of the slaughtering of meat animals which is of very direct concern to the food technologist.

(a) LACTIC ACID

Unless meat contains an appropriate amount of lactic acid it is sticky and flabby and bacteria are liable to multiply in it during storage. This is because a proper degree of acidity restricts bacterial growth. Muscular tissue contains in life about 1% of the starch-like substance, glycogen, which serves as the reserve fuel for muscular activity. This reserve can be depleted in some of the muscles by walking, running or fighting and it may take some time for the glycogen to be restored. When a rested animal is killed, the glycogen in its muscles breaks down and becomes converted into lactic acid, and the meat therefore becomes slightly acid. This acid exerts a preservative effect on the meat. If before it is killed the animal has consumed the glycogen in its muscle, for example, by being driven on foot to the abattoir or by struggling, the final acidity of the meat is very much less and its keeping quality is seriously affected. The acidity, as measured in pH values, for the psoas, the muscle situated below the backbone by which the hind leg is drawn up, for rested and exhausted animals may vary between the following values:

Table 12

	Rested (high acidity)	*Exhausted* (low acidity)
Beef	5·1	6·2
Lamb	5·4	6·7
Pork	5·3	6·9

In order that meat may keep satisfactorily it is essential that the animal should be killed when its muscles contain the maximum concentration of glycogen in them. This implies that beasts should be fully rested before slaughter. If they have been driven to the slaughterhouse on foot, they must be kept quietly for some length of time. For pigs, this may be as long as three days if the percentage of tainted hams is to be kept to a minimum.

Besides reducing the growth of bacteria, both inside the meat and on the surface, which are capable of tainting the meat and causing slime to form, a high concentration of lactic acid will improve the structure of the meat. Meat from rested animals has a more open and less sticky structure.

3. Bacterial infection and meat quality

(*a*) GENERAL INFECTION

Meat is a moist foodstuff and as such is readily susceptible to infection by bacteria and moulds. The degree of infection must be kept to a minimum. The best way to keep down the bacterial count is to ensure clean conditions of transport and storage. The slaughterhouse should be maintained in a sanitary state and the vehicles used for the transport of meat should be designed for the purpose, should be thoroughly cleaned before use and should be cleaned between one load and the next. During the 1939–45 War all kinds of vans, lorries and carts were pressed into service in Great

Britain, some of which were also used for other commodities without proper attention to cleanliness. Under these circumstances, meat infection increased and its keeping quality was reduced.

It has been shown that the storage life of chilled beef is inversely proportional to the logarithm of the number of bacteria per unit area of surface. It has also been found that the nearer the temperature of the chill-room or cold store is to the soil temperature of the place from which the meat-animal came, the greater will be the number of contaminating organisms capable of growing on the meat. It follows, therefore, that chilled beef from the tropics tends to have a longer storage life than chilled beef from more temperate climates.

(b) INFECTION WITH PATHOLOGICAL ORGANISMS

Casual infection due to insanitary transport, storage and handling is bad because it introduces taint and affects keeping quality, but it is not usually harmful to people eating the meat. The danger of eating meat from diseased animals has, however, been recognized in most countries and the flesh of animals which die of themselves is commonly discarded. The following are the principal infective disease organisms which the food technologist must do his best to detect and avoid by a proper system of veterinary inspection.

(i) *Bovine tuberculosis.* This disease can be overcome by a system of regular tuberculin tests and ruthless slaughter of infected animals. Tuberculosis is the principal reason why beef and pig carcasses are condemned as unfit for human consumption. Sheep are virtually immune from the disease.

(ii) *Anthrax.* This is a dramatic and deadly affliction derived from infected cattle. It is rarely found in Great Britain or other industrial countries with a good standard of animal hygiene but it may be found in contaminated meat meal or bone meal imported from Africa or India.

(iii) *Trichiniasis* is commonly among pigs in the United States and is also found in Germany and Poland. It is due to a small worm, *Trichina spiralis,* which is picked up by the pigs from infected food. Rats are thought to carry the infection and to contaminate the pigfood by way of their droppings. The human disease, trichiniasis, is a painful and prolonged one and, since it is difficult to detect the affected pigs, it is always unsafe to eat meat products containing pork that is raw or only lightly cooked. Consequently, certain types of sausages that are commonly eaten raw are a possible source of disease.

(iv) *Tapeworms.* When eaten by cattle the eggs of the human-infecting tapeworm, *Taenia saginata,* liberate a small embryo which works its way into the muscular tissue of the beast, usually the masticatory muscles of the jaw. The encysted embryo, if consumed by human beings, may grow in their intestines up to a length of 20 ft. and has been known to remain in the same individual for 35 years. Tapeworm infection from meat has been by no means uncommon in Denmark, Germany, Holland and in Great Britain during recent years and underlies the importance of the adequate heating of meat products during the course of manufacture. Tapeworms may also be disseminated by certain kinds of fish, including pike, perch and trout.

(c) BACTERIAL CONTAMINATION AND MEAT STORAGE

Bacterial infection can affect meat both on the surface and within the meat structure itself. The following points are of particular importance:

(i) *Bone taint.* This is caused by the internal growth of bacteria which may gain entry from the intestines of the animal. The flesh of beasts that are fatigued or frightened is, as has already been pointed out, particularly susceptible to bacterial invasion of this sort. Meat can also be infected if a dirty knife is used to cut it up. Temperature affects the final bacterial load; rapid chilling has been shown to reduce bone taint.

(ii) *Surface contamination.* The organisms that infect the surface of stored meat are mostly derived from soil and when the soil is cool and its temperature near that of the cold-store, infection is most likely. High humidity also favours the proliferation of surface bacteria and moulds.

4. Storage and transport of meat under refrigeration

A major part of the technology of meat is concerned with its preservation under cool conditions. The object of the reduced temperature is to arrest the processes which would otherwise cause deterioration and decay, namely:

(i) *Enzyme changes.* Enzymes are chemical substances which when the animal is alive facilitate the complex series of reactions by which life is maintained. These enzymes survive after the animal is killed and are present in meat. *Fat-splitting* enzymes produce rancidity, *oxidative* enzymes allow oxygen from the atmosphere to react with meat fat and produce bleaching and tallowy flavours. *Proteolytic* enzymes cause softening of protein and, since they make meat more tender, their effect is desirable. The action of all enzymes, desirable and undesirable alike, is slowed down by reduced temperature, namely, rapid cooling followed by cool or cold storage.

(ii) *Increase of micro-organisms.* Slime, offensive odours and mould growth are due to the proliferation of micro-organisms. These can be checked by reducing the temperature towards freezing and stopped altogether by deep-freeze conditions.

(iii) *Shrinkage and evaporation.* Stored meat shrinks due to the evaporation of moisture even when the meat is frozen. Shrinkage can be reduced if the atmosphere of the store is humid, but this encourages bacteria and mould unless the temperature is well below freezing. Evaporation can be reduced by wrapping, provided the wrapper is close enough to the meat to prevent ice forming inside.

(a) CHILLED MEAT

The structure of the muscular tissue of meat is irrevocably changed at a temperature of 23–25°F (−3 to −4°C), so frozen meat does not possess quite such a good flavour and consistency as fresh meat. It has been found, however, that beef 'chilled' to a temperature of 29·5°F (−1·4°C) can be kept in good condition sufficiently long to withstand quite long sea-voyages in properly constructed ships, or equivalent periods of storage. The following conditions must be maintained:

(i) The meat must be carefully prepared under the most hygienic conditions in order to keep bacterial contamination to a minimum.
(ii) The meat must be hung, not stacked.
(iii) It must be maintained at 29·5F (−1·4°C).
(iv) Storage life can be extended from about 30 to about 50 days if a level of 10 to 12% of carbon dioxide gas is maintained in the atmosphere of the cold store.

(b) FROZEN MEAT

About 25% of the water in the meat is frozen when it is held in chilled storage at 24°F. This gives firmness without excessive hardness and does not disrupt the normal structure of the muscle fibres. For longer storage, however, it is necessary to use a store below 14°F (−10°C) at which temperature microbiological growth is almost entirely stopped. Enzyme action is very much slowed at −10°C although a distinct change in flavour is apparent after, say, 12 months' storage. Freezing temperatures, however, change the structure of the protein molecules and affect their capacity to retain moisture. It follows, therefore, that when frozen meat is thawed it has a tendency to drip and its quality deteriorates.

The limit of storage time even at −10°C is the appearance of 'freezer burn', due to drying out of the meat and the development of a corky appearance.

5. Tenderness and tenderizing

As has already been mentioned, meat naturally contains proteolytic enzymes which are capable, when meat is hung, of breaking down to some degree the structure of the muscle fibres and making the meat more tender. The idea of treating tough meat with artificial preparations of enzymes is of some antiquity. Cortez, 400 years ago, commented on the fact that the Mexican Indians wrapped tough meat in leaves from the papaya tree which are now known to contain proteolytic enzymes.

A number of attempts have been made by food technologists to tenderize tough meat artificially by using specially prepared enzyme solutions. The difficulty in practice is to get the enzyme to penetrate sufficiently into the meat; the outside tends to become mushy before the inside is affected at all. The normal method of operation is to immerse the meat for a short time—say one minute—in the solution and then immediately place it in freezing storage to check and control the enzyme action. Enzymes for tenderizing meat have been obtained from the following sources:

Table 13

Enzyme	*Source*
Papain	The papaya tree
Bromelin	Pineapples
Ficin	Figs
Microbiological proteases	Fermentation

6. Some general principles of meat processing

A very large number of different types of meat products are manufactured to meet the tastes and customs of people living in different localities. These range through an infinity of sausages—in which finely chopped meat mixed with cereal, spices and diverse other ingredients is encased in a covering made either from the intestines of the animal used for meat or from a synthetic membrane—pies, pressed meat, and such specialized articles as haggis and faggots.

Numerous specialized machines have been designed for the manufacture of these meat products. The types of machine include grinders, cutters and choppers; disintegrators capable of producing complete homogenization of meat; machines for filling sausage skins; presses; and diverse kinds of ovens.

(a) BACTERIAL INFECTION

Skill and experience are required to produce on a large scale palatable articles suited to the special tastes of different groups of people. Underlying the skills needed to blend and combine ingredients to produce all these different commodities there is one important scientific principle, and it is this:

Of all foods, manufactured meat products are the most dangerous vehicles of pathological bacteria capable of causing food poisoning.

In a single year (1956), out of 268 outbreaks of food poisoning for which information was available, processed and made-up meat was the vehicle in 181, that is in 67% of all outbreaks. Details of the kind of meat products concerned and the types of micro-organisms causing the poisoning are shown in Table 14 (p. 94). Nor have things improved significantly during later years.

(i) *Salmonella* cause diarrhoea in people eating infected food. The sources of *Salmonella* infection in food are:

(a) Infected pigs, which themselves infect the floors of their pens.
(b) Infected cattle: droppings and liver may be sources of the organism.
(c) Sheep. They are much less often infected with *Salmonella.*
(d) Rats and mice, which are frequent carriers of infection.
(e) Ducks' eggs and bulked dried and frozen hens' eggs, which may be a source of infection in meat products of which they are ingredients.

FISH. 28: Freshly caught fish being cleaned. 29: Fresh fish being filleted before being frozen.

FISH. 30: Trays of herrings being loaded onto a trolley for smoking. 31: Herrings going into a smoking kiln.

CHICKENS. 32: Chicken-house for twenty-four birds. Modern technology may make this scale of operation uneconomic. 33: Chicken-house for 40,000 birds run by one man.

POULTRY. The large-scale processing of poultry. 34: Poultry being attached to the conveyor. 35: Automatic killing machine. 36: Automatic eviscerator. 37: Meat inspectors examining birds on the line.

(*f*) Human beings, who may carry *Salmonella* for prolonged periods and can infect their hands when passing stools.

(ii) *Staphylococcus* if allowed to grow in infected meat products can cause serious food poisoning. It may be derived from the following sources:

(*a*) Human noses: about 30% of all people harbour the organism.
(*b*) Infected cuts and abrasions, spots, boils and pustules.
(*c*) Cattle suffering from mastitis.

Table 14
Types of meat products causing food poisoning in England and Wales in a single year and the kind of micro-organisms involved

1. *Type of manufactured meat product*	*Number of outbreaks*
Re-heated meat	48
Meat pies	45
Cold meat, ham	25
Brawn, meat in gelatin etc.	16
Pressed meat	15
Sausages	8
Other products, stew, meat sandwiches etc.	24
	181

2. *Types of bacterial infection*

	Salmonella	*Staphylococcus*	*Clostridium*	*Others*
Sausages	2	2	—	4
Meat pies	7	5	12	21
Pressed meat	2	9	1	3
Brawn, meat in gelatin, meat roll, potted meat	4	6	2	4

(iii) *Clostridium.* These organisms do not cause poisoning by their immediate presence in the food eaten but by their ability to produce a toxin which may be present after the organisms from which they were derived have themselves been killed. A common strain, *Clostridium welchii,* can cause diarrhoea and vomiting; a strain which is fortunately less common, *Clostridium botulinum,* produces an extremely virulent toxin which may cause rapid, dramatic and painful death. The principal sources of *Clostridium* are:

Clostridium welchii: (*a*) Animal faeces.
(*b*) Human stools.
(*c*) Soil and dust.

Clostridium botulinum: (*a*) Soil.
(*b*) Vegetables contaminated with soil, leafy vegetables, green beans, etc.
(*c*) The intestines of pigs and some other animals.
(*d*) Fish.

7. Maintenance of hygiene and avoidance of infection in the manufacture of meat products

There are three principles that must be followed by food technologists who are concerned with the manufacture of meat products to ensure that these may be safe from organisms capable of causing food poisoning.

(*a*) DESIGN AND MAINTENANCE OF THE WORK-PLACE AND EQUIPMENT

In order to manufacture meat products safely the work must be done with much the same precautions as those used in an operating theatre. Walls must be washable and, if possible, tiled. Floors also must be washable and impervious to water. Windows should be double glazed to avoid the condensation of drops of moisture when steam is produced. Ceilings also should be easily cleaned and free from obstructions such as cold-water pipes which might cause drips. Tables, knives and other utensils, and all machinery must be capable of being completely cleaned and sterilized either with hypochlorite solution giving 100 p.p.m. of chlorine or by being boiled for 10 minutes.

The entry of dirt and infection must be rigorously avoided. There must be no direct entry between the work-room and a lavatory. Flies and vermin such as black beetles, mice and rats must be kept out.

(*b*) AVOIDING INFECTION BY WORK-PEOPLE

It must always be remembered as a basic principle of meat technology that *human beings are serious sources of danger.* Workers must wear clean overalls and a washable head-covering and ought also to wear a gauze mask over their mouths. Before starting work they should scrub their hands and arms like a surgeon does and *must always wash their hands and dry them on a clean towel* after using the lavatory.* Operators must not be allowed to work in a meat-product plant when suffering from boils or infections on their hands or from diarrhoea. Knives and utensils used on raw meat must never be used for cooled or processed meat products.

(c) DESTRUCTION OF HARMFUL BACTERIA

The consumption of uncooked meat, particularly pork, is always potentially dangerous. Whenever the nature of the article permits, therefore, the ingredients should be subjected to the heat of cooking. But even after they have been cooked, meat products are very susceptible to infection. They should, therefore, if they cannot be eaten soon after cooking, be kept at as low a temperature as possible before being eaten and never be touched with bare hands.

(Note: Canning and dehydration are discussed in Chapter 9.)

8. Manufacture of bacon and ham

(a) Bacon. Although the manufacture of bacon is today carried out under modern industrial conditions, the process of curing bacon and ham is based on traditional techniques for preserving meat. The scientific principles upon which bacon curing is based are, firstly, the partial drying of the meat brought about by soaking it in brine. The high concentration of salt in the brine draws out the moisture by the process of *osmosis.* By traditional practice, saltpetre, potassium nitrate, is incorporated in the brine 'pickle'. This serves two functions; micro-organisms which grow in the pickle change potassium nitrate (KNO_3) into potassium nitrite (KNO_2). This has a preservative effect by inhibiting certain decay-producing bacteria and food-poisoning organisms such as *Clostridium botulinum.* The possible implication of nitrite with trace concentrations of potentially carcinogenic nitrosamines is discussed in Chapter 9. It also combines with the red haemoglobin present in uncooked meat to produce nitroso-haemoglobin which gives the cured bacon its characteristic dark colour. This desirable red colour is gradually lost as the pigments are oxidized. This is why bacon is packed in airtight

* Disposable paper towels or long roller towels of which a clean, unused portion is exposed for each worker are ideal.

packagings to prolong its shelf-life. Finally, the bacon is dried further in the smoke of burning hickory or oak sawdust. The tars derived from the smoke together with soluble protein dried by the heat provide a protective covering to the meat.

While the original bacon-making process was designed as a primitive method of preservation, variants of the process which are used today are mainly designed to provide the taste and consistency most acceptable in different markets. For example, in the United States bacon made from the pig's belly contains more fat and salt than other varieties. In Canada, the fleshy part of the loin is commonly used, while in the United Kingdom, 'Wiltshire' bacon is prepared from sides of pigs carefully grown for the purpose.

The stages of bacon manufacture are as follows:

(i) The meat is placed in a brine made up of about 25% of salt and 1% of saltpetre. Sugar is sometimes included as well. The solution is, however, more complex since it is used for more than one batch of bacon and will therefore contain soluble materials extracted from the meat. The duration of the 'curing' process, usually done at a temperature of 38°F (3°C), depends on the size of the pieces of meat. In the United States, 2½ days per lb. of meat is allowed.

(ii) The bacon is removed from the brine, allowed to drain, and then kept in a cool place for one or two weeks to 'mature'. This allows the salt, saltpetre and sugar, if used, to penetrate more uniformly. It also allows the micro-organisms to convert the nitrate of the saltpetre into nitrite and to produce flavour and aroma.

(iii) The cured bacon is hung in a smokehouse and submitted to a controlled concentration of smoke. The amount of smoke can be regulated in modern plants by arranging for a separate combustion chamber and bringing in the smoke through a series of dampers by means of a fan. Originally, the bacon was partially cooked and smoked simultaneously by the burning sawdust. The present practice is to heat it in the smokehouse by steam coils or electric heaters and use the smoke solely for its content of phenolic combustion compounds. Modern processes go further and make use of 'liquid smoke' in which smoke flavours are applied by spraying the surface of the bacon.

More recently, the entire 3-stage process has been superseded by processes designed for speed of production and greater conrol over quality. Production lines for the continuous processing of sliced bacon are now available with capacities of up to one ton per hour. Pork bellies are cured by having the curing solution injected into them through a large number of fine needles. The meat is then transferred to a conveyor and passed through continuous cookers, coolers and brine-spray chillers before being moulded, sliced and vacuum packed. The whole process takes less than 3 days.

(b) Ham. In principle, the manufacture of ham is similar to the manufacture of bacon. Again, the process involves curing in brine followed by smoking. Since a ham is thicker than a side of bacon, it is usually the practice to force the brine solution, which as for bacon will contain saltpetre and possibly sugar, into the tissues by injecting it under pressure into an artery. This operation is called 'pumping'. The ham can then be immersed in 'pickle' for, say, 21 days. Smoking a 15 lb. ham may take up to 60 days depending on the particular flavour required. Once more, modern processes using injection curing and liquid smoking have been introduced. These have been combined with the tumble curing of boned hams to achieve a remarkable reduction in processing times and improvement in yields. Tumble curing involves holding injection-cured hams in rotating tanks with paddles or baffles which work or massage the meat to speed up the even distribution of the curing solution. The addition of phosphates or soya protein to the curing solution before tumbling helps reduce cooking loss, prevents shrinkage and improves colour and other desirable properties such as sliceability. A typical modern process is shown schematically in Figure 14.

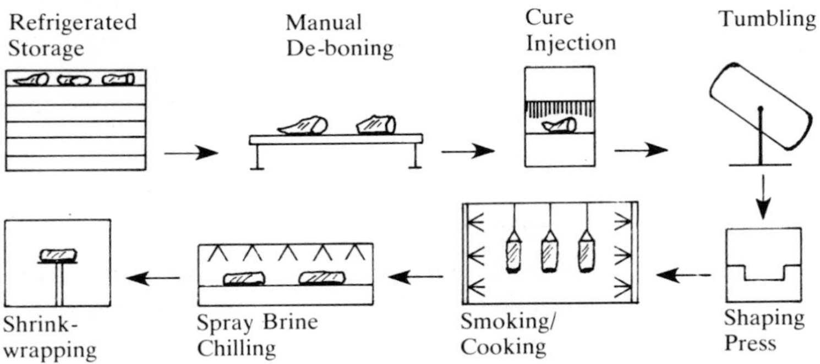

Fig. 14. Simplified diagram of a modern process for curing hams.

(i) Hams to be cured are held in refrigerated storage.
(ii) Bones are removed by hand before the curing solution is applied by direct injection.
(iii) The hams are tumbled to massage the meat and promote rapid distribution of the curing solution.
(iv) The hams are then put into a process casing and are pressed into a uniform shape.
(v) They are then cooked in an oven and liquid smoke is applied via atomizers.
(vi) The hams are cooled by a spray of brine and held overnight in a refrigerated room to allow equilibration of temperature throughout the mass.
(vii) The process casing is then removed and the final product shrinkwrapped in a plastic film for distribution and sale.

9. Sausages

Sausages are one of the oldest forms of preserved meat and were referred to by the classical poet, Homer. Basically, they are ground-up meat, either fresh or smoked, mixed with cereal and other ingredients and spices and usually packed in a casing made of the intestines of a sheep, pig or of plastic film. Fresh sausages are common in North America and the United Kingdom, but various types of sausage made from cooked meat, including liver sausage and blood sausage, are also made. Salami comprise ground meat and other ingredients allowed to cure for 48 hours, encased, cooked in hot smoke and then allowed a further period of air drying.

Skinless sausages are made by filling the mixture into plastic casing, passing the filled pipe of casing through a machine which ties it at regular intervals, passing the string of sausages thus formed into hot water which partially cooks them and then into cold water. They are then drawn over a knife which cuts the casing lengthwise and allows the now firm sausages to fall out of their skins on to a tray.

B. FISH

1. Varieties and structure

Sea fish fall into two main groups: the *pelagic fish*, which live in the middle and surface layers of the sea, and the *demersal fish*, which inhabit the bottom of the sea. Pelagic fish, which include herrings and mackerel, feed on the plankton which grows in the sea much as vegetation grows on land. Demersal fish, which include cod, haddock, whiting and flat fish, while they start their lives eating diatoms and plankton, subsequently live by preying on crabs and other medium-sized crustacea and later on small fish, herrings and sprats. The principal difference in composition and food value between pelagic and demersal fish is that the pelagic fish contain up to 20% of fat while the fat content of demersal fish ranges from about 0·5% for cod, haddock and whiting, about 2% for plaice, megrim, lemon sole and bass, and up to 5% for halibut, mullet and dogfish. The fat content, particularly of the pelagic fish, varies with the age and state of development of the fish. The figures given below show the variation to be expected in herrings:

Table 15

Season	*Fat content of herrings* %
April	8
June	13
July	20
October	15

The most important property of fish for the food technologist is that it is extremely perishable. Carp and some other varieties are kept in carp-ponds, and certain species have recently been farmed in irrigation canals, but on the whole fish is an anomaly in the modern world by being the only remaining wild animal which is hunted by civilized man for use as a major foodstuff. And for this reason much of the sea fish coming into the hands of the processor is—up until the present time at least—already stale by the time it arrives.

2. The effect of advances in fish technology on the quality of the fish marketed

The technical advances in ships and gear, together with electronic devices for locating fish, have led to an immense increase in the destructiveness of modern fishing fleets to the fish population of at least the North Atlantic, North Sea and other waters surrounded by heavily populated lands. Over-fishing and the consequent depletion of the nearer fishing grounds has led to the use of larger and more powerful trawlers capable of travelling into Arctic waters in voyages of three weeks' duration or more. Catches by individual ships can be anything from 50 to 200 tons of fish. The effect of these large-scale operations has been that mostly coarse fish are caught, three-quarters of which is cod, and none of it is improved by lying for three weeks or more in a ship's hold. It follows from all this that one effect of modern advances in fishing technology has been a deterioration in quality where the caught fish are merely stored in ice until the ship reaches land. Ice storage retards the deterioration of fish but does not stop it. The recent development of ships equipped with machinery for processing fish actually at sea has come about to counteract this trend.

(a) WHY FISH GOES BAD

There are two main reasons why fish goes bad more readily than meat:

(i) Because it is not possible to stop fish struggling before they die, the lactic acid content of their muscles becomes depleted.

(ii) Fish flesh contains between 0·2 to 2·0% of a nitrogenous compound, trimethylamine-oxide. After death, bacteria break down this substance into trimethylamine and other compounds. It is the trimethylamine which contributes the characteristic smell of bad fish.

The deterioration that occurs in haddock muscle due to the combined effect of proteinase enzymes and bacterial activity, even when the fish is stored in ice, is shown in Fig. 15 (p. 102).

When this knowledge of the deterioration of fish in ice was fully appreciated and when at the same time fishing technology had reached the point when, as is now the case, trawlers or the depot ships accompanying them to the fishing grounds were themselves equipped with refrigeration machinery, the advance in technology could clearly be seen to have improved the quality of the fish marketed.

(b) PRESERVING THE QUALITY OF FISH

The principles involved to ensure good quality are as follows:

(i) Scrupulous cleanliness and hygiene in handling the fish caught.

(ii) Immediate freezing to at least −10°C (14°F); the freezing time not to exceed two hours.

(iii) 'Glazing', that is arranging for a film of ice to form on each fish, to prevent drying.
(iv) Storage of the frozen fish well below −16°C (3°F).

If these conditions are maintained, gutted white fish can be stored for four months and ungutted herrings for three months without change in quality. These storage times can be doubled if a storage temperature of −30°C(−22°F) is used.

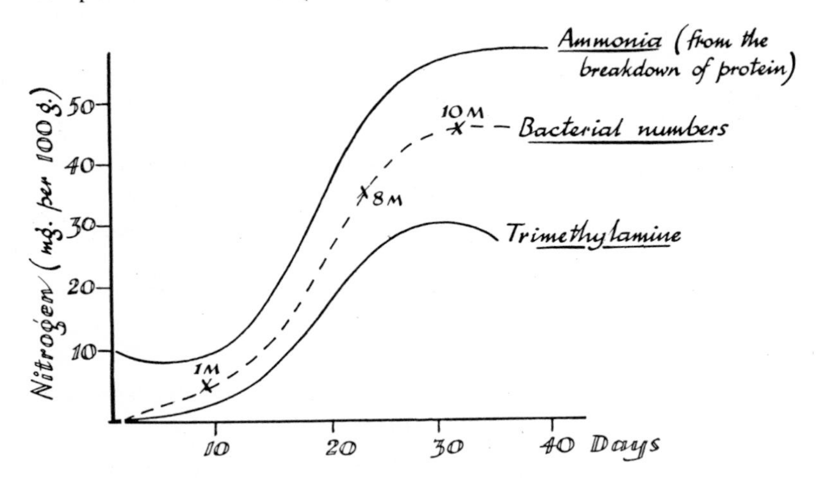

Fig. 15. The graphs show the increase in bacterial numbers and the corresponding increase in trimethylamine and ammonia in haddock stored in ice.

3. Curing

(a) SMOKING

The preparation of kippers, from herring, and finnans, from haddock is similar in principle. Two separate stages are involved:

(i) The fish is split and eviscerated and then steeped in brine composed of 70–80% saturated salt solution. This reduces the water content of the fish and also causes the surface layer of protein to coagulate to some degree. The brine in then allowed to drain away. Nowadays a brown dye is sometimes added to the brine to darken the finished article.

(ii) After treatment with brine, the fish is hung on racks in a kiln and exposed to smoke from burning wood or peat. This fuel may either be burned directly in the kiln or in a supplementary device equipped with forced draught to provide a controlled flow of smoke. The effect of the smoke is as follows:

(*a*) The tar and phenols from the smoke produce a desirable colour.

(*b*) The phenols and volatile acids provide flavour and odour.

(*c*) Formaldehyde and phenols convert the coagulated surface layer into a smooth, resinous pellicle which has a preservative effect.

When a smoke temperature of 25–32°C (77–90°F) is used there is a loss of moisture of about 15–20%. More highly smoked fish may be produced with a smoke temperature of 100–120°C (212–248°F). This produces a 'hot-smoked' product which has been partially cooked by the smoking process; such preparations are tasty and popular in several European countries. As with freezing, the quality of cured fish is affected by the freshness of the original fish and its sanitary state. During finnan curing, the bacterial numbers originally present are reduced by 85–90%.

(*b*) SALTING

This is a useful method of preserving fish. It depends on reducing the moisture content—salt fish is, in effect, partially dried. In addition the high salt content discourages the growth of micro-organisms which otherwise would cause decay. The flavour of salt fish is, however, strong and it is not to everybody's taste. Now that the more technologically sophisticated processes of dehydration and quick freezing are available, giving a product more closely resembling fresh fish, consumers are very much less willing to accept salt fish.

(i) *Dried salted white fish* (cod, ling, saithe, etc.)

The process of salting involves the following stages:

(*a*) The fish is split, most of the backbone is removed, and the split fish laid in piles with salt interspersed between the layers. The pile of fish and salt is left for up to a month or more, although the salt penetrates into the flesh in about 15 days. As the penetration occurs the process known as *plasmolysis* occurs. This is the tendency for the concentration of the solution inside and outside a semi-permeable cell to come to equilibrium. The high concentration of salt outside the fish causes the liquor inside to be drawn out and when it does so, it drains away. This extracted fluid is called a 'pickle'. The fish at this stage is called 'green cured' and its water content has been reduced from 82% to about 54%.

(b) The 'green cured' fish is next exposed on racks to dry in the sun and wind. It may also be hung up and dried artificially over a coke fire. The moisture of the finished article may be varied from 23% for 'hard dried' salt cod to 38% for 'hard dried' Canadian salt cod, to as much as 50% for less fully dried fish. Its salt content is about 28%.

(ii) *Salt herring*

The higher concentration of fat in herrings, their more variable composition with the changing seasons and the different consistency of their skin, which does not behave as a normal semi-permeable membrane, makes it necessary to process them differently from white fish. The following operations are usually adopted:

(a) The fish are sprinkled with coarse salt to remove surface slime and are then freed from their gills and guts.

(b) They are then packed into barrels with a layer of salt between each layer of herrings. After about 10 days the liquid extracted by plasmolysis, called 'blood pickle', is run off and the space left in the barrel tightly packed with cured fish from another barrel. The spaces between the fish are further filled in by returning as much of the 'blood pickle' as the barrel will hold. The net effect of the salting process is to reduce the original water content of the fish from about 62% to 50% and to reduce the fat content from, say, 22% to 15%. The salt content may reach about 12%.

Table 16

The stability of cured fish

	Stored at 0°C (32°F)	*Stored at* 15°C (59°F)
	(approx. number of days remaining in good condition)	
Fresh fish	2	1
Finnan haddock	6	2
Kippers	6	2
Salt herring	1 year or more	3–4 months
Dried salt cod	1 year or more	4–6 months

(Note: Dehydration and *deep freezing* are discussed in Chapter 8.)

C. POULTRY

1. Principles

The modern technology of poultry processing is a good example of the way in which quite complex machinery is being applied to the handling of large numbers of uniform items, the items being young birds grown intensively from standardized day-old chicks. The scientific principles involved are these:

(*a*) The use of uniform birds which are, therefore, all of similar chemical composition.

(*b*) Rapid killing, processing and cooling of the carcasses to reduce enzymic changes to a minimum. The need for a period of delay for 'tenderizing' changes to occur is avoided by the use of young birds.

(*c*) The maintenance of rigidly sanitary conditions and the quick freezing of the processed birds avoids the possibility of micro-biological infection.

An example of a modern process is shown in the diagram on p. 106:

2. Processing

The birds, which have not been fed for 12 hours in order to ensure that their crops are empty, are attached to the conveyor and stunned with an electric stunner. Low-tension alternating current at 90 volts is usually employed. Two cuts are then made through the roof of the mouth to sever the blood-vessels and nerve trunk. When the blood has drained out, the conveyor passes the birds through a scalding tank to facilitate the subsequent plucking. If the scalding is too severe, fat is dissolved and yellow pigment may be brought to the surface. A temperature of exactly 61°C (142°F) for 18 to 30 seconds is usually chosen; this is sometimes described as 'semi-scalding'. The best conditions for scalding will vary depending on the age and condition of the birds.

The machines for wet-plucking consist of revolving drums fitted with short lengths of rubber—called fingers—which project from it. Other drums have attached to them rubber flails. The combined action of the 'fingers' and the flails as the birds are exposed first one way up and then the other ensures the complete removal of the feathers.

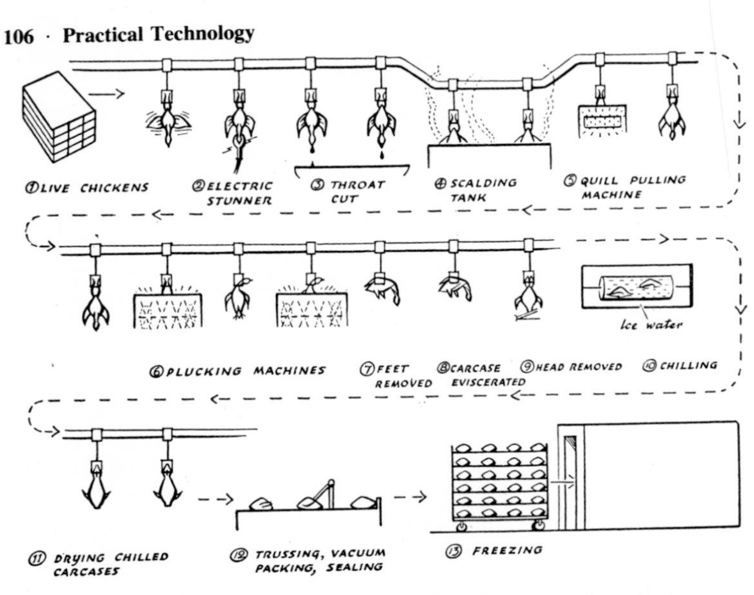

Fig. 16. Simplified flow-diagram of poultry processing plant.

The plucked carcasses next undergo (i) the removal of feet, (ii) evisceration, (iii) decapitation, (iv) cooling in a revolving drum, (v) trussing, (vi) packing in a plastic wrapper, to which a vacuum is applied to ensure its close adherence to the flesh and, finally, (vii) freezing.

Chickens which are raised on general mixed farms or in country chicken-houses are usually hung uneviscerated after being killed. The decomposition products formed in their guts diffuse into the carcass and give it a more pronounced flavour than that of birds processed by up-to-date technological methods.

5

Milk, cheese and eggs

A. MILK

Milk is a remarkable fluid in which the wide diversity of compounds necessary for the nourishment of a young animal are combined as a homogeneous mixture. The fat is in the form of globules which are surrounded by a membrane of lipo-protein (a combination of protein and fat), which prevents their coalescing. The aqueous part of the milk in which the fat is suspended is a water solution of protein, sugar (lactose), calcium salts and other minor components.

1. Food value

Milk is a food of high nutritional value. Its importance is based on three principal scientific facts:

(*a*) It is an exceptionally good source of protein which is of high biological value in promoting the growth of children.

(*b*) It is the best source of calcium in the diet and consequently encourages sound bone and tooth development.

(*c*) It contains a useful miscellany of vitamins, including vitamins A, thiamin (vitamin B_1), riboflavin, pyridoxin (vitamin B_6), biotin, niacin, pantothenic acid, vitamin D, etc.

In addition, the fat content is prized both as cream and as the main component of butter.

2. Possibilities of infection

The rich nutritional composition of milk, combined with the fact that it is a liquid made up of an emulsion of fat droplets each surrounded by a membrane of lipo-protein (combined fat and protein) to prevent its coalescing with its neighbour, suspended in an aqueous solution of protein, lactose (milk sugar), mineral salts and vitamins, gives rise to its main disadvantage from the point of view of the food technologist, and this is that milk is readily infected by micro-organisms. These are derived from:

(i) The cow, or other producing animal.
(ii) The equipment and utensils in which it is processed.
(iii) The people who handle it.
(iv) The atmosphere.

3. The composition of milk

The milk most commonly handled by food technologists is derived from the cow. The composition of cow's milk in comparison with that derived from other sources is shown in Table 17.

Table 17

The composition of milk from different animals

	Carbohydrate %	*Protein* %	*Fat* %
Human	6·2–7·6	0·6–2·0	2·0–6·2
Cow	4·2–6·8	2·5–4·0	3·0–6·0
Buffalo	4·5	4·3	7·5
Goat	4·5	3·7	4·8
Sheep	4·9	6·5	6·9
Mare	5·7	1·3	1·2

The composition of cow's milk depends on two factors: the breed of the cow, and the conditions of husbandry under which it is maintained. The so-called Channel Island breeds, Jerseys and Guernseys, produce milk containing 4½% of fat or more, whereas Friesian (also called Holstein) breeds can be made to give very large yields of milk containing 3% of butter-fat or less. For the full nutritional composition of the milk to be maintained it is important that the cow should be fed supplementary rations before the birth of her calf and for food to be supplied subsequently in proportion to the amount of milk yield. Furthermore, the colour of the milk and its content of vitamin A and vitamin A-active carotene are dependent on the amount of green herbage in the cow's diet. It has been shown that the feeding of properly prepared dried grass to cows during the winter months maintains an adequate nutritional standard in the milk produced.

4. Liquid milk technology

(*a*) PASTEURIZATION

The pasteurization of milk is carried out either by the 'holder process', in which the milk is heated to 63–65°C (145–150°F), held at this temperature for 30 minutes and then cooled, or by the 'flash process', when it is heated to 72°C (162°F) for 15 seconds before being cooled again. *Pasteurization,* or sterilization which is discussed below, *is an essential part of all processes of milk technology where large quantities of milk are handled.*

Pasteurization has the following effects:

(a) It destroys any tuberculosis infection derived from the cow and also other bovine infections such as *Brucella abortus* capable of producing undulant fever and *Streptococcus pyogenes* causing septic sore throat and scarlet fever.

(b) It reduces the number of milk-souring organisms and other bacteria causing milk to 'go bad'; the process consequently prolongs the useful life of the milk.

(c) It destroys bacteria accidentally derived from equipment, utensils and milk handlers.

(d) Extensive studies have shown that pasteurization properly carried out has no significant effect on the chemical composition and the flavour of milk to counterbalance its great importance as a safety measure. In only one respect, pasteurization produces a material change: it reduces the small amount of vitamin C that milk naturally contains. Providing infants with orange juice or some other source of vitamin C, which is now general paediatric practice, is thus doubly important when pasteurized milk is used as the major component of a baby's diet.

(i) *Holder-process pasteurization*

This may be arranged as the simplest form of pasteurization. The milk is pumped through a stainless steel heat-exchanger in which it passes across one side of a series of plates which are in contact with hot water on the other side. The milk emerges from the heat-exchanger and passes into a stirred tank in which it is held for 30 minutes at 65°C. This tank is preferably fitted with a temperature recorder coupled to a clock to ensure that the temperature is maintained long enough to destroy the bacteria but not so long that the milk flavour is impaired. At the end of the 30 minutes, the milk is run out over a surface cooler or through another heat-exchanger in which cold water is run counter-current to the milk on the reverse side of the plates.

(ii) *Flash pasteurization*

Short-time, high-temperature pasteurization may be used to treat a continuous flow of milk. Pasteurizing units can be constructed in

MILK. 38: Traditional milk-bottling plant. 39: Aseptic filler capable of filling 5,000 cartons of long life milk per hour.

MILK. 40: Modern automated rotary milking system capable of handling 24 cows at one time.

CHEESE. Stages in the modern manufacture of cheese. 41: Cheese vats, containing 13,000 litres (3,000 gallons), where milk is separated into curds and whey. 42: The curd, formed in the cheese vats, rests for 1½ hours in the cheddaring tower before being milled into 'chips'.

CHEESE. 43: Salted, milled curd passing along a conveyor-belt to the cheese-presses. 44: Curd being fed into a 1-tonne cheese-press.

such a way that the required conditions of 72°C for 15 seconds are safely maintained under automatic control. A system of operation is shown in the diagram below.

The raw milk flows through a first heat-exchanger 'a' (the 'regenerator') through which the already pasteurized milk is flowing on the reverse side of the plates. This serves to warm the incoming raw milk. The raw milk then passes through a second heat-exchanger 'b' (the 'heater') which brings its temperature up to 72°C. It is then pumped through the holding tube 'c' which is of such a length and diameter in relation to the capacity of the pump that each particle of milk takes 15 seconds to pass through. At the end of this pipe there is a thermostatically controlled valve 'd' so adjusted that, should the temperature of the emerging milk be more than 0·3°C (0·5°F) below 72°C, it is deflected from the pasteurized-milk pipeline back into the raw milk flow. If the temperature has been maintained, however, the milk passes through the 'regenerator' heat-exchanger 'a', but on the reverse side of the plates, and thence to a third heat-exchanger 'e', which is the 'cooler'.

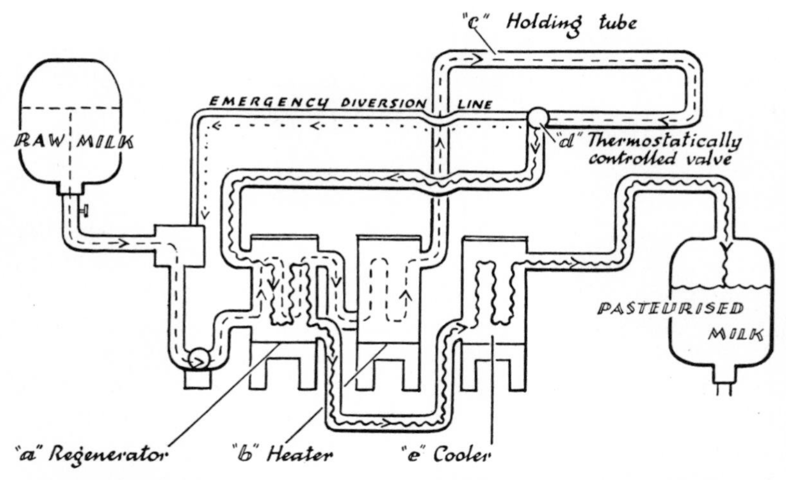

Fig. 17. Simplified flow-diagram of flash-pasteurizing plant. The raw milk passes first through the regenerator, where it is partly heated by the milk that has already been pasteurized and which is flowing across the other sides of the heat-exchanger plates. Next, the milk is raised to pasteurizing temperature as it passes through the heater unit and remains at this temperature for the time it takes to flow through the holding tubes. It is then cooled, first by passing through the regenerator and then through the cooler.

(b) BOTTLING

The basic scientific principles upon which the technology of milk handling is based are: (i) that to avoid bacterial contamination the milk must be kept clean and away from infected dirt of all sorts; (ii) to avoid the multiplication of those bacteria that will inevitably be present, it must be kept cool; and (iii) the materials with which it is brought in contact must be inert. Glass and stainless steel are particularly suitable; *even small traces of copper are particularly harmful.* The importance of pasteurization to destroy pathogenic bacteria has already been emphasized.

To conform to these principles, the following routine must be followed:

(i) *Milk supply*

Modern methods of milk collection have led to the almost complete disappearance of the milk churn as a storage vessel. Milk from the cow is collected on the farm in refrigerated tanks which are capable of holding two or three milkings. It is then transferred to bulk road tankers for transportation to the dairy or milk factory. Mobile bulk tanks of 50–100 gallon (225–450 litre) capacity, capable of being connected to refrigeration systems on the farm, are also available. These may be left at the junction of the farm road and the highway to be collected by road tankers. A new development is the introduction of large heavy-duty polythene bags of up to 200 gallon (900 litre) capacity for the storage of milk on farms when collection is impossible in exceptionally bad weather or to avoid week-end collections.

It is of the greatest importance that milking should be done under clean conditions. The milk should be strained and transported in clean, sterilized vessels. When it is to be handled by the technologist in any quantity, it is good modern practice for supplies to be received at the processing plant in stainless steel or glass-lined tankers. Arrangements must be made to permit the milk to be stirred before it is discharged to avoid an uneven distribution of cream.

(ii) *Holding tanks*

Milk received at a processing plant must be cooled as soon as possible. This can be done by pumping it over a cooler or through a heat-exchanger into holding tanks, or by using tanks fitted with coils or jackets through which chilled brine can be circulated. These tanks need to be fitted with stirrers.

(iii) *Filtration*

In order to remove dirt and sediment or any other foreign matter that may be present when large amounts of milk are mixed together, it is good practice to filter the milk supply. This can be done either while the milk is still cool or after it has been partially heated for the processes of pasteurization or sterilization.

(iv) *Homogenization*

The butter-fat in milk normally occurs as small globules suspended in the fluid of the milk. Because fat is lighter than water—in scientific terms, it is said to have a lower *specific gravity*—it tends to rise to the top. In some communities there is a preference for milk of uniform composition in which such separation of cream does not occur. This is achieved by forcing the milk under a pressure of 2000 lbs./sq. in. through small holes. The fat globules are subdivided by this process into such minute particles that they remain as a homogeneous suspension within the milk for an indefinite length of time.

(v) *Pasteurization*

The filtered milk is pasteurized either directly or after homogenization when homogenized milk is desired.

(vi) *Bottling*

Before they are filled, the bottles themselves must be washed clean and sterilized. Numerous automatic bottling machines are produced by dairy engineers. The milk may be measured automatically into twenty-four bottles at a time.

(vii) *Sterilization*

Besides killing pathological bacteria, pasteurization also reduces the number of the bacteria which cause milk spoilage. However, the temperature used in pasteurizing milk is not sufficient to render it sterile and, although the useful life of the milk is extended, it nevertheless remains a perishable commodity. In some places, however, a market exists for completely sterilized milk which is a great deal more stable. The temperature required to achieve sterilization does change the flavour and this is not universally acceptable.

To achieve sterilization, the filled bottles of milk, which must be closed by a crown closure, a screw top or a spring cap, are loaded into pressure vessels—autoclaves—the temperature raised to 112°C (235°F) by steam under pressure, and this temperature maintained for 15 minutes. The bottles are cooled to 80°C (175°F) or so by a water spray and are then removed from the autoclave and allowed to cool to atmospheric temperature.

A milk-bottling plant is illustrated in plate 38.

(viii) *The UHT (ultra-high-temperature) process*

Long-keeping milk capable of being stored for 6 months at room temperature without going bad or material loss of palatability can be prepared if fresh milk is heated to 132°C (270°F) for 1 second. This can be done either by passing it through a heat-exchanger or by the direct injection of live steam. If steam is used, the added water which it represents must be evaporated as the heated milk is being cooled. After milk has been subjected to UHT treatment it must be packed under sterile conditions. A Swedish device for packing UHT milk in sterile cartons is the so-called 'Tetrapak process'.

(c) CLEANING AND STERILIZING EQUIPMENT

It is extremely important that every part of the receptacles and equipment with which milk comes in contact during processing should be clean and sterile. Even a small area of contamination in a pump or pipeline can quickly infect a large bulk of milk. The process of cleaning and sterilization involves the following steps:

(i) *Washing*

As soon as a piece of equipment has been used it should be thoroughly washed with cold or lukewarm water. Water should be pumped through pipelines, pasteurizers, heat-exchangers and tanks to prevent the possibility of milk residues drying on their surfaces. More intricate equipment needs to be dismantled and washed.

(ii) *Sterilization*

A. *Steam sterilization.* Where equipment, such as pipelines, coolers, etc. are set up as closed systems, live steam can be passed through. It is important to ensure that as the steam passes through all air is ejected, otherwise the high temperature necessary for efficient sterilization will not be attained. When steam sterilization is used, the steam must be able to flow through the entire system.

B. *Hot-water sterilization.* Sterilization can be achieved by pumping hot water through equipment provided that the temperature of the water never falls below 75°C (167°F).

C. *Sterilization with chlorine.* Clean equipment can effectively be sterilized by sodium hypochlorite solution of sufficient strength to provide 100 p.p.m. of available chlorine. This solution is also pumped through pasteurizers and coolers. Stronger solutions containing up to 250 p.p.m. of chlorine are sometimes sprayed on to the surface of transporter and storage tanks. When chlorine solutions are used for sterilization it is important that the vessels and equipment should already be clean.

5. Evaporated milk

Milk is a bulky and perishable foodstuff of which about 86 to 88% is water. As long ago as 1856 a process was developed by which part of the water was removed by evaporation. Under modern conditions, evaporated milk is concentrated under vacuum in order to avoid the necessity to boil it at atmospheric pressure, which tends to produce an undesirable 'boiled' flavour. Evaporation may be carried out under a vacuum of 28 in. of mercury at a temperature of 50–55°C (122–127°F) and continued until the water content has been reduced to 74%. It has been found that if *calcium chloride, disodium phosphate* or *sodium citrate* are added in a small amount not exceeding 0·1% of the final evaporated milk, its consistency is improved. Sometimes a small amount of concentrate of vitamin D is also added to provide 7·5 international units of vitamin D per oz. of evaporated milk.

Evaporated milk is usually packed in cans and is sterilized by being autoclaved at 112°C for 15 minutes.

If the evaporated milk is restored to the volume of the original milk from which it was derived by dilution of water, its nutritional value is approximately the same as that of fresh, pasteurized milk and it can be used for infant feeding. Occasionally skimmed milk, from which the fat has been removed to make butter, is processed into *evaporated skimmed milk*. This is a useful source of protein but, since its butter-fat content is missing, it is nutritionally defective as an infant food.

6. Condensed milk

The term 'condensed milk' usually implies whole milk which has been partially evaporated and to which a proportion of sugar has been added. Condensed milk is a valuable food because it contains the nutrients from the milk and the presence of the comparatively high concentration of sugar keeps it from 'going bad' for a considerable length of time after the can or other container in which it is packed has been opened. A characteristic composition of condensed milk is:

Table 18

	%
Protein	8·1
Butter-fat	8·5
Mineral content	1·7
Lactose plus added sugar	54·7
Water	27·0

The technical operations of making condensed milk are usually carried out as follows:

(a) Pasteurizing. The milk is pasteurized without subsequent cooling.

(b) Evaporation. The milk, still hot, is run into an evaporator and a sugar syrup containing about 60% of sugar is added at the same time. The proportion of sugar is usually adjusted in proportion to the fat composition of the particular batch of milk. Evaporation is carried out under a vacuum of 29 in. of mercury at a temperature of 50–55°C (122–127°F).

(c) Agitation and cooling. When the required concentration has been reached, as determined with a *refractometer,* the condensed milk is pumped into an agitated vessel and cooled. It is important that the evaporation, agitation and cooling are carried out in such a way that the lactose in the milk crystallizes as small crystals, otherwise the condensed milk will have a sandy texture.

(d) Packing. If hygienic conditions are maintained in carrying out the process, the condensed milk can safely be packed into sterile cans or other receptacles without further heating or sterilization.

7. Filled milk

Filled milk is a development of the food technologist. It consists of either partly or completely skimmed milk in which part of the butter-fat has been replaced by a vegetable oil, which may be enriched with vitamin concentrate to compensate for the vitamin A and D naturally present in the butter-fat fraction of whole milk. Filled milk has an important function under the following circumstances:

(a) In countries where supplies of whole milk and butter are inadequate, part of the milk fat may be made available for the

manufacture of butter or ghee; the skim milk, which still contains the milk-protein, mineral contents and water-soluble vitamins, is then restored to its original food-value as whole milk by the addition of vegetable oil of which there may be more ample supplies.

(b) In prosperous countries, there is evidence to suggest that the susceptibility of older men to coronary heart disease is linked in some way with the consumption of large amounts of 'saturated' fats, in which category is butter-fat. The substitution of butter-fat in milk by selected vegetable oil, which is less 'saturated', may therefore be beneficial.

A typical filled milk developed by Professor Malmros in Sweden was a homogenized emulsion of corn oil in skim milk.

In certain countries, including the United States and Great Britain, where powerful dairying interests have exerted pressure on the legislature, the manufacture of filled milk has been hampered by restrictive labelling regulations.

8. Dried milk

The high nutritional content of milk—its specially nutritious protein, its calcium, the group of B-vitamins and the vitamins A and D from its butter-fat—can most conveniently be preserved by drying it. Dried milk also forms a useful and palatable culinary ingredient.

(a) Roller-drying is the simplest method. Milk is caused to run, either as whole milk or after having been condensed, in a thin film on to a heated roller. The film of milk is dried almost instantaneously and is scraped off as the roller slowly turns. The roller is usually heated by steam; it must be hot enough and must revolve at the appropriate speed; the film of milk must be of the right thinness to obtain adequate drying; yet the temperature must not be too high, nor the drying period too long, or the dried product will have a cooked flavour, the nutritional value of the protein will be reduced and the solubility of the milk powder will be damaged. Even under the best possible conditions there is some loss of solubility and a certain amount of insoluble residue remains when the dried milk is reconstituted with water. Roller-dried milk, however, is a food of excellent nutritional value, as can be seen from the table in Appendix 2 on p. 289, and is extensively used as an infant food. For this purpose it is usually fortified by the addition of synthetic vitamin D as a prophylactic against rickets. This enrichment is not necessary if it is to be used in tropical countries, where adequate vitamin

D-activity is produced naturally by the action of sunlight on the infants' skin.

(b) Spray-drying is a second method somewhat superior to roller-drying. The milk is injected as a fine spray into a chamber through which a stream of hot air is blown. The droplets of milk are immediately dried and fall to the bottom of the apparatus as powder. Spray-dried milk, efficiently manufactured, does not suffer from the partial insolubility which is a weakness of roller-dried milk and its protein is also of slightly higher nutritional value. On the other hand, the spray-dried powder is bulkier than roller-dried powder and the cost of packing, storing and transporting is, therefore, somewhat higher.

The steps taken in spray drying are commonly as follows:

(i) *Preheating.* Preheating the raw milk to 63°C (145°F) for half an hour, or to 107°C (225°F) for a few seconds has been found to produce 'anti-oxidants' which delay the development of rancid flavours in the dried milk.

(ii) *Condensing.* Water is evaporated more economically under vacuum than it is at atmospheric pressure in the spray-drier itself. It is customary, therefore, to condense the milk until its moisture content has been reduced to 60%. If skim milk is being dried instead of whole milk, the moisture content can only safely be reduced to 65% before spray-drying (82% before roller-drying).

(iii) *Spray-drying.* A number of spray-driers are available. Most consist essentially of a chamber in the shape of an inverted cone. The milk is sprayed from the broad base of the cone at the top and the powder collects below at the narrow point of the vessel. Dry air at temperatures up to 150°C (302°F) can be used.

(c) Easily reconstituted powdered skim-milk. Lactose, the sugar naturally present in milk, is not very readily soluble when it is entirely freed from combination with water. The 'wetability' of powdered skim-milk is greatly improved if, after it has been initially dried, it is damped and then re-dried. This restores the 'water of hydration' to the lactose and makes it much more readily soluble.

(d) The storage of dried milk. Dried milk can deteriorate in three ways:

(i) The presence of oxygen can accelerate the development of rancid flavours by oxidizing the fat.

EGGS. 45: Eggs awaiting packing. 46: An egg being candled.

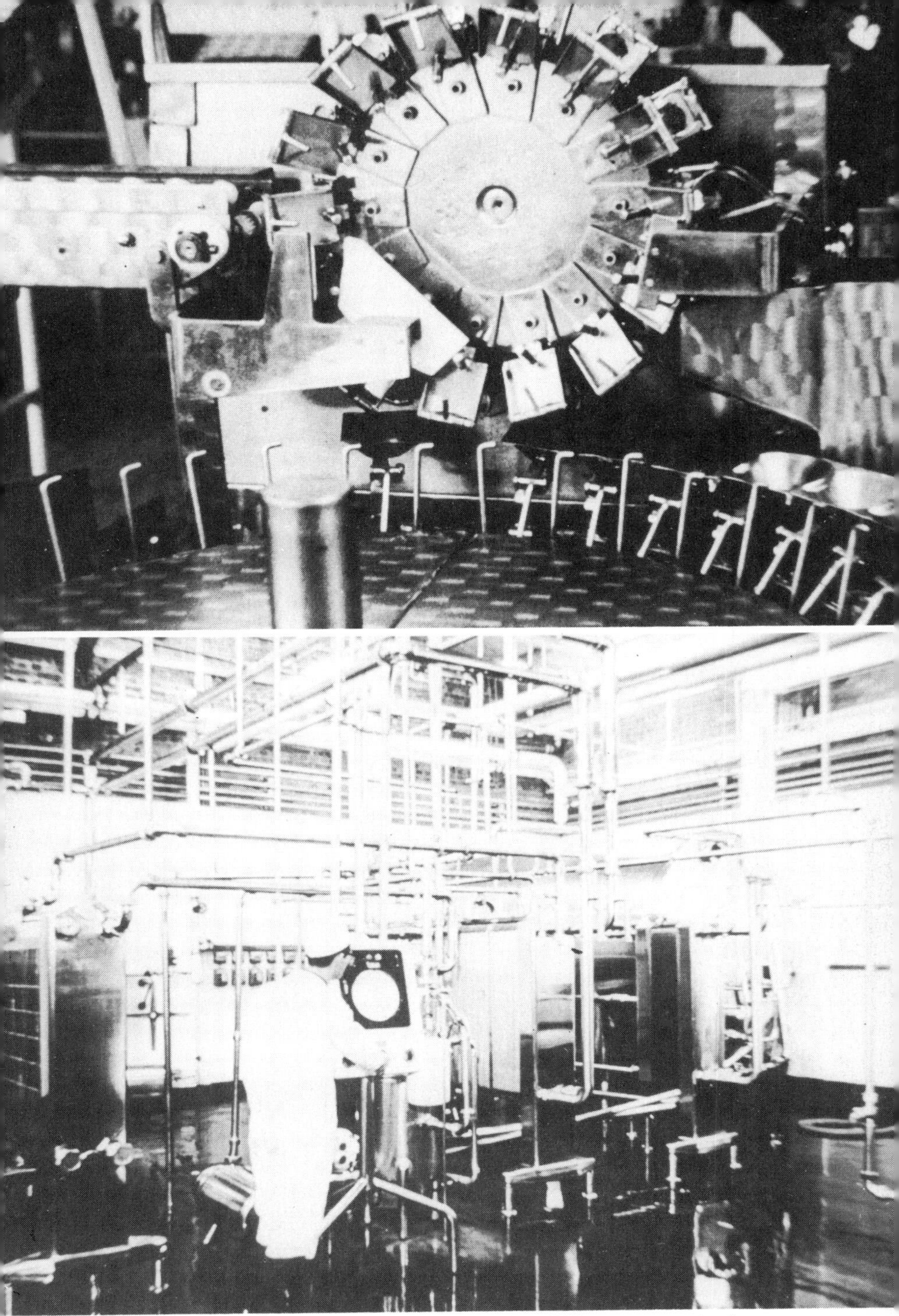

EGGS. 47: SANOVO egg-breaking machine. 48: APV egg pasteurization equipment.

EGGS. 49: Egg frozen in large slabs in plate freezer. 50: Egg frozen in small slabs in GRAM freezer.

EGGS. 51: Spray-drier for the production of dried milk or egg products. The process workers indicate the scale of the equipment.

(ii) In the presence of moisture a combination between protein and the milk-sugar, lactose, can occur. This is called the 'browning reaction'. It causes a 'stale' flavour, reduces the solubility of the milk powder and seriously damages its nutritional value.

(iii) Too high a moisture content can also lead to caking of the dried milk due to a change in the crystalline state of the lactose.

In view of the above facts, dried milk should be packed in air-tight drums or cans in an atmosphere of nitrogen and at a moisture content preferably not exceeding 3%, but certainly not above 5%, and should if possible be stored in a cool place.

Note: The stability of dried milk during storage can be markedly increased by the use of certain 'additives'. These are described in Chapter 9.

9. Yoghurt

(a) ORIGIN

Yoghurt is the Turkish name for a fermented milk product originating in the Middle East and the Balkans and traditionally popular from Italy to India. Over the last decade it has achieved great popularity throughout the western world largely as a result of the addition of sugar and various combinations of fruits, nuts and flavours. This practice has modified the characteristically acid flavour of the traditional product which was not particularly attractive to the occidental palate.

(b) THE FERMENTATION PROCESS

The tradition of using a mixed culture of *Lactobacillus bulgaricus* and *Streptococcus thermophilus,* usually in equal proportions, to ferment milk is still considered the most desirable practice. There are two popular methods for the large-scale production of yoghurt: set yoghurt, in which the fermentation is allowed to take place in the carton in which it is to be sold, and stirred yoghurt, which is fermented in bulk and subsequently filled into retail containers. The process begins with the pasteurization and homogenization of fresh milk. Milk powders are sometimes added to the milk, particularly if set yoghurt is being produced. The milk is then cooled to the

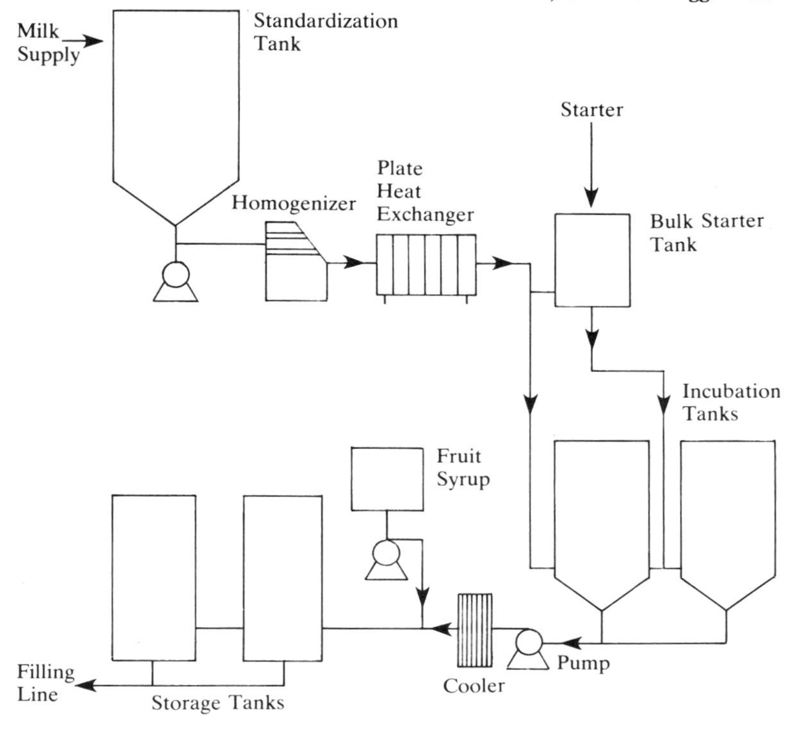

Fig. 18. The manufacture of stirred yoghurt.

(i) Bulk milk is standardized to the correct fat level.
(ii) It is then homogenized and pasteurized in a plate heat-exchanger and cooled to the incubation temperature before being pumped to fermentation vessels fitted with stirrers.
(iii) Starter cultures are prepared in bulk in milk, added as required to the incubation tanks and mixed. During the fermentation process, lactic acid is produced and as the acidity of the milk increases it coagulates and sets.
(iv) When incubation is complete, the coagulum is broken by stirring and rapidly pumped to holding tanks through a cooler to prevent further fermentation.
(v) If fruit or fruit pulp is to be added it can be metered into the yoghurt at this stage.
(vi) The product is then filled into retail containers, packed in cases or trays and stored under refrigeration.

incubation temperature of 35–48°C and the mixed starter culture is added. The temperature of fermentation is controlled at this level, whether the process takes place in bulk or in cartons. When the product has reached a titratable acidity of 0·8–1·0% (ph 4·0–4.4) it is rapidly cooled to between 3 and 8°C to stop fermentation. If the product is fermented in bulk it is stirred before filling. Yoghurt must be stored at refrigerated temperatures and has a shelf life of about two weeks. If desired, 3–5% sugar and 15–18% fruit may be added before fermentation. Stabilizers are now also commonly added to improve consistency—this applies particularly to bulk-fermented fruit yoghurts. Long-life versions of yoghurt have been successfully produced by a variety of methods including drying, freezing and pasteurization, but are as yet of little commercial importance. A simplified schematic diagram of the manufacturing process for stirred yoghurt is shown in Figure 18.

B. CHEESE

1. The chemistry of cheese-making

The manufacture of cheese represented in its original form a process for preserving milk nutrients for the winter when milk production was a seasonal operation largely confined to the spring and summer. As was described in Chapter 1, protein has a highly complex chemistry. In milk, protein only retains its solubility under certain conditions. When the natural acidity of the milk rises, the protein curdles, that is to say it forms into a curd. This 'precipitation' of protein is most complete at a precise degree of acidity called the *isoelectric* point. Part of the difficulty of making good cheese lies in the need to attain exactly this level of acidity. A supplementary agent used in cheese-making is an enzyme, rennet, isolated from calves' stomachs, which also brings about the intra-molecular chemical change associated with coagulation.

The acidification of milk to make cheese is nearly always brought about by inoculating the milk with strains of lactic-acid-producing bacteria. Different types of bacteria produce different amounts of lactic acid as well as a number of other chemical substances. These differences are the main cause for the wide variety of cheeses produced in different places, but differences are also due to the use of whole milk of varying composition, skim milk, milk from animals other than cows, and variations in the cheese-making process.

2. Cheddar cheese manufacture

The basic process for making Cheddar-type cheese is as follows:

(*a*) INITIAL COAGULATION

In modern technological practice, pasteurizated milk is placed in a rectangular stainless-steel vat equipped with an outer water-jacket. A culture of selected lactic-acid-producing bacteria is added. This culture is called the 'starter'. Colouring matter may also be added. The milk is brought to *c*. 30°C (84—88°F) and its acid concentration, reckoned as lactic acid, allowed to rise until it reaches 0·17–0·20%. A measured amount of rennet concentrate is then added, selected so as to give complete coagulation in about 20 minutes.

(*b*) PREPARATION OF CURD

The appropriate modification of the protein molecules, which is the object of the cheese-making process, is a matter of some complexity. To obtain the desired result, the curd, now floating in the liquid whey, is cut into cubes of about 0·5 in. sides by a series of wires fixed on to a frame. The temperature is raised to 37–40°C (98–104°F) in a period of 30–40 minutes, causing the pieces of curd to contract. The liquid whey is drained off and the curd cubes allowed to coalesce.

(*c*) CHEDDARING AND MILLING

When the curd has settled into a firm mass, it is cut into slabs. These are piled up, six slabs high or so and are turned every 15 minutes or thereabouts. This treatment, which is called 'cheddaring', allows the protein structure to attain the desired firmness and consistency. The curd is then chopped into pieces about ½ in. wide and 2 in. long in a 'mill' to allow more moisture to escape. Afterwards, salt, at the rate of 1 to 2½ lb. per 1000 lb. of the original milk used, is mixed into the mass of milled curd.

(*d*) PRESSING AND CURING

The salted curd is filled into cheesecloth wrappings and placed in a circular mould where gradually increasing pressure is applied for about 48 hours. The cheese is usually removed from the press and re-wrapped after 24 hours. Pressed 'green' cheese—as the new cheese is called—is sometimes coated with wax. The final 'curing' is carried out by storing the cheese in a well-ventilated place kept at about 13°C (55°F).

Much of the cheese-making process as described above can be carried out automatically. In Holland, equipment has been developed in which, after the milk has been coagulated by lactic acid fermentation and the addition of rennet, the whey is drained away from the curd on a moving band. The curd blocks are cut to size as they move on, are then pressed into the required form, and put into cheesecloth or plastic covers while still moving forward on the conveyor belts.

C. EGGS

1. Qualities

Eggs possess two groups of characteristics that make them valuable as foodstuffs.

(a) They are high in nutritional value, since:
  (i) Their protein is of excellent biological value.
  (ii) They are rich in fat.
  (iii) They contain vitamins A and D.
  (iv) They are one of the best dietary sources of iron.

(b) The soluble protein has great technical usefulness is giving desirable structure and coherence to confectionery and to other types of food.

2. Hens' eggs

The eggs which are by far the most commonly used as human food are hens' eggs. A hen's egg is a rather unstable system. The edible part is made up of 12·6% of protein and 11·3% of fat; the remaining 74·1% is water. This is contained in a shell which, in its natural state, is comparatively resistant to bacterial attack although it is permeable to moisture, air and carbon dioxide. The main problem for the food technologists is to store eggs and prevent them from deteriorating. Under commercial practice, eggs can be stored at –1 to 0°C (29–32°F) for periods up to nine months during which they will remain in a state not grossly dissimilar from fresh eggs. The object of the food technologist is to delay or arrest the natural changes that occur during storage and to prevent harm by external agencies and particularly by invading micro-organisms. It is important that normal changes should be prevented as quickly as possible, for not only do they proceed at an increasing rate once they start, but they also facilitate attack by moulds and bacteria.

3. Changes in eggs during storage

(a) LOSS OF CARBON DIOXIDE GAS THROUGH THE SHELL

This makes the white less acid or, in technical terms, it causes the pH to rise. The rise in pH has two effects: it changes the structure of the protein of the egg-white, which appears as 'staleness'; on the other hand, after about 3 days the pH may rise to 9·3 or more and even render the egg less susceptible to bacterial infection. Changes due to loss of carbon dioxide can be held back by 'gas storage', where $2\frac{1}{2}$% of carbon dioxide is added to the atmosphere of the store.

(b) EVAPORATION OF MOISTURE

During storage eggs lose water through their shells by evaporation and the air-space naturally present at the big end increases. When eggs are examined by being 'candled' in front of a strong light in a darkened room, the examiner can make a good estimate of their age from the size of the air-space. Evaporation can be delayed by increasing the humidity of the store but this increases the danger of mould growth.

(c) MOVEMENT OF WATER WITHIN THE EGG

In parallel with the loss of moisture from the egg through the shell, there is a movement of water from the white into the yolk. Thus, in eggs which have been stored for any considerable length of time, the yolks become 'flabby' or 'runny'. The eggs consequently become difficult to poach or fry satisfactorily. These changes can be delayed in two ways: by efficient handling to ensure that eggs reach the cool store as quickly as possible, and by 'gas storage' in an atmosphere containing carbon dioxide.

(d) CHEMICAL CHANGES IN THE EGG

Changes gradually occur in the internal molecular structure of the egg-white protein. The normal firmness of the egg-white becomes lost and 'watery whites' appear. A similar change affects the protein membrane surrounding the yolk and makes it liable to rupture. These changes increase the susceptibility to infection. They can again be checked by maintaining a low temperature throughout the storage life of the egg and by 'gas storage'.

4. Storage factors

The defences of an egg against the micro-organisms that surround it are:

(i) The membrane layers under the shell.
(ii) The degree of impermeability inherent in the shell itself.
(iii) The anti-bacterial effect of the marked rise in the pH of the egg white.
(iv) A group of antibiotic substances in the white which are known to be hostile to invading organisms.

(a) CONDITIONS FOR KEEPING

In order to ensure good keeping quality, the following points must be borne in mind:

(i) The egg-producer must ensure that his hens are maintained under hygienic conditions to avoid heavy infection of the egg-shells.
(ii) Washing eggs by the very fact of making them wet increases the likelihood of their being invaded by micro-organisms. Eggs must not be washed.
(iii) Hens which lay eggs with particularly porous shells should be discarded.
(iv) Stale eggs should not be stored in contact with fresh eggs; since their yolks become liable to break out of their sacs they form a particularly favourable medium for the growth of infection.

(b) MICRO-ORGANISMS

The principal micro-organisms which the food technologist must guard against are:

(i) *Pseudomonas*—bacteria derived from soil and water causing green rot and a smell of cabbage water.
(ii) *Sporotrichum*—causing 'pink rot' of the egg-white and decay of the yolk.
(iii) *Cladosporium*—causing black spots and rapid decay of the yolk.
(iv) *Proteus*—producing the 'black rots' of really rotten eggs; gas sometimes causes infected eggs to burst when the shell is cracked.

(v) *Achromobacter*—causing musty eggs.
(vi) *Coliform organisms*—producing fishy flavours.

(c) MICROBIAL INFECTION OF EGGS CAUSING FOOD POISONING AND ILLNESS

Unlike pigs, sheep and cattle, hens suffer from few infections that can be passed on in their eggs to produce pathological symptoms in man. There is, however, one group of micro-organisms which may be harmful: the *Salmonella*.

Hens can pass *Salmonella* infection into their eggs and thus cause food poisoning but the incidence of infection is comparatively low. Fresh hens' eggs or eggs after cool storage are not very likely to cause much harm, since an individual egg is only likely to be eaten by at most a few people if it is used in an omelette or other lightly cooked dish. However, when large numbers of eggs are mixed together for processing into dried egg, as discussed below, a single infected egg can contaminate a large bulk and form a major source of danger.

Ducks are much more susceptible to Salmonella infection and due to this their eggs are a common source of food poisoning.

5. Frozen liquid egg

Those hens' eggs whose shells have been dirtied, or small and irregularly shaped eggs can very well be processed into frozen egg. Indeed, certain specialized poultry farms find it convenient and economic to process all their eggs in this manner. Cracked eggs are best processed into liquid egg for immediate use.

Frozen egg is processed as follows:

(a) PREPARATION AND EXAMINATION OF THE EGGS

Every precaution must be taken to ensure that the bacteriological contamination of the final product is reduced to the lowest possible level. The eggs should therefore be kept cool before they are handled. It is also necessary to wash them and sanitize them by spraying with a solution containing 100–200 p.p.m. chlorine or some other suitable sanitizing agent. They are then broken into clean pans and examined. All unsatisfactory eggs must be discarded and the pans into which they were broken immediately washed and sterilized.

The development of machines for breaking and separating eggs automatically has had a major effect on the efficiency of what was once a manual operation. Eggs are washed, sanitized, cracked and separated individually at very high speed. If whole liquid egg is required, the two liquid streams are combined and mixed in a tank. One operator using the most up-to-date can process over 1000 dozen eggs per hour.

(b) PASTEURIZATION

Sound eggs, handled and broken in a hygienic manner, should contain only a few bacteria. Pasteurization is, however, an added precaution. It can be done by heating the liquid eggs to 63°C (145°F) for one minute without affecting their culinary qualities.

(c) PACKING

The broken eggs are passed through a fine sieve to remove any fine pieces of shell or chalazae (the membrane strings that hold the yolk in position within the shell). The liquid egg is then filled into a variety of packs. Until recently the preferred container was a 30 lb. can in which it was frozen by being left at −16°C (3°F) for 77 hours. If a cold air blast freezer is available the freezing time is reduced to 36 hours. Modern trends have seen the introduction of plastic pails, paperboard cartons and plastic bags held in boxes.

Defrosted frozen whole egg is used by bakers and confectioners for any purpose for which they might otherwise use fresh egg. The technological preparation of the frozen product enables eggs to be used when they are most plentiful and consequently cheapest. The cans of egg can be stored frozen for prolonged periods without deterioration and can be transported without damage provided refrigerated vehicles or ships are available.

If egg-yolk is frozen separately from the white, it tends to thicken if it is stored frozen for more than a few weeks. This change can be prevented by adding up to 10% of salt or 10% of sugar to the egg-yolk. Salted yolk is acceptable to manufacturers of mayonnaise, and sugared yolk to confectioners.

6. Dried egg

An alternative to freezing is spray-drying. The same stringent precautions need to be taken to maintain the highest degree of sanitary and bacteriological purity. It is particularly important to use eggs from healthy birds to avoid contamination with *Salmonella* organisms. The liquid egg should be pasteurized and spray-dried as quickly as possible to limit the time available for the multiplication of any contaminating micro-organisms that may be present.

The same type of spray-drier is used for eggs as for spray-drying milk. The production of a high-quality article of good flavour is not altogether easy since it is obviously undesirable to use too high a temperature in the drying process.

Where the dried egg is to be used for confectionery, sugar may be added to the liquid egg before drying since it has been found that the dried egg then reconstitutes easier when water is added.

The moisture content of the dried egg must not exceed 5% and, indeed, improved stability is obtained by adjusting the pH of the liquid egg to 6·5 and then drying to less than 1% moisture.

7. Egg substitutes

Various proteins are used to provide the same technical properties as egg in making flour confectionery and in other processes where the peculiar binding properties of egg are required.

(a) Fish protein. Fillets of cod or haddock, carefully washed, de-fatted by extraction in alcohol or trichlorethylene, dried and heated with caustic soda give a protein solution which, after being neutralized with acetic acid, can be spray-dried and used, like dried egg, in aerated bakery products, etc.

(b) Milk protein. Skim milk partially concentrated and then treated with caustic soda or lime will also give a protein behaving similarly to egg when used in baking. This material also is most conveniently used as a spray-dried powder.

(c) Blood protein. Plasma, the clear yellow fluid in which the red corpuscles of blood are suspended, contains a soluble protein which is similar in its chemistry to that of egg-white. As might be expected, therefore, it behaves in the same way when used to make meringues or other articles in which the technical properties of egg-white play a part. The process followed in preparing a marketable egg-substitute from blood is to arrange with the slaughterhouse for the fresh blood to be collected in vessels containing a small amount of sodium citrate to prevent it from coagulating. The red corpuscles can then be removed by centrifuging and the liquid plasma spray-dried. The dry powder may be mixed with a proportion of starch and a little locust kernel gum to give it the right stickiness before being sold to the bakery and grocery trades.

OILS. 52: Break rolls, which crack the oil-bearing seeds. 53: Flaking rolls for the converssion of seeds to flake form.

OILS. 54: Low-pressure expeller, which removes part of the oil from the flaked seed. 55: Rotocel solvent extractor, which extracts residual oil from the expeller cake with hexane.

BUTTER. 56: Modern stainless steel churns which convert cream into butter.

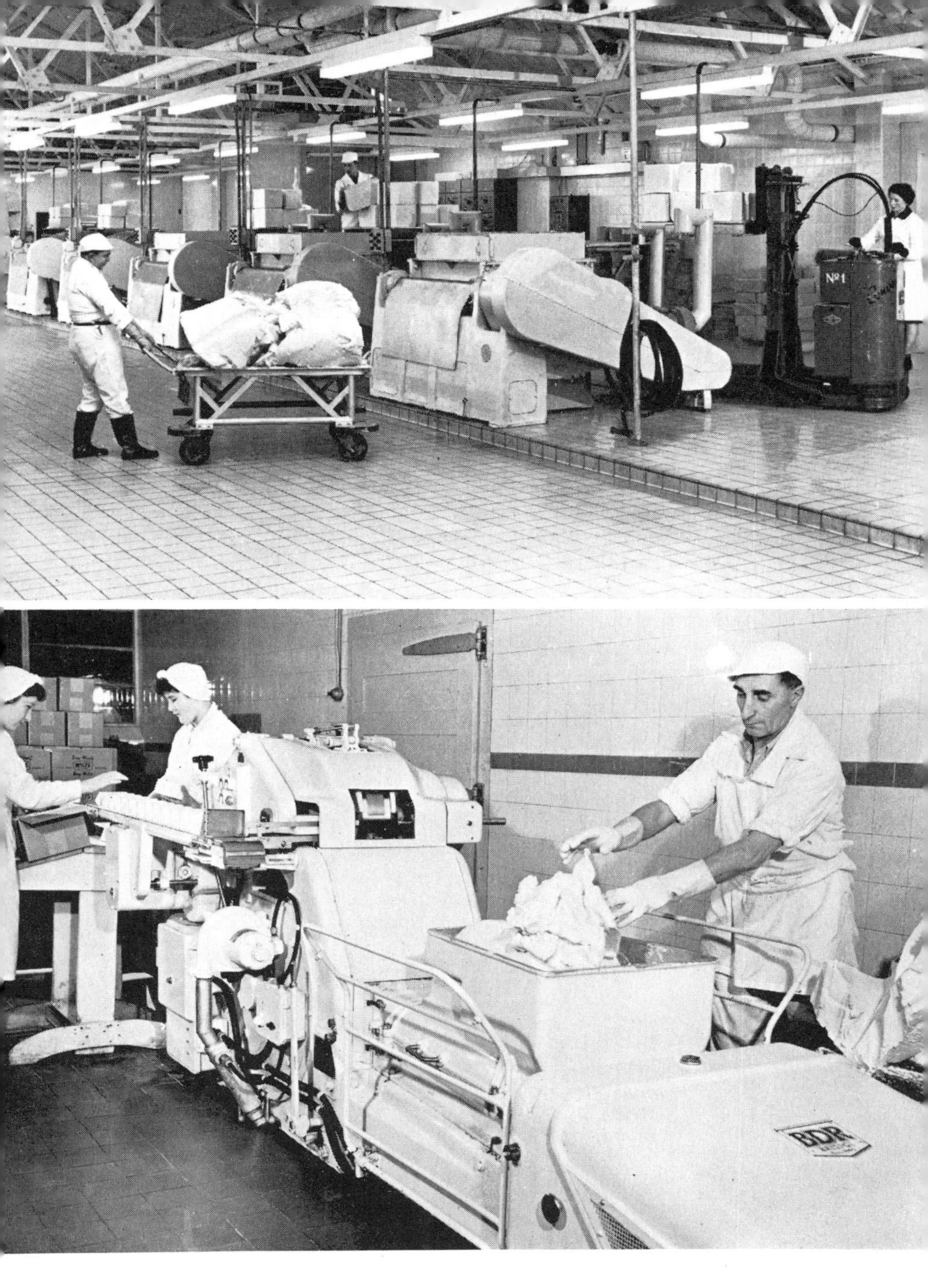

BUTTER. 57: Blending butters. 58: A machine for packaging butter.

6

Fats and oils

Fats and oils are valuable in the diet for three reasons: (i) They are the most concentrated of all sources of Calories. For this reason, a high proportion of fat enables a hard-working person who is expending a large amount of muscular energy to obtain his daily needs without having to consume an undue bulk of food. (ii) Fats are a source of the fat-soluble vitamins A and D and of the natural anti-oxidant, vitamin E. (iii) Fats make the diet more palatable; bread-and-butter, besides being richer in Calories than dry bread, is more agreeable to eat; cake is, in its proper place, more agreeable still; fried fish and chips make a more attractive dish than boiled fish and boiled potatoes; and mayonnaise adds to the dietetic pleasures of green salad.

The edible fats and oils on the world markets are largely derived from the following sources:

Table 19

	Approx. percentage of the total
Vegetable oils	
Cottonseed, groundnut, coconut, soya bean	32
Olive, sesame, palm, sunflower seed, etc.	17
Animal fats	
Butter, ghee	24
Lard, beef-fat, mutton-fat	22
Marine oils	
Whale oil	3
Fish oil	2

In modern industrial countries, food technologists are able to select from the world's supplies the diverse kinds of fats and oils listed above and convert them into forms suitable for use in shortening, confectionery coatings, in recipe products such as mayonnaise and salad dressings, as cooking fat and in butter and margarine. In this way, maximum advantage can be taken of fluctuations in prices, and supply problems are overcome. Oils for salads and salad dressings are selected for blandness of flavour and stability against rancidity. Naturally suitable oils such as maize or sunflower are expensive and soya oil treated by hydrogenation to improve its properties has been developed as a less costly alternative.

Shortening for use in baked goods was traditionally made from lard or beef fat, but the technologist has so improved the plasticity and the ability to incorporate air of more plentiful vegetable oils, such as cottonseed and soya, that they can be used instead. Many different types and combinations are thus now readily available to suit products as diverse as batters and sponges.

Cocoa butter, because of the pleasant way it melts in the mouth, is ideal for confectionery coatings. However, it is very expensive and substitutes derived from cottonseed, coconut and palm-kernel oils have been developed. No less ingenuity has been applied to the conversion of such varied starting materials as whale oil and palm oil into a standardized product such as margarine. All of these developments rely basically on applied chemistry, but before such chemistry can be applied it is first necessary to extract the fat from its source and purify it.

A. VEGETABLE OILS

1. Extraction

The oils and fats are extracted from vegetable sources by processes based on two main principles: (i) *mechanical expression,* which depends on the disruption of the plant cells containing the fat, usually by means of heat, followed by crushing under high pressures; (ii) *solvent extraction*, involving the immersion of the oil seeds in a liquid, which may be a petroleum fraction or a non-flammable fluid, commonly a chlorinated hydrocarbon, in which fat dissolves. The solvent is subsequently boiled off and the extracted fat recovered.

(a) HYDRAULIC PRESSING

(i) The seeds are cleaned and sifted and extraneous portions, such as the fibres attached to cotton seed, are removed. It is usual also to pass the seeds over magnetic separators to remove any metal contaminants.

(ii) When the seeds possess husks, these are removed by passing the seeds through a system of revolving knives and beaters and then over a series of screens and aspirators. This process is called *decortication*.

(iii) The decorticated material is either ground into a meal or alternatively rolled into flakes by being passed between heavy smooth steel rollers.

(iv) If oil of the highest quality is required, with pale colour and minimum flavour, the ground or flaked material is passed immediately to a press. To extract the maximum amount of oil, however, it is necessary to heat the prepared oil-seed for, say, 90 minutes in steam at 110°C (230°F) or for 15–20 minutes at 127°C (260°F). This makes the cells permeable to the passage of oil but at the same time tends to darken the oil and emphasize the flavour.

(v) The modern hydraulic press consists of a stack of horizontal plates, upon each of which is placed a batch of the oil-seed meal or flakes wrapped in cloth. The space between each plate is formed into a 'box' by means of angle-iron side walls. The stack of 'boxes' is compressed by a hydraulic ram capable of producing a pressure of 2000 lb./sq. in. on the cake. The oil runs out through openings in each 'box'. The residual cake is usually used for animal food. It contains between 4% and 6% of oil depending on the length of time it is allowed to drain in the press.

(b) EXPELLER PRESSING

The expeller or screw-type press is of great antiquity but in its modern form can be made to operate at a good level of efficiency. It can also be operated as a continuous process. However, for an expeller press to be efficiently used it is necessary to heat the oil-seed meal to about 115°C (240°F).

In essentials, an expeller press consists of a screw, similar to that found in a mincing machine. This screw is contained in a slotted housing and operates against a restricted opening. The oil-seed cake becomes compressed as it is forced through the housing by the screw and a pressure up to 15–20 tons/sq. in. (30,000 to 40,000 lb./sq. in.) may be developed. The oil escapes through slots in the housing. The residual cake contains 4% to 5% of oil.

(c) SOLVENT EXTRACTION

Solvent extraction is different in principle from mechanical expression. It depends upon the fact that fat, although it is insoluble in water, is readily soluble in a number of organic liquids. A characteristic type of solvent-extraction apparatus is shown in the diagram below.

Fig. 19 illustrates the recovery of oil from soya beans. The beans, shown in the figure entering at the bottom, are passed through cracking rolls and are then heated to 66°C (150°F) while being conveyed through a steam-jacketed 'tempering tube'. Thence they are passed through flaking rolls. The flaked soya beans are conveyed up by an elevator into the extraction apparatus. This is primarily a pipe along which they pass—to the right, as drawn in the

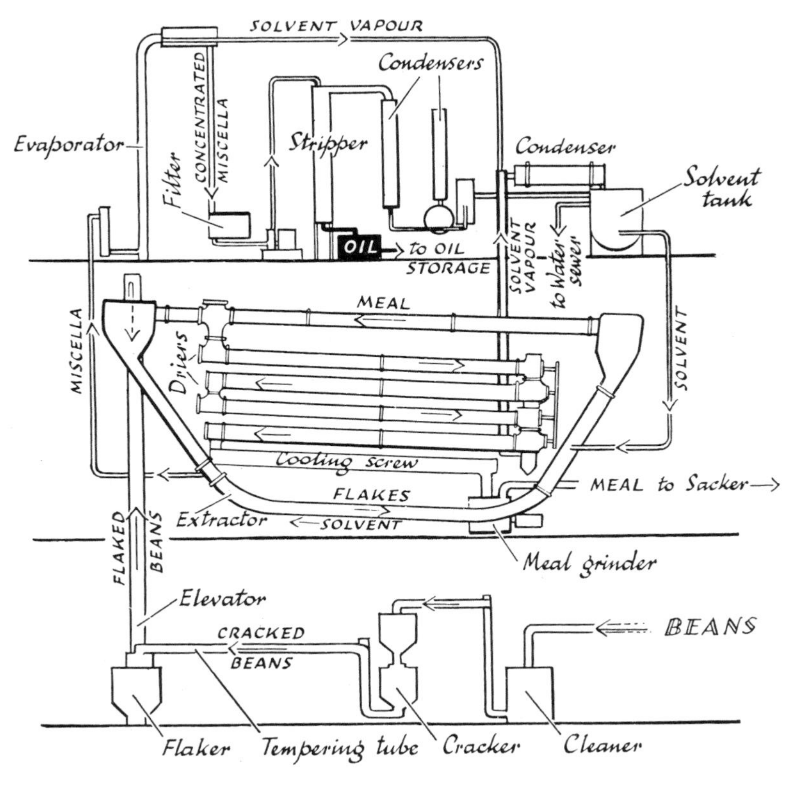

Fig. 19. Simplified flow-diagram of the solvent extraction of oil from soya bean.

diagram—while the trichlorethylene used as solvent passes to the left. The solvent, now containing extracted oil—and called 'miscella'—is pumped up to the evaporator where the trichlorethylene is recovered and the oil freed from solvent.

The soya bean flakes, after being conveyed through the solvent in the extractor pipe, are then carried on through a further series of heated pipes in order to drive off solvent. The evaporated solvent vapour is condensed for re-use and the extracted meal is ground for sale as a feeding-stuff or for technical purposes.

The mechanical oil-extraction processes are capable of removing all but 4 to 5% of the oil originally present; solvent extraction only leaves 1% or less of the oil behind. However, solvent-extraction plants require a larger capital investment than mechanical expression and it is important that they are run efficiently in order to avoid the expense involved should a significant amount of solvent be lost during the operation of the process.

2. Refining

A crude vegetable oil, such as soya-bean oil or ground-nut oil, obtained by a process of mechanical expression or solvent extraction, will not consist solely of fat, as chemically defined in Chapter 1. It will be contaminated with water, resins, gums and various decomposition products and not all of the fatty acids in it will be combined with the glycerol, as they should be as an entire, unbroken fat molecule, capable of being described as a good quality 'neutral' oil or fat. Some of the fatty acids will be separated and uncombined. A crude oil contaminated in this way, whether it is from vegetable or animal sources, is cloudy and sour and rapidly deteriorates and becomes rancid.

To refine a crude oil, the following procedures are adopted:

(*a*) The first stage of the process of refining is to treat the crude oil with an alkali. Caustic soda ($NaOH$) or soda ash (Na_2CO_3) is commonly used. The mixture is heated by steam coils and the alkali combines with the free fatty-acids and converts them into soap.

(*b*) The emulsion of fat, soap and water derived from the alkali solution is heated to an appropriate temperature dependent on the nature and condition of the oil, and passed through a centrifuge to separate the oil from the soaps.

(*c*) The refined oil is mixed with water to wash out residual traces of contamination and soap and centrifuged again. The washed oil is dried by being passed through a flash separator under vacuum.

Successful refining requires the proper adjustment of alkali strength, temperature and time to deal with the degree of contamination and the amount of free fatty acids present, without bringing about saponification of the fat itself. When crude oils are comparatively pure in the first place, refining may be satisfactorily achieved by simple steam distillation which will remove free fatty acids by evaporation.

3. Bleaching

For most technological processes, it is considered desirable to remove the colour from oils and fats no matter what their source. It is an odd reflection, in these modern times, to note that the process for bleaching fats used today, which makes use of the special properties of fuller's earth, is in principle identical with that referred to in the Bible where it is stated: 'And his raiment became shining, exceeding white as snow; so as no fuller on earth can white them' (St Mark 9:3).

From 0·5% to 5% of fuller's earth is added to the oil and the temperature raised to about 120°C (250°F) while a vacuum is maintained. The oil is then cooled to about 70°C (160°F) and filtered to remove the fuller's earth together with the colour adsorbed on it. In some plants, the oil is bleached continuously by feeding the fuller's earth steadily into a vacuum chamber.

Fuller's earth is a particular type of clay which is either mined or dug in the open and then dried and ground. Although a number of physico-chemical theories have been developed to explain its remarkable ability to adsorb the dark and coloured constituents of oil, leaving behind the colourless components, the reason for its activity is not fully understood. Other clays of the same montmorillonite group can be found possessing an identical chemical composition yet without the adsorbent activity.

4. Deodorizing

It is often essential to remove undesirable odours and flavours from many natural oils. This process of deodorization is normally accomplished by steam distillation under vacuum by which means the volatile flavour compounds are removed by evaporation.

5. Winterizing

Where fats or oils are to be used in liquid products which may be stored at low temperatures, they are first subjected to a low temperature or 'winterizing' treatment. They are held at 5°C to allow crystallization of the low melting fractions which are subsequently separated by filtration. This treatment is frequently applied to cottonseed oil or hydrogenated soya bean oil and prevents cloudiness in salad oil and the breakdown of salad dressing emulsions.

B. BUTTER

1. Manufacture

Milk is a watery solution in which about 3·5% of fat is incorporated as fine globules. The mixture of very finely divided fat globules in water is called a *colloidal suspension*. But this suspension is not very stable and, as is well known, if milk is allowed to stand, the fat gradually rises to the surface as cream. Very large amounts of milk are processed into cream, which itself is used as the raw material for the production of butter.

(a) THE BATCH PROCESS

(i) *Separation of cream*

Cream is separated from milk in modern establishments by means of a cream separator. The milk is run into the top of a system of rapidly revolving discs. The specific gravity of the globules of butter-fat is 0·930 at 15°C (60°F) compared to a specific gravity of 1·032 for whole milk. Consequently, the non-fatty parts of the milk tend to be thrown to the outside of the separator by centrifugal force while the butter-fat gravitates to the centre. The cream that is run off usually contains 30–35% of butter-fat.

(ii) *Preparation of the cream*

For the manufacture of 'sweet' butter, the fresh cream is directly pasteurized. When it is desired to produce butter with the flavour described as 'sour', the cream is allowed to sour and the acidity is standardized to about 0·25% lactic acid by adding sodium carbonate or lime; it is then pasteurized. The flavour of 'sour' butter can be further modified by inoculating the pasteurized cream with a culture of *Streptococcus lactis.*

(iii) *Churning*

The churning of cream into butter depends on the fact that cream consists of a colloidal suspension of small globules of fat suspended

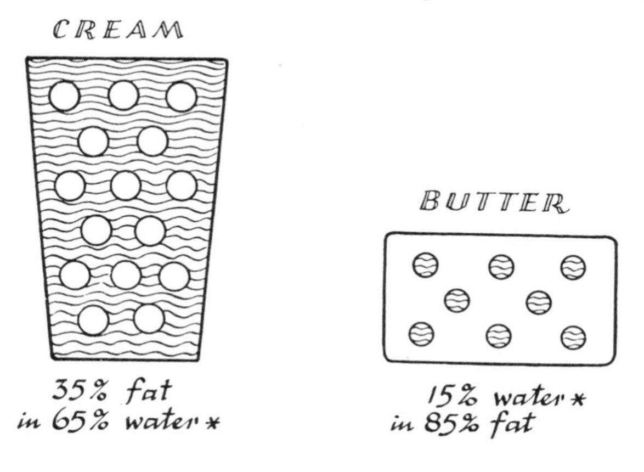

Fig. 20. Diagram illustrating the 'inversion' of a colloid. Cream is a suspension of fat globules in water, whereas butter is a suspension of water droplets in fat.

in a watery solution. When this suspension is subjected to the appropriate amount of mechanical agitation at a temperature of 10°C (50°F), the suspension becomes 'inverted'. That is to say, the fat and a proportion of the aqueous solution separate as granules of butter and the remainder of the watery portion of the cream can be drawn off as fat-free buttermilk. The process is shown diagrammatically in Fig. 20.

It can be seen what was meant above by saying the colloid had become 'inverted'. Whereas cream is a suspension of fat globules in a watery fluid, butter is a suspension of watery globules in fat.

(iv) *Washing and adding salt*

After the buttermilk has been drawn off, the granules of butter are washed with water and anything from 2·5 to 13% of salt mixed in. Salt improves the flavour of the butter and also serves the technological purpose of inhibiting infection by yeasts and moulds and by proteolytic and lipolytic bacteria. The keeping quality of the butter is also improved if the water globules in it are reduced to a very small size. Some modern butter-making procedures consequently introduce a machine to homogenize the butter and hence subdivide the globules of water in it.

(v) *Packing*

In order to obtain the most satisfactory keeping quality it is desirable to pack butter immediately after salt has been added and the butter 'worked'. Under modern conditions, the butter is forced by a worm conveyor through a shaping machine from whence it is extruded in a continuous flow, and divided into appropriately sized pieces, often by an automatic weight-controlled packing machine in which the individual blocks of butter may also be wrapped in paper.

(b) CONTINUOUS BUTTER-MAKING

In recent years a number of machines have been developed for making butter by a continuous process. As in the older batch process, it is important to ensure that the cream used as starting material contains a uniform standardized content of butter-fat, that its bacterial content is satisfactorily low—in most instances the cream is pasteurized as was described above—and that its temperature and acidity are also at a fixed uniform level. The inversion of the colloid, from a fat suspension in water to a water suspension in fat, is brought about by mechanical mixers as the cream passes through the butter-making machine. Considerable study has been given to the principles underlying the mixing and blending of butter. It appears that the quality and consistency of the butter produced depends on the fineness and uniformity of the droplets of moisture suspended in the fat. It has been found that the way the butter is worked, whether it is rolled on a flat surface or pressed through a perforated plate, affects the end result. For example, the moisture globules are more effectively reduced in size if the butter is pressed through numerous small perforations rather than through fewer larger ones.

2. Ghee

In India and other tropical countries butter is 'clarified' and converted into ghee. The process can conveniently be done on an industrial scale by melting the butter and passing the liquid obtained through a centrifuge. The resulting oil is almost completely free from water and water-soluble proteins and other components and it consequently keeps very much better than butter. When ghee is made from buffalo milk, the butter is clarified by boiling followed by filtration. This gives a clear oil which is highly resistant to rancidity.

C. MARGARINE

1. Manufacture

Margarine was one of the earlier products of food technology. It was invented in 1870 by a Frenchman named Mèges-Mouriès. It was originally made by melting down and clarifying various animal fats, that of the ox being chiefly employed. These fats were at first churned with a proportion of cream in order to simulate as closely as possible the making of butter. Today, margarine is a manufactured imitation of butter made by mixing a variety of fats that may include whale oil or vegetable oils, hydrogenated to an appropriate degree as described in detail on p. 154, with lecithin or some other stabilizer, an oil soluble dye and a proportion of soured skimmed milk to supply flavour.

(a) MIXING THE FATS

The various fats to be used in the manufacture of margarine are raised to their melting points, piped into a weighing tank and thence pumped into a 'composition tank'. The fat mixture is then heated to a temperature varying from 26°C (80°F) to 40°C (104°F) and kept stirred before being submitted to emulsification. An example of characteristic blends is shown in Table 20.

Soft margarines, or those designated to spread straight from the

Table 20

Blends of fats for margarine manufacture

	%		%		%
Coconut oil	50–60	Palmkernel oil	50	Hydrogenated groundnut oil	70
Hydrogenated vegetable fat	20–25	Hydrogenated palm oil	20	Coconut oil	10
Oil*	20–25	Oil	30	Oil	20
Hydrogenated whale oil	25	Hydrogenated whale oil	20	Beef-fat	25
Coconut oil	50	Palm oil	15	Coconut oil	35
Oil	25	Coconut oil	20	Oil	40
		Palmkernel oil	20		
		Oil	20		

* Often clarified animal oils from which the solid stearins have been separated; or vegetable oil.

MARGARINE. 59: 'Starter' being added to the skim-milk component of margarine.
60: 'Compounding panel' where the ingredients for a margarine mix are selected.

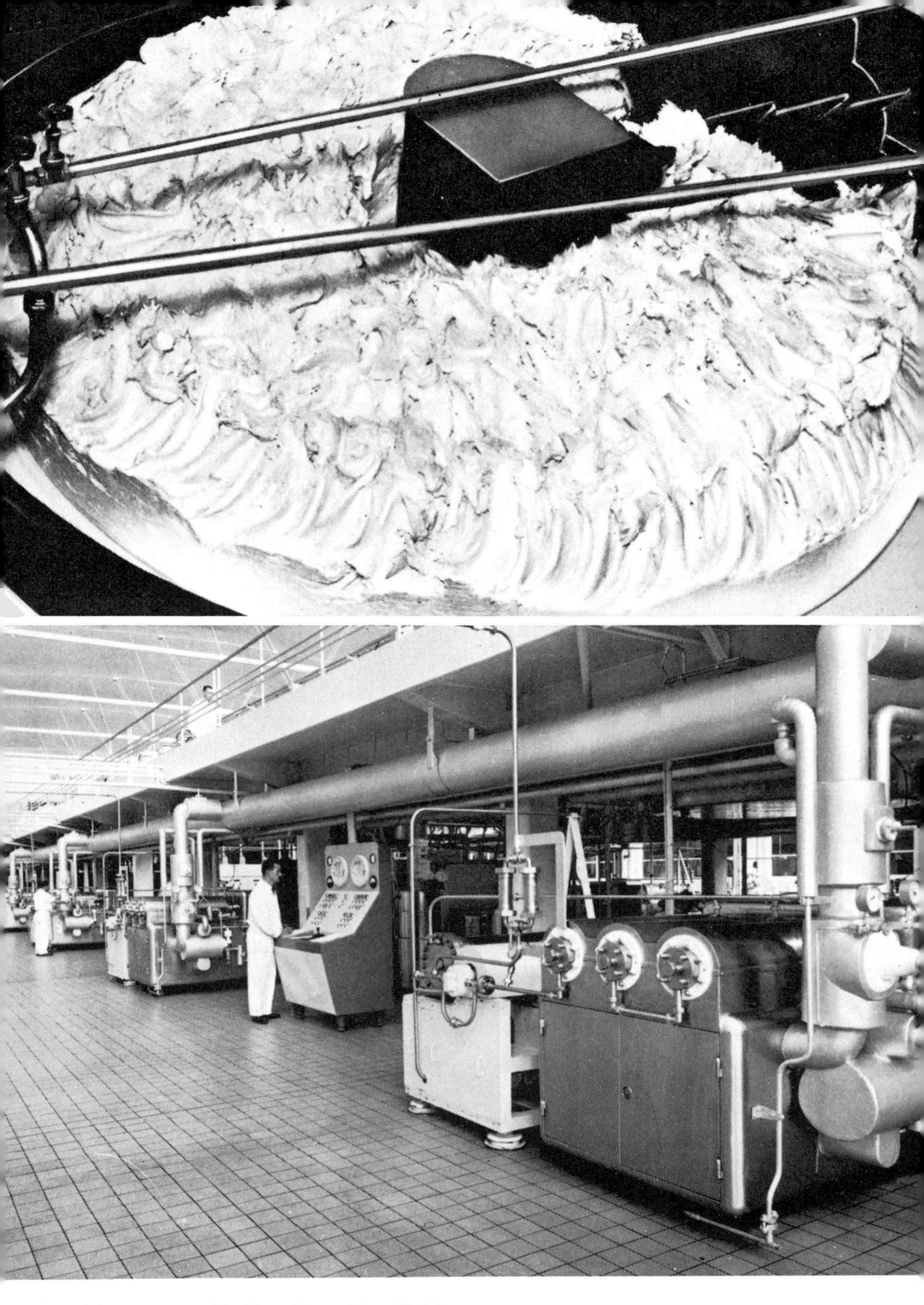

MARGARINE. 61: Kneading table. 62: Votators.

OILS. 63: Cracking rolls through which oil seeds are passed prior to the oil extraction process.

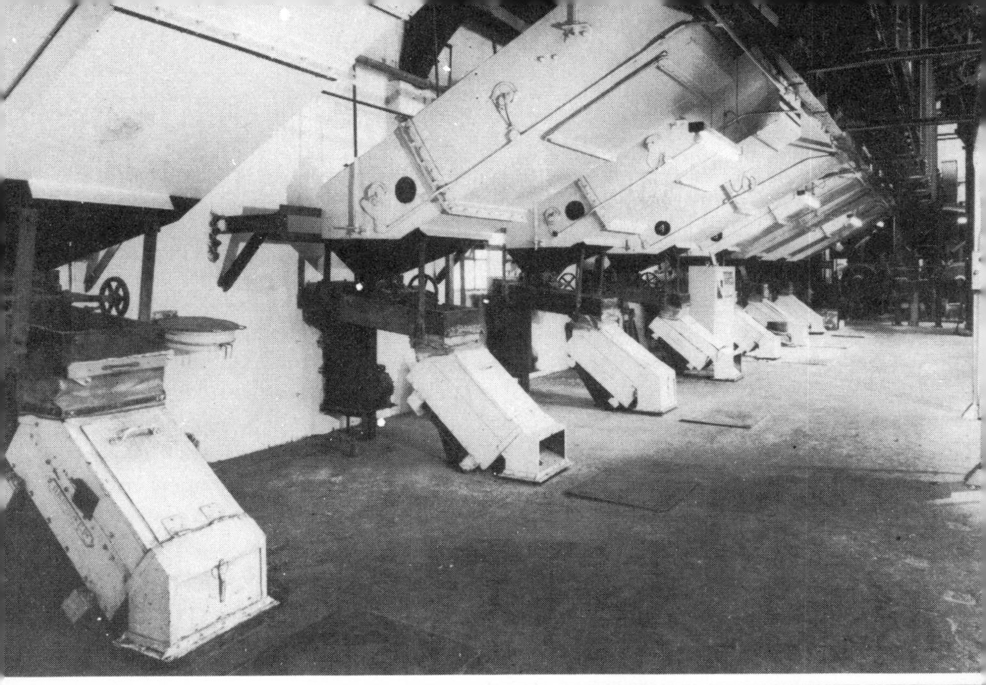

OILS. 64: Vibratory trash dressers and magnets for cleaning seeds before they go to the processing plant. 65: Vessels in which oils are hardened by being stirred in the presence of a catalyst and hydrogen under pressure.

fridge, are prepared from blends of oils specially selected or modified to contain reduced proportions of high-melting fractions.

(b) PREPARATION OF WATER-SOLUBLE COMPONENTS

Margarine, like butter, contains a proportion of water. It has been found that a good flavour can be given to margarine if its watery component is made up of skimmed milk which has been 'ripened', or soured, by the action of a specially selected culture of micro-organisms. This operation is commonly carried out in a 'ripening vat'. This is a stainless-steel tank fitted with a water-jacket to regulate the temperature and an oscillating motor-driven coil for stirring. About 1% of the starter culture of *Streptococcus lactis* or *Streptococcus cremoris* is added to the pasteurized skim milk and the whole agitated at 20–25°C (68–77°F) for 18–24 hours. This should produce the required aroma. If the ripened skim milk is not immediately required for use, it must be cooled to 8°C (46°F).

(c) EMULSIFICATION

The basic technology of margarine-making depends on the preparation of an appropriate emulsion of fat of the right consistency in which the watery component is dispersed just as it is in butter. The operation can be done either batch-wise or continuously.

For batch manufacture, the fat blend, comprising 80–83% of the whole, is run into the *emulsion churn* at a temperature of 32–35°C (90–95°F) which is arranged to be 2–3°C above its melting-point. The ripened skim milk, comprising the remaining 17–20% of the mixture, is run in simultaneously at a very much cooler temperature which may be as low as 3–4°C (37–39°F) but is more commonly 7–10°C (45–50°F). Salt is usually added to margarine in the proportion of about 2%; this concentration is most conveniently obtained by dissolving 13% of salt in the skim milk solution.

When the ingredients have been pumped in, the water-jacket of the churn is set at about 35°C and the agitators are run at a high speed of 150–200 r.p.m. to give a fine dispersion of water in oil. The presence of 'stabilizers', of which *soya-bean lecithin* is widely used at the rate of say 0·2%, affects the character of the emulsion. There are numerous stabilizers or emulsifiers in use—special soaps, glyceride derivatives, glyceryl-monostearate (GMS), monostearin sulphoacetate, 'polymerized oxidized oil' and many more.

After the mixture has been rapidly agitated for 10–15 minutes, the temperature of the water-jacket surrounding the churn is reduced. This causes the margarine to become more viscous. Eventually, the fat can be seen to crystallize.

When this stage is reached, the emulsion is warmed a few degrees to about 30–32°C (86–90°F) by raising the temperature of the water-jacket. This produces fat crystals of small and regular size and hence improves the consistency of the margarine. When the appropriate temperature is reached, the speed of the agitators is reduced to 60–70 r.p.m.

As an alternative to batch operation, a number of manufacturers have installed machines called 'votators' in which the emulsification and the subsequent conditioning processes are carried out continuously. A votator is a machine in which margarine can be manufactured in a single continuous operation. The oils first enter a cooling cylinder; they then pass into a pre-crystallizing chamber and on into a post-crystallizing chamber. From these they emerge in a semi-solid condition and in this form they can be pumped directly to a butter-wrapping machine. By suitable adjustment of the degree of cooling and of the speed at which the machine is operated, margarines of differing quality and consistency can be produced.

(*d*) COOLING AND CRYSTALLIZATION

The emulsified margarine mixture is very rapidly cooled by being run out of the emulsion churn on to the surface of a revolving, refrigerated drum. The drum is usually made of stainless steel and is cooled by refrigerated calcium-chloride brine at −15°C (5°F) which is passed through an annular space inside it. The solidified emulsion is carried round on the surface of the revolving drum until it is removed by a fixed scraper.

(*e*) KNEADING AND ROLLING

The chilled flakes of crystalline margarine are allowed to 'mature' for a short time, often while being transported in shallow trays to the kneading plant. It is found that this period of gradual re-warming allows the crystalline structure to adjust itself so that an appropriate consistency is obtained after kneading.

The rolling process in margarine manufacture is carried out by passing the flakes between horizontal rollers, arranged something after the fashion of an old-fashioned mangle. A large variety of rollers is used: these may consist of smooth rollers or fluted rolls;

single pairs; two pairs one above the other (called 'duplex') or 'multiplex', comprising several sets of rollers and conveyor-screws. In order to obtain a uniform, smooth consistency most types of margarine, after having been passed through the rollers, are next submitted to a kneading process. This is usually carried out on a machine called a 'kneading table'. It consists of a circular table which is arranged to rotate slowly under a revolving fluted roller of a conical shape that corresponds to the flat conical surface of the table, and can be adjusted vertically so that the distance between the roller and the table can be varied depending on the amount of margarine being worked.

(*f*) PACKING AND WRAPPING

The rolled and kneaded margarine is packed and wrapped in the same way as butter.

The entire elaborate process of margarine manufacture, of which the foregoing paragraphs only give a short description, is designed (*a*) to produce an emulsion of water droplets in fat, (*b*) to obtain a consistency equivalent to that of butter, and (*c*) to obtain, by the use of ripened skim milk as the water component, a flavour the same as that of butter. Numerous 'additives' may be used; besides the emulsifiers that have already been mentioned, they may also include colouring materials, flavours, anti-mould agents and vitamins. These are discussed in Chapter 8.

The whole margarine-manufacturing process is summarized diagrammatically in the figure on p. 157.

D. HYDROGENATION OF OILS

Vegetable fats, such as olive oil or cotton-seed oil, and animal fats, such as cod-liver oil, are customarily considered to be *oils* rather than fats, since they are generally liquid at room temperature. On the other hand, fats which melt at higher temperatures, such as cacao-butter, suet, lard and whale blubber, are customarily classified as *fats*.

It will be recalled from Chapter 1 that chemically fats are mainly composed of a combination of a molecule of glycerol combined with three molecules of one or more of a variety of fatty acids. These fatty acids consist in the main of a chain of linked carbon atoms of which the free linkages, not otherwise occupied in linking one carbon atom with another, are attached to atoms of hydrogen.

Among the commonest fatty acids are *palmitic acid* ($C_{16}H_{32}O_2$) and *stearic acid* ($C_{18}H_{36}O_2$) although numerous other fatty acids occur, some of which are of shorter carbon-chain length, notably *butyric acid* ($C_4H_8O_2$) present in butter. But among the C_{18}-fatty acids, besides stearic acid, the carbon atoms of which are fully 'saturated'

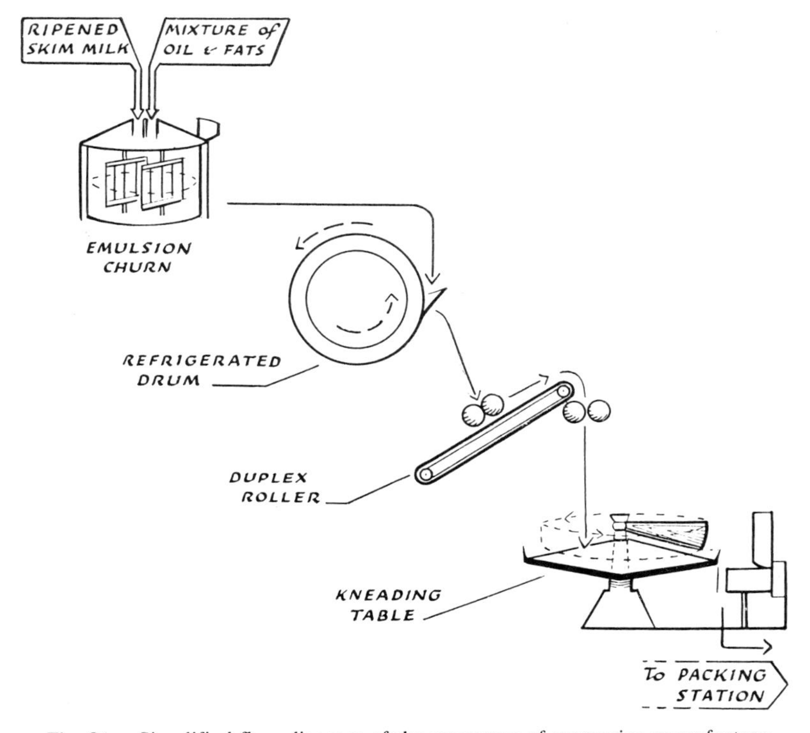

Fig. 21. Simplified flow-diagram of the processes of margarine manufacture.

with hydrogen, there also occur *oleic acid* ($C_{18}H_{34}O_2$), *linoleic acid* ($C_{18}H_{32}O_2$), and *linolenic acid* ($C_{18}H_{30}O_2$). It will be noted that these fatty acids contain to an increasingly marked degree less hydrogen than the fully saturated C_{18}-fatty acid, stearic acid. They are, in fact, 'unsaturated'. This chemical difference is related to a physical difference in their properties, namely, that they possess lower melting-points. It follows, therefore, that fats containing increased proportions of unsaturated fatty acids tend to be liquid at room temperature. Hence, by introducing hydrogen into their molecules—that is, by *hydrogenation*—these fatty acids can be made more saturated and the oils of which they form a part will consequently be *hardened*.

In many parts of the world, there is a strong demand for solid fats—'hard' fats, as they are called—rather than liquid oils. In industrialized countries most of the cooking is done with lard-like fats rather than with oils. One of the major developments in modern food technology has been the use of controlled hydrogenation to convert liquid oils of all sorts into uniform cooking fats and margarine.

1. The process of hydrogenation (hardening)

The conversion of a liquid unsaturated oil into a solid fat is brought about as follows. The oil is heated, a solid catalyst is stirred with it and hydrogen gas is bubbled in under pressure. Under these conditions, the hydrogen is gradually taken into the molecules of the unsaturated fatty acids. The rate at which this chemical reaction takes place and the exact course it follows depend on a number of factors:

(i) The temperature at which the hydrogenation process is carried out.
(ii) The pressure under which the hydrogen is injected into the heated oil.
(iii) The purity of the hydrogen gas.
(iv) The nature and purity of the catalyst.
(v) The composition of the oil that is being treated.

Variations in the conditions of the process may cause $C_{18}H_{30}O_2$ to become $C_{18}H_{32}O_2$; alternatively the change may be that the $C_{18}H_{32}O_2$ becomes $C_{18}H_{34}O_2$, or the reaction may cause the $C_{18}H_{34}O_2$ to go to the fully saturated $C_{18}H_{36}O_2$. More complicated still, however, is the fact that whereas in nature the molecules of the various unsaturated acids such as linolenic, linoleic and oleic acids are doubled back on themselves in a particular configuration, the same chemical combinations produced in the course of artificial hydrogenation may possess molecules that are folded differently. This has some effect on the hardness of the oil or fat produced; it may, however, have a parallel effect on the nutritional value of the fat. This matter is still being investigated. Although the conclusions are not yet clear, it is a matter that must be borne in mind by food technologists.

2. Industrial process

The process of hydrogenation may be carried out as follows:

(a) Heating. About 10 tons of, say, refined cotton-seed oil is heated to 120°C (250°F) under vacuum, in the presence of 0·05% of a nickel catalyst.

(b) Hydrogenation. The heated oil is stirred, the vacuum shut off and hydrogen admitted into the vessel at a pressure of 40 lb./sq. in. This pressure is maintained as the hydrogen is absorbed by the oil. The absorption of hydrogen is accompanied by the production of heat. The temperature of the reactor is kept at 120°C by running cold water through an outer jacket.

(c) Cooling. When the oil is considered to be hydrogenated sufficiently (this is measured chemically by determining the 'iodine number'), the flow of hydrogen is stopped, the residual gas vented, the vacuum reapplied and the oil cooled to about 80°C (176°F). The nickel catalyst is then removed from the hydrogenated fat by filtration.

E. RANCIDITY

The taste and smell of fats can be spoiled, and they can consequently become rancid, for a number of reasons. Each kind of spoilage is, as a general rule, due to a particular chemical or biological cause.

(a) ABSORPTION OF ODOURS

Many odours are due to very small traces of chemical substances which are soluble in fat. It follows that such smells—for example, those of paint, petroleum oils, boxes made from unseasoned resinous wood—will be absorbed by fats. Clearly, therefore, edible oils, fats and fatty foods must not be stored where such smells are likely to be present.

(b) ENZYMIC BREAKDOWN

The living animal and vegetable cells in which fats occur in nature contain enzymes, *lipases,* which possess the ability to split the chemical molecule of the fat into its component parts, namely, glycerol and fatty acids. Lipases are protein compounds and may remain as contaminants in unrefined fats and oils. If fats are to be stored for any length of time, it is therefore important to ensure that they are efficiently refined and substantially free from moisture in which lipases could occur. *Lipoxidases* are also widely distributed in plants and animals. These enzymes cause rancidity by oxidizing the fat molecule.

(c) MICROBIOLOGICAL ATTACK

Moulds, yeasts and bacteria, in the presence of moisture and nutrients, can all cause chemical deterioration of fats. It is important, therefore, to ensure that animal tissues and vegetable sources from which fats and oils are to be extracted should be as free from microbiological contamination as possible. For example, it has been shown that beef fat from a freshly killed animal had only 0·1% of free fatty acid whereas fat from tissues allowed to remain for three days in a humid atmosphere contained 2·6% of free acid and had a tainted flavour. Fats after being refined must be kept free from moisture. Microbial growth has been shown to occur on lard containing as little as 0·3% moisture.

(d) OXIDATIVE RANCIDITY

One of the commonest and most disagreeable forms of rancidity is not due either to enzymic breakdown or to the action of micro-organisms. It is the development of tallowy, 'rancid' flavours in perfectly well-refined and water-free fats. This is due to chemical reaction with the oxygen of the air. In the main, the action takes place most readily when the fats contain a proportion of unsaturated fatty acid in their molecule. The CH_2-group adjacent to the double bond may become a *hydroperoxide* ($-CH{=}CH-\underset{\displaystyle OOH}{\underset{|}{CH}}-$) or a *peroxide* may be formed thus:

$$\begin{array}{cccccc} H & H & & & H & H \\ | & | & & & | & | \\ -C- & C- & C= & C- & C- & C- \\ | & | & | & | & | & | \\ H & H & H & H & H & H \end{array} \rightarrow \begin{array}{cccccc} H & H & O- & O & H & H \\ | & | & | & | & | & | \\ -C- & C- & C- & C- & C- & C- \\ | & | & | & | & | & | \\ H & H & H & H & H & H \end{array}$$

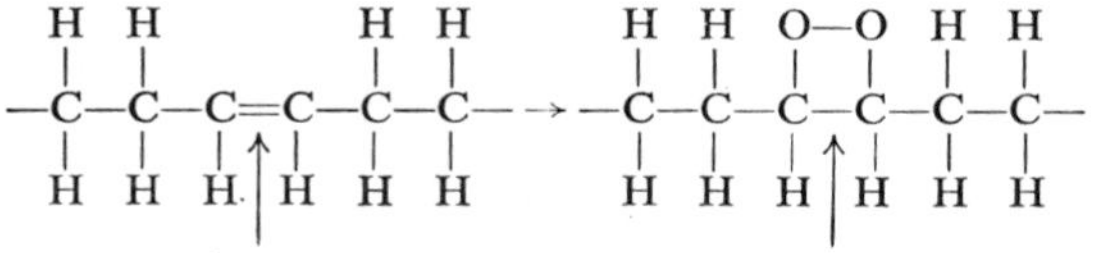

Point of unsaturation *Formation of peroxide*

Besides being produced by oxygen itself, rancidity due to the formation of peroxides is encouraged by a number of agents. Among these are:

(i) *Light.* It is common knowledge that fats exposed to strong light, particularly sunlight, are peculiarly liable to oxidative rancidity. Ultra-violet light and light at the blue end of the spectrum have an especially potent effect.

(ii) *Peroxides.* Chemical substances containing peroxides catalyse the development of rancidity. Among these are such materials as turpentine or benzoyl peroxide; but of more direct importance, a small proportion of rancid fat will itself initiate rancidity in a larger bulk with which it may be mixed.

(iii) *Metals.* Traces of metallic contamination, particularly copper and also iron, which may be derived from containers or equipment will start the process of oxidative rancidity. Fats should, therefore, be stored away from metal. Even bright tin-plate has been shown to affect the flavour of fats compared with non-metallic surfaces such as lacquered tin or glass.

(*e*) REVERSION

Some fats contain very small amounts of substances whose molecules possess more than two double bonds. These substances may undergo molecular rearrangement which affects the flavour of the fat. In some instances this may improve flavour. For example, part of the creamy taste in butter due to such 'reversion' in contact with air is due to the formation of a substance, 4-cis-heptenal, $CH_3{\cdot}CH_2{\cdot}CH{=}CH{\cdot}CH_2{\cdot}CH_2{\cdot}CHO$, of which only a few parts per 1000 million may be present.

7

Sugar, syrup and soft drinks

One of the most striking features of the growth of industrialization in a society is the increase in the amount of sugar and soft drinks which accompanies it. The manufacture and processing of sugar are similar in principle to the production of fat which must first be extracted and then refined. Sugar is a component of cane or beet; it must first be extracted and, after having been separated, must then be refined.

1. The manufacture of raw cane sugar

Sugar cane from the tropics contains from 14 to 17% of sugar. The cut cane is fed into a machine which cuts it into chips. These pass through a crusher in which two deeply grooved rollers express more than half the juice. Next, the cane goes through a battery of mills, in each of which are large steel rollers arranged in sets of three. These mills exert pressures of from 200 to 500 tons. To increase the extraction, juice or water is sprayed over the partly ground cane entering the last sets of rollers. The cane residues, or bagasse, are used as fuel for the boilers.

The raw juice is strained through a fine screen, sufficient lime is added to neutralize organic acids, the temperature raised to boiling point and the 'mud' allowed to settle in a clarifier. This is a vessel with a conical bottom in which the sediment collects. It is run off and dewatered in a filter press. The decanted clarified juice is concentrated to a syrup in a multiple-effect evaporator. The concentrated syrup, or massacuite, containing 55–70% solids, is transferred to the final mixer or crystallizer. The exact conditions of supersaturation at which the 'strike' is made and crystallization occurs are critical. The rate of cooling and stirring, among other factors, determine the amount and nature of the eventual sugar crystals obtained. The unrefined, commercial sugar is finally separated from the mother

SUGAR. 66: Cutting sugar cane by hand. 67: Cut cane on its way to the crushing mill.

SUGAR. 68: Cane being crushed. 69: Crushed cane being washed. 70: Vacuum pans where the sugar is boiled for crystallization. 71: White sugar centrifuge – sugar is seen entering the centrifuge prior to the separation of crystals.

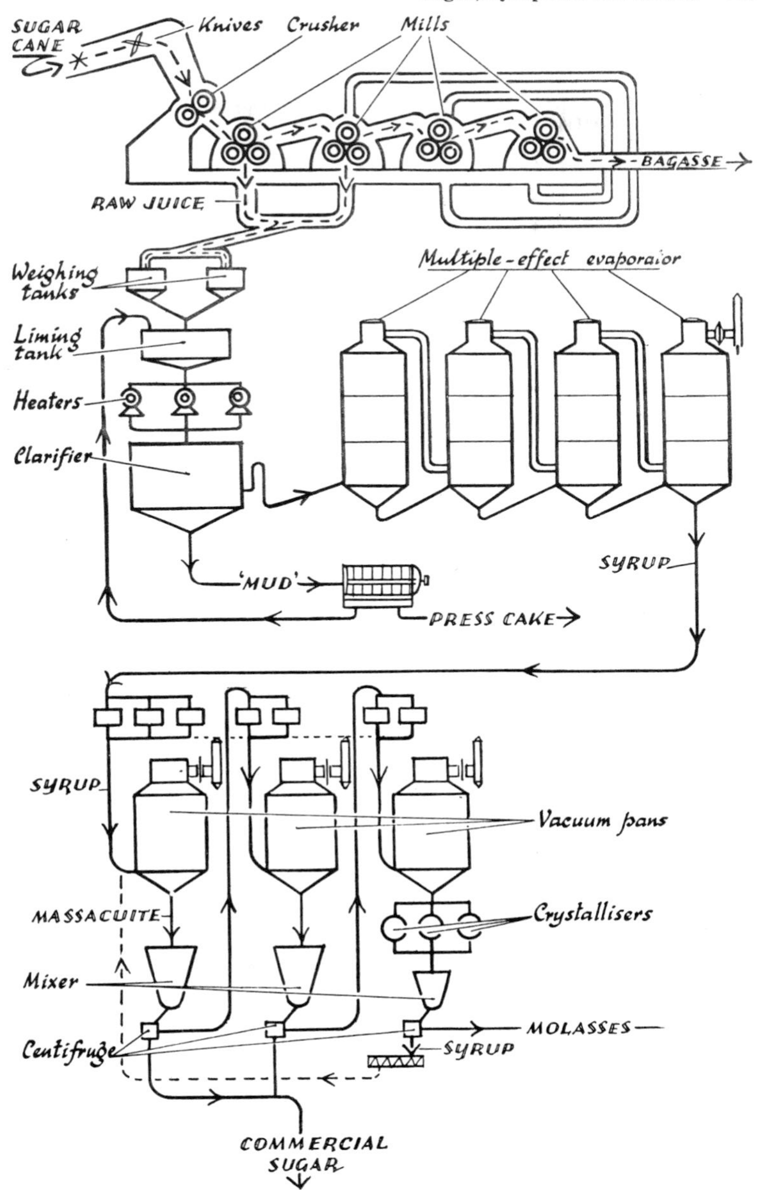

Fig. 22. Flow-diagram of cane sugar manufacture.

liquor, or molasses, by means of a centrifuge. Figure 22 is a diagram of the process.

2. Refining raw cane sugar

The raw sugar crystals are mixed with heavy syrup and centrifuged and at the same time the crystals are washed with a spray of hot water while they are still in the centrifuge basket. The washed crystals are then transferred into a melter and treated with steam and hot water; the heavy syrup separated by the centrifuge is mixed with the next batch of raw sugar. The melted sugar, now converted into a syrup at 150°F, goes to the carbonation vessel where lime is added and carbon dioxide injected, converting the lime to calcium carbonate which traps waxes, gums and other impurities. The sediment of impurities and calcium carbonate is removed by filtration. Final purification is achieved by passing the syrup through granulated bone char. The material, produced by charring granules of animal bone and hence forming a porous substance composed of calcium phosphate on which there is a layer of charcoal, has been used since antiquity. Batches of bone char can be re-used many times if they are washed and then heated to 1000°F. The purified syrup is boiled in vacuum pans until crystals of the required size are obtained. The crystals are finally washed, dried, sifted and packed. The whole operation is shown diagrammatically in Figure 23.

3. The manufacture of beet sugar

Sugar beet is the source of about a third of the world's supply of sugar. Botanists and plant geneticists have achieved significant advances in breeding high-yielding varieties of beet, and agronomists have worked out cultural conditions to obtain maximum concentrations of sugar. The sugar content of the harvested beet is of the order of 18%. The main difference in principle in recovering the sugar from beet rather than from cane is that, whereas the juice is mainly crushed out of cane, it is washed out of beet by extraction with hot water.

Beets brought in from the fields are first washed in a rapid stream of water to remove soil and dirt. They are then cut up into small V-shaped pieces by very sharp knives set on the inner side of a revolving drum. The chopped beet is then extracted in hot water at 185°F in a series of 'diffusers'. This operation may be carried out continuously. The beet in long perforated trays is carried through vertical chambers. The fresh hot water enters the compartment out of which the exhausted beet pulp is being discharged and flows in the opposite direction so that the concentrated juices eventually emerge from the chamber into which the unextracted chopped beet first enters.

Although there are certain differences in detail, in principle the evaporation and concentration of the beet juice, the crystallization of the sugar and its subsequent refining is similar to the procedure used for cane.

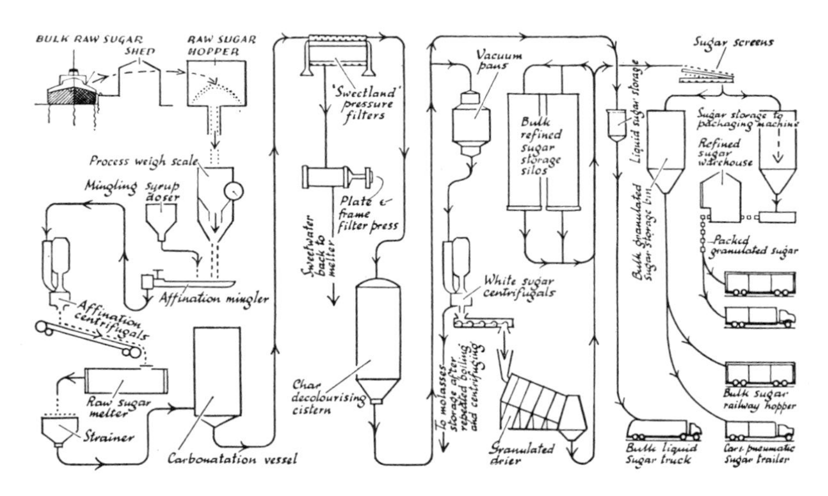

Fig. 23. Flow-diagram of cane sugar refining.

4. Golden syrup

Sugar, which in chemical terms is sucrose, a compound of glucose and fructose, is not very soluble in water. It is, therefore, not possible to prepare a concentrated syrup which will be stable in use. The sucrose will always tend to crystallize out. The popularity of golden syrup is due to the fact that crystallization does not take place. This is achieved by mixing a sugar syrup with a proportion of the more soluble 'invert sugar'. Invert sugar is itself a mixture of glucose and fructose which has been obtained by breaking the chemical bonds by which these two sugars are combined to form sucrose. Invert sugar is made by adding hydrochloric acid to a 96% sugar solution to bring the pH to 3–4. The enzyme, invertase, prepared from yeast, is then introduced. When the reaction is complete, the mixture is neutralized with sodium carbonate. Sucrose can also be converted to invert sugar by treatment with acid at an elevated temperature.

Golden syrup is usually made from the mother liquor from the second or third massacuite stage in the process of sugar manufacture. Invert sugar is then added and the mixture canned (see illustration 91).

5. Soft drinks

Sugar syrup, commonly containing from 55 to 65% of sugar by weight, is one of the main constituents of soft drinks which are increasingly popular all over the world. Such drinks may be manufactured in a form suitable for direct consumption or as a concentrate which is intended to be diluted four times with water before being drunk.

(a) DRINKS FOR DIRECT CONSUMPTION

It is good practice to heat the sugar syrup to pasteurize it. Acid is commonly added, either as citric acid or as a mixture of citric, phosphoric and tartaric acids, sometimes with lactic and malic acids as well. Colours and flavour are also added and the syrup mixture clarified by being passed through a filter. The central feature of the manufacturing process is the filling machine. This, in modern factories, is an engineering product of considerable complexity. It is designed to dispense the syrup into washed and sterilized bottles, add water into which carbon-dioxide gas has previously been injected in a carbonator, and then cap and label the bottles. About 4 volumes of carbon dioxide per volume of liquid, giving a pressure of approximately 30 lb. per sq. in. inside the bottle, are customarily used. The water for soft drink manufacture must be free from chlorine and is usually de-ionized before being used. Sulphur dioxide and benzoic acid are commonly permitted to be added as preservatives. Carbonated soft drinks may vary in flavour and appearance to suit the taste of their consumers but are usually made to contain about 10% of sugar by weight.

Fruit beverages of this sort are frequently made by passing lemon, orange or grapefruit juice, either unconcentrated or after concentration, through a sieving machine to remove pips and large cells and then mixing them with the filtered and sterilized sugar syrup. Fruit essences, citric acid and sometimes saccharine are also included. The syrup mixture is usually adjusted to contain 25–30% of juice. The final carbonated beverage commonly contains 70 p.p.m. of sulphur dioxide as a preservative.

(*b*) SQUASHES

These are most commonly manufactured from 'comminuted' citrus fruit. The whole oranges, lemons or grapefruit are milled in a machine between rapidly revolving carborundum wheels and quickly pasteurized, partly to prevent the growth of micro-organisms and partly to inactivate enzymes which would otherwise damage the flavour and consistency of the juice. The comminuted fruit is then thoroughly mixed with sugar syrup, flavouring essences and a proportion of saccharine, and the acidity adjusted in order to achieve the desired taste and character. When the drink is intended to be consumed without dilution, the final composition is commonly 2 lb. of fruit in 10 gallons, i.e. 2% and 4·5 lb. sugar, equivalent to 4·5%. The maximum permissible content of saccharine is 80 p.p.m. Squashes that are intended to be drunk after dilution with 4 volumes of water are made to contain 10% by weight of fruit, 22·5% of sugar, with a maximum of 400 p.p.m. of saccharine. Benzoic acid, added at concentrations of 160 and 800 p.p.m. respectively, is used as a preservative in fruit squashes.

8

Fruit and vegetables

In a book of modest size such as this it is impossible to review, one by one, all the different types of fruit, and all the different varieties of vegetables, and describe in detail every different process to which they may be subjected. Apart from the inordinate length which so much description would require, many of the different processes do not represent any separate scientific principle, nor do they necessarily involve any special technological novelty. I give only a brief description of the main scientific factors that must be considered in handling fruit and vegetables—the fact that they are alive and consequently in a state of constant change, the fact that they may be affected by the atmosphere surrounding them, and that they may be susceptible to quite moderate variations in temperature. And the way these principles are made use of in handling the major different categories of fruit and vegetables: apples, tropical fruit such as bananas, and citrus fruit; green vegetables, fresh and dried peas, and—representing a root crop—potatoes.

I. FRUIT

A. GENERAL PRINCIPLES OF TECHNOLOGY

Fresh fruit and vegetables are different in two respects from most of the foods so far discussed. First, they do not under normal circumstances constitute a significant source of the major nutritional components, protein, carbohydrate and fat—and hence Calories. Their dietetic significance is, instead, restricted to providing a minor component, namely vitamin C, and freshness, flavour and variety. Secondly, they are alive. This implies that the food technologist whose business it is to handle fruit and vegetables must always bear in mind the need to allow for their respiration.

(a) RESPIRATION

All fruit are living entities which absorb oxygen, produce carbon dioxide and generate heat while doing so. Storage life and rate of ripening are affected by the composition of the atmosphere in the store. Appropriate conditions can be achieved by the use of a gas-proof room equipped with a fan to circulate the atmosphere through the boxes of fruit. The oxygen content falls due to the natural respiration of the fruit and the carbon-dioxide content, which tends to rise, can be limited to any desired level by conducting the atmosphere through a caustic scrubber that absorbs carbon dioxide. Excess carbon dioxide may 'stifle' fruit and can cause 'brownheart' and 'invasive' alcohol poisoning in apples and pears. Recent investigations suggest that very low carbon-dioxide concentrations associated with reduced oxygen may be particularly suitable for certain varieties of fruit. On the other hand, raised concentrations of carbon dioxide up to 25% or even 50% have been used successfully for cherries, raspberries and blackcurrants.

Respiration may cause trouble when fruit is pre-packed in plastic wrappers for self-service stores and it is prudent to provide such wrappers with perforation holes.

(b) TEMPERATURE

Transport and storage of many kinds of fruit is more successfully achieved when the fruit is cooled and its natural heat of respiration is removed by refrigeration. Too low temperatures, however, are damaging and the temperature must not be allowed to fall below freezing-point. (Quick-freezing is discussed in Chapter 8.) Bananas are particularly sensitive to cold and may more often require warming—to 13°C (55°F)—rather than cooling. This sensitivity to cold is shared by a number of other tropical fruits, including mangoes, avocados, pineapples and also tomatoes and many melons.

(c) RIPENING

In any population of fruit some individuals will be found to ripen faster than others. It was observed some time ago that these early ripening fruit give off a gas, ethylene. This is a comparatively simple organic compound with the chemical structure

$$\begin{array}{c} \text{H}\quad\text{H} \\ |\quad\;| \\ \text{H}-\text{C}=\text{C}-\text{H} \end{array}$$

It can be produced in petroleum refining and is used industrially in the manufacture of plastics. But its characteristic that is of particular interest to the food technologist is that when present in very low concentration it accelerates ripening. Consequently a single early ripening fruit in a bulk store will stimulate the ripening of the rest. The effect may be used to advantage in commercial practice, since by introducing ethylene into the store chamber ripening can be accelerated.

However, the effect of ethylene is somewhat complex and different fruit may behave differently. For example, although ethylene hastens the development of colour in plums, it does not affect the rate of sweetening or the development of flavour.

(d) INFECTION AND ROTTING

In spite of the variety of troubles which can afflict fruit in storage, some of which may be due to an unsatisfactory atmosphere perhaps containing too much carbon dioxide, or to too low a temperature, and in spite of loss due to 'bitter pit' of apples and other ills probably due to abnormality in the uptake of minerals while the fruit are still on the tree, the most serious wastage with which the food technologist has to deal is due to infection by micro-organisms, particularly fungi. Rotting is due to the invasion of the tissues of fruit by mould mycelium. Two basic principles are, therefore, involved in preventing it, firstly, to minimize the level of mould infection by good housekeeping and by ruthless segregation and destruction of already infected fruit and, secondly, by taking all possible steps to protect the fruit from mechanical damage so that they may be able to resist attack.

B. APPLES

When apples are picked they may still contain starch, together with the sugars, sucrose, fructose and glucose, and the organic acid, malic acid. As they ripen in store, the starch quickly disappears, followed by most of the sucrose; glucose disappears at a slow steady rate; fructose remains for a while and then, after some weeks, it too begins to disappear, while the malic acid is used up at a continuously accelerating rate. The whole time, the fruit is 'breathing in' oxygen from the atmosphere and 'breathing out' carbon-dioxide gas. This is the process of respiration.

The rate of respiration, which can be measured by recording the amount of carbon dioxide produced, is quite rapid when the fruit is picked. At first the respiration rate of the freshly picked fruit falls until, just before ripening begins, it rises again quite rapidly to a peak. This stage is called the 'climacteric'. After the 'climacteric' is reached the respiration rate falls off continuously as the fruit ages in storage. It is at the 'climacteric', or shortly after, that fruit acquire their characteristic odours and flavours. Pears, bananas and many other fruit besides apples, also show this 'climacteric' peak in their rate of respiration as they approach ripeness.

It is from information such as this, derived from scientific studies of the biology of 'senescence' in fruit, that appropriate technological conditions have been worked out for the handling of apples and other fruits.

(a) TEMPERATURE OF STORAGE

As in all living organisms, the rate of change in apples is more rapid at raised temperature. Consequently, they can be stored for longer periods at reduced temperature. For cold storage, the lowest practicable temperature is −2°–0°C (29–31°F) provided the relative humidity is 85–88%. For certain varieties of apples, however, the lowest safe temperature is 2°–3°C (35–38°F).

(b) GAS STORAGE

The rate of respiratory activity of apples, and consequently the rapidity with which they first become ripe and then become old, is controllable by altering the concentration of oxygen and of carbon dioxide in the atmosphere in which they are stored. As the concentration of oxygen is reduced from about 20%, as normally present in air, the rate of respiration falls until at a definite point the lowest level is reached; less oxygen still would cause respiration to increase rather than decrease further. This critical concentration varies somewhat from one variety of fruit to another. For example, for Canadian McIntosh apples the value is from 2–3% oxygen at a temperature of 4°C (40°F).

The rate of respiration is affected by carbon-dioxide gas as well as by oxygen. For carbon dioxide, however, the effect is that respiratory activity is reduced as the concentration of carbon dioxide rises to a certain specific limit. The optimum level, again using McIntosh apples as an example, is 5%. Consequently, the atmosphere allowing the longest storage of these fruit should be made up of 2–3%

oxygen and 5% carbon dioxide with the remainder nitrogen. In air, the nitrogen content is normally about 80%.

Depending upon the qualities of the particular fruit being handled, these techniques may extend the life of fruit in store by several months.

(c) ETHYLENE RIPENING

It has been found that 0·1% of ethylene introduced into an apple store will accelerate ripening by about 14 days.

C. BANANAS

Bananas, like apples, are living entities right up to the time they are eaten. Considerable changes take place in their composition during the process of ripening: the sugar content increases from 2% in green bananas to 20% when they are fully ripe.

(a) TEMPERATURE

The most important scientific discovery about the physiology of the banana that enabled it to be transported all over the world and, in particular, to be marketed and enjoyed in non-tropical countries was that it cannot tolerate a temperature lower than 13°C (55°F). If unripe bananas are exposed to a cold draught in a greengrocer's shop on a wintry day, even for a short time, they become chilled, their skin becomes a muddy khaki colour, they fail to ripen and are uneatable. The technologist who has to handle bananas must ensure that they are kept at an even temperature throughout their journey on sea and land and at every point where they need to be held; whether in bulk storage or in a retail shop, they must be put into a temperature-controlled 'banana room'.

(b) RIPENING

Ethylene may be introduced into banana-ripening rooms to accelerate ripening and to ensure that all the fruit become ripe at about the same time. The same concentration (0·1%) as that used for apples has been found to be most satisfactory.

(c) HISTORY

Successful food technology always tends towards standardization and the production and marketing of a uniform article. The history of the banana industry in Jamaica shows that this may sometimes employed since they can resist the corrosive effect of acidity. In packing juice, the cans are sterilized and the juice run in hot from the pasteurizer. A method of excluding traces of air capable of damaging the flavour and destroying a proportion of the vitamin C is to inject live steam into the head-space of the can immediately before it is sealed. When the cans are sealed they must be cooled to avoid any deterioration in flavour which will occur if the juice is kept hot too long.

An alternative method of treatment is to fill cans nine-tenths full with unpasteurized juice, seal them, heat the filled cans to pasteurizing temperature, making sure that sufficient time has been allowed to heat the entire bulk, and then cool them as rapidly as possible.

An increasing quantity of fruit juice is being stabilized and marketed frozen. This can allow the production of an article with especially fine flavour.

2. Contamination

The combination of low pH and of the particular organic acids naturally present in most fruit juices is quite remarkably corrosive. It is, therefore, important that all the equipment with which juices come in contact is inert. Most modern plant is fabricated from stainless steel but even when this is so it is prudent to carry out trials to ensure that the quality of the stainless steel used is resistant under the conditions to which it is to be subjected. Special care must be taken to avoid contamination with copper which, besides being capable of spoiling the colour and flavour of juices, also acts as a catalyst for the destruction of vitamin C.

The canning and quick-freezing of fruit are discussed in Chapter 9.

II. VEGETABLES

Vegetables comprise several principal types of foods. Firstly, there are the green, leafy plants of which the members of the Brassica, the cabbage family, are the commonest. These include, beside cabbage itself, cauliflower and brussels sprouts. There are, however, a number of other commonly used leaves, such as turnip greens, spinach and watercress. A second group of green vegetables comprises green peas and beans eaten green or in the form of green unripe pods. Next can be included root vegetables which must be subdivided into (*a*) the yellow, vitamin A-active roots, carrots and

FRUIT. 72: Apple rot due to infection by a mould. 73: Rotten orange infected by *Penicillium digitatum*.

FRUIT. 74: Harvesting bananas. 75: After being harvested bananas are washed, wrapped in plastic and the cut stalk sealed to protect them from damage and infection during shipment.

FRUIT. 76: Bananas ripening in an electrically heated store under thermostatic control.

FRUIT. 77: The 'jump test' for cranberries. This is an ingenious yet simple device for separating firm berries of good quality from over-ripe or damaged ones. Only those which bounce over the 4-in. barrier are selected.

sweet potatoes, and (*b*) roots such as turnips, swedes and also, perhaps, onions, which have no vitamin-A activity. Potatoes deserve to be considered by themselves as a separate category. The last important group of items which are—probably mistakenly—considered to be 'vegetables' are the dried pulses, dried peas, beans and lentils.

A. GREEN VEGETABLES

Green vegetables, like fruit, are living entities and when they are freshly harvested are respiring. Consequently, if cabbages or other similar green foods are to be stored before being marketed or subjected to processing, they should be kept in a cool atmosphere, near but not below freezing-point, and at sufficiently high relative humidity to prevent drying out. It is also important to ensure that the store is satisfactorily ventilated.

The leaves of green vegetables are made up of a honeycomb of living cells. While these cells are vigorously alive, their outer membranes are capable of maintaining a considerable 'osmotic' pressure within the cells. This pressure gives the whole leaf of a living plant—or a 'fresh' vegetable—a degree of crisp stiffness which is characteristic of freshness. Under unsatisfactory storage conditions, or when the life of the vegetable even under good storage is approaching its end, the leaf cell membranes gradually lose their integrity and are unable to maintain the osmotic pressure of the freshly harvested plant. Consequently, the leaves begin to wilt. At this stage also, the vitamin C content of the leaves begins to dwindle away as the structure of the living cells becomes disorganized.

Green vegetables may be dehydrated or quick-frozen; these processes are discussed in Chapter 9.

(*a*) SAUERKRAUT

A traditional process for preserving cabbage is to convert it into sauerkraut by adding 1·5 to 2·5 lb. of salt per 100 lb. of shredded cabbage, which largely disrupts the cells, and allows the natural bacteria on the leaves to ferment the juice. These bacteria produce up to 1·5% of lactic acid. Fermentation is usually carried out in quite full, closed vats kept at 16°–23°C (60–75°F) for about six months. The vitamin C content of sauerkraut is about 3 to 4 mg./oz. compared with 20 mg./oz. in fresh cabbage.

B. PEAS

Peas are a vegetable to which science and technology have been applied in several ways; they can be eaten as two quite different foods; that is, as green peas or as dried peas. What is apparently a third type, namely, 'processed' peas, consists, in fact, of dried peas processed so as to simulate green peas.

1. Green peas

(a) COMPOSITION

Green peas contain about 85% of moisture and 15% of dry matter. This is a substantially less water and more dry matter than the 94% of moisture and 6% of dry matter present in cabbage; but green peas can, nevertheless, be classified as a green vegetable, the principal nutritional function of which is to contribute vitamin C and vitamin A to the diet. They also provide freshness and their characteristic flavour owes much to the fact that they contain a significant amount of sugar.

(b) HARVESTING

The composition of peas growing on the vine changes quite quickly so that it is of the utmost importance to the technologist that he obtains his supplies at the precise time when the peas attain the desired degree of maturity. Small, immature peas contain the highest *concentration* of sugar, amounting to 33% of the dry matter of the shelled peas. But the state usually accepted as best for processing is when the peas have reached their full size and contain the largest *amount* of sugar per pea. If this stage is missed, even by a day or two, the amount of sugar falls and the amount of starch rises in proportion. Another factor underlining the technological importance of handling green peas at precisely the appropriate time in their development and also of processing them with the maximum speed when they are harvested is the fact that once the peas are removed from their pods, the sugar in them very quickly changes to starch. Whereas at room temperature the sugar content of unshelled peas will fall by 10% in 24 hours, in shelled peas the loss of sugar will amount to up to 18%.

The best guidance that scientific knowledge can give to the technologist handling green peas is to obtain them at precisely the right degree of freshness, transport them to the processing plant as quickly as possible, and carry out whatever processing is to be done immediately.

(c) STORAGE

Green peas can be stored for up to two weeks if they are held at 0°C (32°F) in a moist store with a relative humidity of 85–90%. Storage can be prolonged by a significant length of time if 5% of carbon dioxide is provided in the atmosphere of the store.

Canning and quick-freezing of peas are discussed in Chapter 9.

(d) THE TENDEROMETER

It is worth considering the use of a technological device, the 'tenderometer', to measure and standardize the exact degree of maturity of green peas. Clearly, it is not always possible in practice to carry out chemical analyses of the sugar content of the peas to ensure that they are processed at precisely the right moment. In place of a chemical measurement, therefore, a physical measurement has been chosen as a means of assessing their condition. As is well known from practical experience, the complex biochemical changes associated with ripening, the initial increase in sugar concentration followed by a gradual fall and a parallel increase in starch content, all these are associated with a change in the physical structure of the peas and in their degree of tenderness. A machine, the 'tenderometer', was therefore developed to measure tenderness in as objective and precise a way as possible. In many places, the payment made to growers for quality, as well as the operation of a pea-canning or freezing plant, is based on 'tenderometer' readings.

The 'tenderometer' consists of a 'mashing grid' comprising two sets of flat metal strips that mesh into one another. The lower set is mounted on a shaft which is counterbalanced by a lever on which one, two or three counter-weights can be hung. The upper set is revolved by an electric motor. About 6 oz. of the peas to be tested are put into the space provided when the two sets of strips are disengaged. The cover of the machine is closed and the motor put in motion. The upper set of strips starts to revolve and crushes the peas against the lower set. The resistance of the peas being crushed pushes round the lower set of strips against the counter-weights on the lever fixed to its shaft. The distance this shaft is moved round before the peas are finally disintegrated is measured by an indicator on a scale. The 'tenderometer' mashing grid is illustrated in Plate 80.

The 'tenderometer' is an example of a machine designed to measure in as precise quantitative terms as possible what is, in fact, a highly complex biological condition. The complexity of what is being measured becomes apparent when attempts are made to standardize a number of different 'tenderometers'. So far, it has not been found possible to select any absolute physical measurement, or to find any substance of known softness, such as plastic or rubber—even cigarettes have been tried as a standard measure of 'tenderness', but without success. Each season it is necessary for the growers and the processors to assess the change of quality of the peas as they ripen, by chemical or other means, and then to select an agreed 'tenderometer' figure as a standard.

2. Processed peas

The most significant feature of the food value of green vegetables in general and, therefore, of green peas, whether fresh, canned or frozen, is that they provide vitamin C, which is only present in fresh vegetables and in fruit. When peas are allowed to ripen, they gradually dry and their vitamin C content falls to zero. Whereas green peas contain 85% of moisture, 6% of protein and 30 mg. of vitamin C per 100 g., dried peas may contain only about 5–8% of moisture, 25% of protein but no vitamin C at all. They are, in colloquial terms, not a 'vegetable' any more but can be eaten as pease-pudding or pea soup as a source of protein and calories to satisfy hunger. On the other hand, dried peas can be processed and canned so that they almost seem to the eater to be green peas. The similarity extends to consistency, colour—as an added dye—and taste, but not, of course, to nutritional value, since the vitamin C is lacking.

The basic technological operations involved in the manufacture of processed peas involve:

(*a*) *Washing* the peas to free them from extraneous matter, earth and other dirt.

(*b*) *Sizing*. Next, the peas are sifted so that those selected shall be uniform in size.

(*c*) *Sorting*. They are then passed slowly along a travelling belt which carries them under a revolving drum studded with sharp, bent needles. This drum picks up the peas which contain worm holes.

(d) *Soaking and blanching.* The sound ones are allowed to pass to soaking tanks for 18 hours and then blanched. After they are blanched, an edible green dye is added.

(e) *Packing.* They are then packed in cans, sealed and sterilized.

Processed peas can be handled in a cannery during the winter months when otherwise factory plant might be idle and workers unemployed.

C. POTATOES

Potatoes are perhaps the most valuable of all root vegetables. Their culture is remarkably widespread. They are grown in substantial quantities in most of the countries of the Northern Hemisphere including the USSR, Poland, Czechoslovakia, the USA, France, Germany, Spain, Eire, Great Britain and many others. They are also grown in South America, where the plant, *Solanum tuberosum*, originated, and in China.

Potatoes owe their importance as a food to a number of factors: (i) In countries to which their culture is suited, they provide the highest food-value yield (in terms of Calories) per acre. For example, in Great Britain where the yield of wheat is considered to be high, an acre of wheat will only produce about 80% of the yield of Calories from an acre of potatoes—and this does not include whatever Calories a hard-put consumer could expect to obtain from the peel. (ii) Unlike manioc, which is the highest Calorie-yielding root crop in certain tropical countries, potatoes provide a significant contribution of protein as well. (iii) They are a food that consistently and day by day contributes vitamin C to the diet.

1. Storing potatoes

From the point of view of the food technologist, the main problem in handling whole potatoes arises from the fact that they are, like other vegetables, alive and also impermanent. No matter what precautions are taken in storing them, half the vitamin C they contained when they were dug is lost after three months' storage, and three-quarters has disappeared in six months. By the employment of adequate measures, deterioration due to microbiological attack and the onset of sprouting can be deferred for almost a twelvemonth, but unless special technological steps are taken to dehydrate potatoes, as described in Chapter 9, it is impossible to preserve a surplus from one year to the next. Processing potatoes must add substantially to their cost; it is therefore a matter of considerable importance to apply scientific knowledge to obtaining the greatest possible improvement in conditions of storage.

(a) CLAMPS

It is common farm practice to store potatoes in 'clamps'. These are shallow trenches usually lined with straw. The potatoes are piled into them and covered with a layer of earth to protect them from frost. Although this method of storage is reasonably satisfactory, substantial losses may occur and modern practice is to store potatoes in specially constructed buildings.

(b) REDUCTION OF ROTTING

Infection by disease organisms is a serious cause of loss of stored potatoes. Precautions should therefore be taken by spraying growing crops with appropriate fungicides. An additional safeguard is allowing the haulms to die down before the tubers are lifted. As further precaution, the haulms should be destroyed, for example, by spraying them with sulphuric acid. Next, efforts must be made to avoid damaging the potatoes before they are put into store and removing any infected or damaged tubers. The potatoes must also be free from excess moisture and should be maintained at an appropriate temperature.

(c) STORAGE CONDITIONS

Stored potatoes need to be kept cool. Because they are living and respiring they produce heat and at the same time use up their own substance—and consequently lose weight—while doing so. The rate at which they respire depends on their temperature and is about doubled for every 10°C (18°F) rise in temperature. *The best storage temperature is between 5 and 10°C (40–49°F)*. If the temperature is reduced much below 5°C (40°F) the normal process of respiration is upset and the potatoes develop an undesirable sweet taste due to the formation in them of sugar.

It has been found that a ton of potatoes at 5°C (40°F) produces about 1200 B.T.U.s of heat by respiration every 24 hours. Ideally, this should be removed; it can be done by ventilating the store with

VEGETABLES. 78: Spinach being harvested six rows at a time by a food-manufacturing firm to transport to the factory and immediate processing. 79: Modern automatic viner harvesting peas

VEGETABLES. 80: Tenderometer for measuring the maturity of peas. 81: Drums for sorting dried peas. Those with worm-holes are picked up by the fine spikes with which drums are studded.

POTATOES. The manufacture of potato crisps. 82: A bulk potato store in a potato crisp factory. 83: Potato crisps flow from a high-technology cooker.

POTATOES. 84: Potato crisps direct from the cooker pass on to revolving drums, which add salt or other flavours. 85: Crisps being packed.

FRUIT AND VEGETABLES. 86: Spinach being washed prior to processing. 87: Broccoli being sorted. 88: Strawberries being inspected and sorted. 89: Sweet corn brought direct from the field and cut to size prior to blanching and processing.

2000 cu. ft./hour of cool air at 1–2°C (say 35°F) for 2–3 hours. The practice is often followed of using well-insulated stores and applying forced ventilation at night when the outside air is coldest. In order to avoid drying out the potatoes, the atmosphere of the store should be as humid as possible without actually causing a film of water to form on the potatoes, which could encourage bacterial infection.

(d) PREVENTION OF SPROUTING

As the season advances, the loss of potatoes in store tends to increase and as June approaches—still two months prior to the next main crop in temperate countries of the Northern Hemisphere—sprouting may become a serious cause of deterioration. Recent studies have shown that sprouts can be effectively suppressed by spraying vaporized *nonyl alcohol* into the atmosphere of the store as soon as the sprouts are seen to be forming.

```
              H              H
              |              |
          H—C—H      H—C—H
     H        |      H        |        H   H
     |        |      |        |        |   |
H—C———C———C———C———C—C—O—H
     |        |      |        |        |   |
     H        |      H        H        H   H
          H—C—H
              |
              H
```

Nonyl alcohol

The possibility of using radioactivity to check the growth of potato sprouts is discussed on pages 225–6.

2. Processing potatoes

As has already been mentioned, potatoes are low-cost foodstuffs. It has, however, increasingly been found to be an economic proposition to provide them with added value by submitting them to technological processing. For example, considerable progress has been made in developing dehydrated potato; this process is described in Chapter 9. More recent has been the development of frozen potato product, particularly french fried or chipped potatoes, which are the single most important frozen vegetable. The overwhelming appeal of these products is their convenience, which is something upon which changing eating habits places a premium.

3. Crisps

A great deal of technological effort has been devoted to the manufacture of potato crisps, which are nowadays a popular appetizer or dietetic embellishment. The process includes the following stages:

(a) Selection of an appropriate variety of potatoes containing a high percentage of starch and a low percentage of sugar. The sugar content of each batch is usually determined by analysis since it has been found that some adjustment may be necessary in the cooking time for potatoes of varying sugar content. Potato varieties have been selected which accumulate negligible amounts of sugar even after several months' storage. These potatoes produce crisps of good colour. One variety, specially selected for processing in Scotland, is 'Record'.

(b) Cleaning may be accomplished by passing the potatoes first under water sprays and then through a tank of brine in which they float while any stones, which may have been mixed with them during digging, sink to the bottom.

(c) Peeling. The potatoes may be peeled by being agitated in water in a revolving drum lined with carborundum. An alternative process which causes less loss is *lye peeling.* The potatoes are carried on a conveyer first through a system of hot-water sprays and next through sprays of a boiling solution of 1·5 to 2·5% caustic soda. The exact concentration of caustic must be adjusted to suit the quality of potatoes being treated and the time of exposure. After passing through the 'lye' solution, the potatoes must be exposed to a further water wash to remove traces of alkali.

(d) Slicing and washing. Next they are sliced in a cutter carefully adjusted to make each slice exactly $^1/_{32}$ in. thick. After they are cut, the slices are washed under high-pressure jets to remove surface starch which might cause them to stick together during frying. Surplus water is removed by spinning the sliced potato in a centrifuge.

(e) Frying. The potato slices are fried by being carried on a moving conveyor through a trough of oil which is maintained at a predetermined temperature. Various specifications have been drawn up, calling for temperatures from 150°C (300°F) to 166°C (330°F). The exact temperature used depends on the time taken for the conveyor to carry the slices into the hot oil at one end of the trough and out again at the other end. Times varying from 75 to 210

seconds have been recommended.

(f) Packing. After they have been fried, the crisps are centrifuged to free them of extraneous oil, cooled and packed, usually by an elaborate automatic machine, in cellophane bags.

4. Potato starch

Potatoes are an important source of starch for use not only in food but for the paper, textile and adhesive industries as well. While the production of potato starch is a useful means of utilizing sub-standard potatoes and occasional surpluses, special varieties have been developed specifically for the starch industry.

In the modern production of potato starch, potatoes are washed and disintegrated or macerated to a pulp with water. This pulp is subjected to a complex series of washes and centrifugal sievings to remove fibrous materials. This starch 'milk' is then centrifuged to remove the soluble impurities before being dewatered in filters and dried. The drying process is most efficiently carried out in cyclone driers. The modification of starches for use in food products are described in Chapter 9.

D. SWEET POTATOES

Sweet potatoes (*Pomoea batatas*) are extensively grown in the United States, tropical America, the warmer islands in the Pacific, Japan and the USSR. The main fact to be borne in mind by the food technologist handling sweet potatoes is that, like bananas, they are very susceptible to cold. Stores must be maintained between 10°C (50°F) and 13°C (55°F), following a 'curing' period for a week to 10 days after harvesting when the roots are held at a temperature of 29°C (85°F) and a relative humidity of 85 to 90%.

9

Some modern technological processes

A. CANNING

The principles upon which canning is based are: (i) to pack food in an impervious container which, up to the present, is always a steel box lined with tin or some other inert coating, or a glass bottle or jar, but could equally well be a container made of plastic or some other material capable of standing up to the subsequent process of sterilization. When the food has been packed, the second principle involved in canning is (ii) to kill all the contaminating microbiological flora in the food and thus render it sterile. So long as the sterility is maintained, microbiological decay cannot occur and the food becomes relatively permanent. This permanence, however, may have strict limits. Whereas certain historic canned foods have been shown to remain edible for 100 years or more, some foods will deteriorate in flavour if intra-molecular chemical reactions occur and others may eventually corrode the metal of the can.

Nicholas Appert invented the process of bottling, which is, of course, the same as that of canning, at the end of the eighteenth century. He was supplying bottled meats, vegetables, fruit and milk to the French Navy in 1806—that is, long before Pasteur had elucidated the facts of bacterial infection. Although Donkin and Hall's factory in Bermondsey, London, was successfully supplying the Royal Navy with canned meat in 1813, and Gamble & Co were also doing so in 1818, the canned foods supplied by a subsequent manufacturer in 1845 caused disaster to at least one naval expedition. Large amounts went bad owing to the use of containers which were too big and through which the heat designed to sterilize their contents failed to penetrate completely. It is dangerous to operate a technological process without understanding the scientific principles upon which it is based.

The prejudice arising from early failures in canning techniques persisted long beyond the disappearance of the causes giving rise to it. Foods canned under modern conditions may today be less likely to be infected and may be of 'fresher' quality than those marketed fresh, and their nutritional value is substantially the same.

Appert's rules were in general sound. They were (i) to take the product in its prime, (ii) to prepare it as quickly as possible before it had a chance to deteriorate, (iii) to enclose it in a container which could be sealed hermetically, and (iv) to heat the closed container sufficiently to keep its contents good indefinitely. Under modern conditions, the process of canning can be broken down into the following principal operations:

(a) CLEANING AND PREPARATION

Since canned foods are usually intended to be ready to eat when they are removed from their containers, it is obviously important that the articles put into the cans, whether they are fruit, such as pineapples or peaches; vegetables, such as peas; meat; or fish, are free from inedible parts. It is also very important that articles to be canned should be washed to reduce to a minimum the level of microbiological infection and extraneous contamination. Although the sterilization, which is an essential feature of canning, is designed to kill microbiological infection of all sorts, it is clearly prudent to limit as far as possible the chance of the survival of an infecting organism by reducing the numbers of those initially present.

Besides the removal of extraneous matter and the washing or cleaning of foods by some other means, a large number of different preparatory operations may be necessary depending on the nature of the product to be processed. For example, vegetables and fruit may be peeled and cored, the stones of cherries, plums and peaches may be removed or the fruit and vegetables may be strained or made into purées if the canned product is intended for infants, meat may be chopped or compressed, and fish may be cooked and prepared in oil before being canned. These varied operations are frequently carried out mechanically.

(b) BLANCHING

During blanching the foodstuff is scalded for a brief period, either by being immersed in boiling water or by being exposed to live steam. In continuous blanching, the food is passed through a tunnel into which steam is injected. The period of exposure may last from 2 to 10 minutes. One of the principal purposes of blanching, particularly for fruit and vegetables such as peas, is to drive out the air bubbles which are otherwise retained within their structure. Blanching also causes foods to shrink and hence facilitates the packing of the cans. For some foods, notably peas, it improves the flavour and colour of the canned article. Blanching can also be useful by destroying enzymes which may affect the stability of a foodstuff.

(c) FILLING AND EXHAUSTING

In modern cannery practice, the washed, open cans are conveyed mechanically to automatic filling machines which are designed to fill them at high speed with a weighed amount of the product to be canned. In some circumstances, it is possible to fill the cans with hot food coming directly from the cookers. Alternatively, the filled cans may be passed from the filling machine to an 'exhaust-box' in which they are exposed to hot water or steam so that, when the lid is sealed on, an air-free vacuum will form at the top of the can. Another method for ensuring the absence of air is the use of a mechanical exhauster. This is often employed when packing corn-on-the-cob and also salmon. The mechanical exhauster withdraws air and other gases from the cans by means of a high vacuum. The cans are then sealed immediately while still under vacuum.

(d) SEALING

The filled and exhausted cans are passed directly to an automatic sealing machine which may be capable of sealing 250 or more cans a minute by bending over into a 'roll' the edge of the cover and the flange on the can body so that, when the 'roll' is flattened, it forms a hermetic seal. An alternative method of sealing cans is to fix on a cover containing a small vent-hole before the air is exhausted. Then, when the covered can is subjected to the heat of the exhauster or to vacuum, the vent hole is closed with a small blob of solder.

(e) STERILIZING

Foods decay because micro-organisms of one sort or another, as already described in Chapter 2, grow in them. The fundamental scientific principle underlying the whole of canning technology is to kill all those organisms capable of spoiling the canned food by the application of an appropriate degree of heat. The amount of heat required depends on the following factors:

(i) *The size of the can*

Because heat takes longer to penetrate into the centre of a large can than into a smaller one, it is essential to establish that the temperature used and the duration of heating are adequate for the size of container and the nature of the product being canned. This can be done by calculation but the process used ought always to be verified by actual trial.

(ii) *The acidity of the food being canned*

A. *Acid foods.* Bacteria cannot grow in acid foods whose pH is less than 3·7. Consequently it is only necessary to kill yeasts and moulds in these foods. Acid foods include the following: grapefruit, oranges, plums and most other fruits; figs, pineapples, pears and tomatoes are on the border-line as acid foods and their pH may be 4·5 or higher. It is only necessary to heat cans of fruit to boiling point, i.e. 100°C (212°F). Thus the smaller sizes of cans are usually processed at 100°C for 8–16 minutes. Bacterial spores may in fact survive in cans of fruit but since they are unable to grow do no harm.

B. *Non-acid foods.* Bacteria can readily grow in non-acid foods and their heat-resistant spores may grow also. These foods include: meat, fish and vegetables. In order to make sure of killing bacteria and their more heat-resistant spores, it is necessary that all parts of the material within the can are heated to at least 116°C (241°F). The length of time required depends on the size of the can. To achieve this temperature, it is usual to use steam under a pressure of 10 lb./sq. in. The sealed cans are put into an *autoclave*, which is a pressure cooker, or they may be passed through a continuous sterilizer in which high-pressure steam can be applied for the required length of time.

A great deal of study has been given in canning technology to the rate of heat-penetration for different types of cans and for different products. Much work has also been done to assess the death rate of various kinds of micro-organisms. The spores of *Clostridium botulinum* are often used as test organisms, since this bacterium is the most dangerous of all potential contaminants. The figure on p. 202, based on the work of Gillespy, shows the 'thermal death time curve' for the spores of a test organism at temperatures ranging from 104°C (220°F) to 116°C (241°F). The 'z-value' shown in this graph is the number of degrees Fahrenheit increase or decrease for a ten-fold increase or decrease in the death rate (i.e. the 'D-value').

The importance of the steam used for sterilization being free from air is shown in the figures given opposite. It can be seen that whereas steam at 10 lb./sq. in. pressure has a temperature of 115°C (239°F) when it is free from air, its temperature will only be 112°C (234°F) if it is adulterated with 10% of air. The danger of there being a proportion of air present mixed with the steam is made more serious for the canner if, as is likely, the air is not evenly distributed. It might follow, therefore, that the vapour in part of the sterilizing vessel might contain a substantial proportion of the total air adulteration.

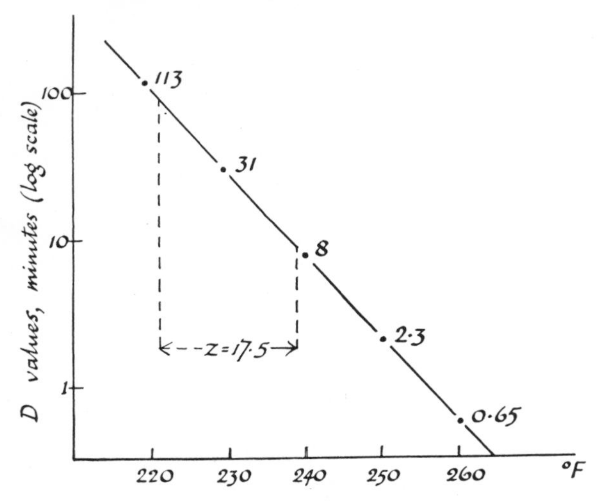

Fig. 24. A 'thermal death time curve' for bacterial spores during the sterilization of a canned food pack. It can be seen that the higher the temperature the shorter is the 'D value' in minutes. For this curve, an increase in temperature 17·5°F (the 'Z value') is accompanied by a tenfold reduction in 'D value'.

(*f*) COOLING, LABELLING AND STORING

Large cans must be cooled slowly by gradually reducing the pressure in the autoclave and then allowing the temperature to fall gradually. This avoids the danger of the cans straining outwards and buckling, which might occur if the steam pressure were suddenly dropped. Smaller cans, however, are commonly cooled by shutting off the steam, opening the autoclave to the atmosphere and admitting cold water. Alternatively, the cans are removed from the autoclave and passed through cold water in a cooling trough. Towards the end of this cooling process a vacuum develops in the cans and they may leak, particularly if they are roughly handled. Although cans ought, if possible, to be sufficiently robust and well made not to leak, the cooling water should be clean and sterile so that if an occasional can should leak the contents will not be infected.

Cooling is only continued until the cans reach 38°C (100°F) so that their warmth may be sufficient to dry the surface and thus avoid the possibility of rusting. Wetness on the outside of a can may become contaminated; it consequently represents a danger since it might be drawn into the can through any minute leak as the contents contract when they are cool. Automatic machinery is used to label the cans when they are dry.

Canned foods, though stable for substantial periods of time, should be stored under dry conditions, again to avoid rust forming and leading to corrosion and leakage.

(g) STERILIZABLE FLEXIBLE PACKAGING

The development of plastic/aluminium foil laminates capable of withstanding retort temperatures of 121°C (250°F) led to the concept of sterilizing food products in flexible pouches as an attractive and less expensive alternative to the can. Flat, rectangular pouches allow for more rapid transfer of heat throughout the product, and reductions in processing times of 30–40% have been achieved. Better quality products with less of the sometimes undesirable cooked flavour of canned foods are thus possible.

Although the technology has been available since the early 1960s, the production of retortable pouch products has grown very slowly. This is largely a result of the high cost of the special laminates required and the comparatively slow speed with which pouches can be filled and sealed. Until the late 1970s filling speeds were restricted to 40–60 packs per minute and although automatic machines are now available speeds are still limited to around 200 packs per minute. This compares unfavourably with high speed canning lines where the robustness and ease of handling of the can

Table 21

The temperature of steam at 10 lb./sq. in. adulterated with air

Mixture of air (% by volume)	*Temperature* °C	°F	*Mixture of air* (% by volume)	*Temperature* °C	°F
0	115	239	50	95	203
5	114	237	60	90	193
10	112	234	70	82	179
20	108	227	80	72	162
30	104	220	90	57	134
40	100	212			

permit filling speeds of 800–1000 cans per minute with relative ease. It is forecast, however, that as consumers find foods packed in pouches increasingly attractive, the development of sophisticated automatic filling equipment, continuous sterilizers suitable for pouches and less expensive laminates will allow the retortable pouch to compete effectively with the can.

(h) HEAT STERILIZATION AND ASEPTIC PACKAGING

Aseptic packaging is the term commonly applied to the production of packaged foodstuffs which have undergone a process of heat sterilization, been cooled and then filled into sterile containers. The conventional canning process described above involves filling product into containers that are subsequently heat sterilized. This process suffers from the major disadvantage of requiring relatively long periods of time for the heat to penetrate throughout the food, especially where large containers are involved. This can result in detrimental changes in the flavour, colour, consistency and nutritional value of the product. It further imposes severe restrictions on the nature of the container itself in view of the robustness required to stand up to the severity of the process. The aseptic process minimizes these problems by the use of high-temperature, short-time (H.T.S.T.) sterilization (see p. 116). Instead of submitting cans of food to temperatures of about 120°C (248°F) for a length of time from 20 minutes to 120 minutes dependent on the size of the cans and other conditions, the food itself is heated very rapidly for periods ranging from 6 minutes down to a few seconds at much higher temperatures from 130°C (266°F) to 150°C (300°F), and immediately cooled again. The sterilized food is then packed and sealed under sterile conditions into previously sterilized cans or other containers. The method of operation of an aseptic canning plant is shown diagrammatically in Figure 25. The heating system employed to sterilize the food is normally a tubular heat exchanger or a scraped surface heat exchanger. Direct injection of superheated steam into the product is also used. Cans are normally sterilized at very high temperatures in a flame box.

There is no restriction on the size of the container that may be filled, from single-serve portions to 55-gallon drums. More important, a wide variety of packaging materials, mostly less expensive than the can or the retortable pouch, may be used. These include foil and plastic sachets, waxed cartons, bag-in-box arrangements, thermoformed aluminium pots and injection-moulded plastics. As these materials could not withstand the temperatures necessary to sterilize cans, they are chemically sterilized with hydrogen peroxide or ethylene oxide.

The first product to be aseptically canned commercially was pea soup in 1949 and since then the technique has been restricted to fluid or near fluid products because of the difficulty of getting rapid heat penetration into large particles such as chunks of meat or diced vegetables. Advances in the design of sterilizing equipment such as thermoscrews and agitating pressure vessels, the development of new filling systems and a better understanding of the microbiology of large particles of food make it virtually certain that the first aseptically packed particulate products will be commercially available in the 1980s.

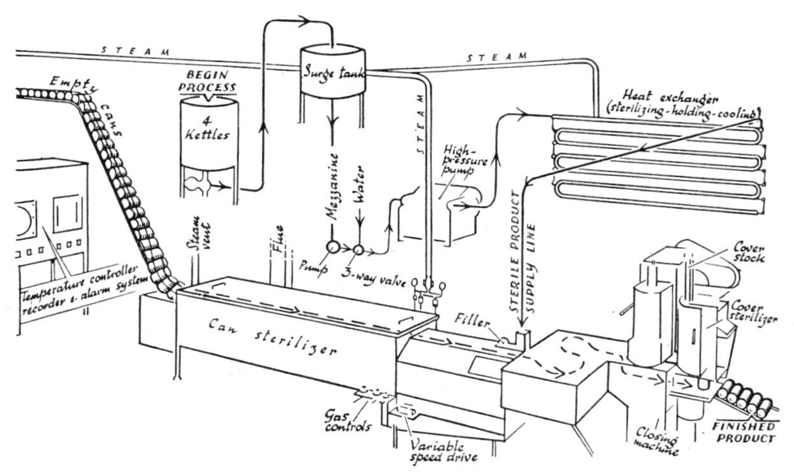

Fig. 25. Flow-diagram of aseptic canning plant.

(*i*) CAUSES OF SPOILAGE OF CANNED FOODS

Canned foods most often spoil because they have not been heated sufficiently long or to a sufficiently high temperature for the heat to penetrate to every part of the can to kill the most resistant type of bacteria present. Alternatively, spoilage may be due to leakage into a badly made can or one insufficiently sealed, or to corrosion either by acid food packed in a can not properly designed to resist it or by rusting and damage due to cans being stored in unsatisfactory conditions. Infected cooling water is a dangerous source of contamination. It may gain access into an already sterile can through a minute pinhole or a defective end. Cooling water should, therefore, always be chlorinated.

There are various types of spoilage caused by specific organisms that have escaped sterilization. They have been classified as follows:

(i) *'Flat sours'*

There are certain types of bacteria—of which *Bacillus stearothermophilus* is a characteristic species—which produce spores that are more resistant to heat than those of other organisms. If, therefore, low-acid foods such as peas or corn are infected with these bacteria and by some means escape the proper sterilizing temperature, the spores will subsequently germinate in the cans and produce acid. This, while not markedly changing the appearance of the contents, gives it a faintly disagreeable smell. These organisms do not produce gas, so the infected cans do not bulge; hence they are called 'flat sours'.

(ii) *Thermophilic gas spoilage*

Bacteria of the type *Clostridium thermosaccharolyticum* are also comparatively resistant to heat. They grow in the absence of air in insufficiently sterilized cans of low-acid foods and produce large amounts of hydrogen gas which cause the cans to bulge and sometimes burst. Swollen cans, in which the contents may become slimy and frothy and where the gas is largely carbon dioxide, are usually infected by non-spore-forming bacteria which have gained access to the cans after sterilization, either through leakage inwards of cooling water or through unsatisfactory sealing procedure.

(iii) *Sulphide spoilage*

Clostridium nigrificans is a third type of heat-resistant micro-organism whose spores may survive incomplete sterilization. It is occasionally a cause of spoilage of non-acid foods. The organism produces hydrogen-sulphide gas which gives the food a smell of bad eggs and may also cause blackening. Insufficient gas is produced to cause the cans to bulge and they remain flat.

The type of micro-organisms which cause gas spoilage and sulphide spoilage do not normally constitute a danger to food canned and used in temperate climates. Canned food which is to be used in tropical countries must be heat treated sufficiently to destroy the spores of these organisms which will otherwise germinate and cause spoilage.

These are only examples of the principal categories of infection that may occur. Numerous other kinds of spoilage have been reported but, in principle, all can be prevented by *(a)* good housekeeping to maintain sanitary conditions in the foods that are prepared for canning, *(b)* effective sterilization, adequate to allow a killing temperature to penetrate to all parts of the container's contents and be maintained for an adequate length of time, and *(c)* the use of efficient equipment, cans of proper construction and a satisfactory technique for obtaining a hermetic seal. Most of the different kinds of micro-organisms likely to escape sterilization are not harmful to health; however they spoil the quality of the food and render it unfit for consumption. Certain organisms, of which *Clostridium botulinum* is the most deadly, are capable of producing very toxic substances in canned food if they are permitted to survive. Spoiled canned food should, therefore, always be discarded.

B. QUICK-FREEZING

The preservation of foods by freezing depends on two principles: *(a)* all types of change that cause decay, whether due to living micro-organisms or to the enzymes naturally present, are slowed down at low temperatures; and *(b)* by freezing the water present in fresh foods it becomes, in effect, withdrawn from the food which can almost be considered, therefore, to have been dried. A further principle underlying the modern process of quick-freezing is that the rapid withdrawal of heat leads to the conversion of the watery fraction of the food into very small crystals which do much less harm to the structure of the commodity frozen than the larger crystals produced when the rate of freezing is slow.

Three types of freezing processes are used in modern food technology:

(a) IMMERSION FREEZING

The foods to be frozen are plunged directly into a very cold solution. At one time brine was employed, particularly for freezing whole fish. Alternative freezing liquids that have more recently come into use are invert sugar solutions, particularly for fruit and vegetables. A variation of immersion freezing is the *indirect contact system* in which the food is placed in a metal container and the container then immersed in a bath of refrigerated brine or some other freezing solution.

(b) CONVECTION FREEZING

This system involves the use of a blast of cold air which, when directed on the foods, quickly freezes them.

(c) 'MULTIPLATE' FREEZER

This is a cabinet with a number of hollow shelves which form the freezing surface. The food to be frozen is placed between the shelves, which press together on to the items to be processed.

(d) CRYOGENIC FREEZING

This method which is being rapidly developed involves the exposure of food to a cooling medium at a very low temperature. Liquid nitrogen at a temperature of −195·8°C has been used successfully on a commercial scale. The principle may be used in a number of ways. For example, strawberries immersed in liquid nitrogen for 30 seconds can be cooled from 72°F (23°C) to 10°F (−12°C). Alternatively, the food to be frozen can be exposed to a spray of liquid nitrogen or to a blast of the very cold nitrogen gas. The rapid freezing achieved by these processes can give products particularly good flavour.

(e) FLUIDIZED-BED FREEZING

In this process, a blast of cold air is blown upwards through a bed of the food to be frozen in such a way that the portions of food bounce up and down in the air flow and the entire mass behaves almost as if it were a liquid. If the bed is slightly sloping, the mass of food will flow along supported on the air stream without the need for conveyor belts which may give mechanical trouble and which require cleaning.

1. Fruit and vegetables

(a) BLANCHING

Although bacterial activity is brought to a halt at the customary temperatures at which quick-frozen foods are held, many of the enzymes present in vegetables remain active. It is, therefore, necessary to *blanch* these foods. Scalding for a short time in boiling water, or brief exposure to live steam destroys most enzymes. For steam-scalding, the washed, trimmed and otherwise prepared fruit or vegetables are conveyed through a steam-tunnel. For water-scalding, the vegetables are passed through a tank of boiling water.

The enzyme *peroxidase* survives heat treatment for longer than many others. It is usual, therefore, when the conditions for quick-freezing a new product are being established, to continue blanching until a negative chemical reaction for peroxidase is obtained. The *Peroxidase test* is done by putting a spot of a freshly made solution of 1% guaiacol mixed with an equal amount of hydrogen peroxide (five volumes strength) on to the food. If peroxidase is still present, a reddish-brown colour appears within 1 minute.

(*b*) FREEZING

For freezing, the food, which may be packed in cartons or wrapped in plastic film, is cooled to −23°C (−10°F) to −35°C (−30°F) in as short a time as possible. Once the food is frozen, it is not necessary to maintain it at these low temperatures.

(*c*) STORAGE

Storage should be at about −20°C (−4°F). Even at this temperature, some changes occur. For example, a loss of up to 20% in the green chlorophyll in frozen green beans may occur in six months, and this loss increases in speed four to five times for each 6°C (10°F) rise in temperature. It follows that it is of much importance for quick-frozen foods to be held at low temperatures. Serious deterioration can occur if, for example, the storage cabinets in retail stores are inefficient, as is sometimes found.

(*d*) VITAMIN C CONTENT

The vitamin C content of properly processed quick-frozen fruit and vegetables is often superior to that of fresh material as obtained in the market, due to the rigorous selection of sound material for freezing. Losses of vitamin C occur as follows:

(i) Blanching may cause a loss of 10–20%.
(ii) Food stored at −20°C (−4°F) will lose 50% of its vitamin C in a year.
(iii) Four- to five-fold loss occurs for each 6°C (10°F) rise in storage temperature.

2. Fish

Frozen foods are of importance in modern food technology because when properly stored at appropriate low temperature they can be kept for a year or sometimes more. But a further advantage is that they are 'foods of convenience'. The carefully chosen and prepared foods which can usually be taken directly from a carton and put into the cooking vessel or, in the case of fruit such as strawberries, simply allowed to thaw and then eaten, avoid the need for any trouble to cook or housewife. Of all unprocessed foods, fish is perhaps the most inconvenient, being of uncertain quality, highly perishable, troublesome to prepare, difficult to cook well and not easy to keep hot if not needed immediately. For this reason, prepared fish portions quick-frozen have become a major article of commerce. They are known as 'fish fingers' in Great Britain and 'fish sticks' in America. They are processed as follows:

(a) PREPARATION OF PORTIONS

Skinned fillets of cod or haddock are tightly packed into rectangular cardboard boxes of standard dimensions; $20 \times 12 \times 1\frac{1}{2}$ in. is a convenient size. The boxes are frozen in a pressure-plate freezer. The blocks of frozen fish are cut up into 'sticks', $4 \times {}^{7}/_{8} \times {}^{5}/_{8}$ in., or into 'portions', $4 \times 2\frac{1}{2} \times {}^{5}/_{8}$ in. Mechanical stainless-steel bandsaws may be used but cause a certain loss of fish as sawdust. This may be avoided by the use of a guillotine.

(b) COATING

The pieces of fish are passed on a mechanical conveyor through a curtain of batter, usually composed of egg, flour and skim milk powder. The operation is similar to the 'enrobing' of biscuits in chocolate. The batter-covered pieces then pass through two further curtains of bread-crumbs and then over a vibrator which shakes off excess crumbs.

(c) FRYING

The coated fish sticks are fried in fat at 190°C (375°F) to 204°C (400°F) for between 40 and 55 seconds, usually in a continuous mechanized fryer. It is important that good-quality fat is used for frying and that equipment of stainless steel or some other inert metal is used to avoid any possibility of contamination, particularly by copper, which might cause rancidity.

(d) FREEZING

An essential step in producing a finished article of good quality is to arrange to cool and freeze the fried fish fingers immediately they are cooked. This may be done by freezing them directly as they leave the fryer in a blast of cold air sufficient to maintain a temperature of −40°C (−40°F) for about an hour. Alternatively, they can be cooled, packed in cartons and the cartons then frozen in a pressure-plate freezer.

3. Poultry

Dressed poultry may be packed in a plastic container and frozen as described in Chapter 4. Or, on the other hand, the birds can be cut into portions, boiled and then coated, fried and frozen in the same way as fish fingers.

C. ACCELERATED FREEZE-DRYING

If a foodstuff is frozen so that the natural moisture in it is turned into ice and then placed in a chamber under a high vacuum and heated, the ice will evaporate directly as vapour without ever turning back into moisture. In principle, frozen food is, as was mentioned before, dehydrated because its moisture is immobilized as ice crystals. It only retains its stability, however, so long as it is kept frozen. On the other hand food that has been subjected to 'accelerated freeze-drying' and from which the ice crystals have been removed by evaporation will remain stable so long as it is kept dry and protected from air. Another very substantial advantage of accelerated freeze-drying is that the structure and quality of the food is well maintained, so that when it is unpacked and moistened again it becomes a food of high quality and good flavour. The main disadvantage of accelerated freeze-drying is that it requires quite elaborate machinery and is consequently expensive, and it requires a high degree of technical competence from the people who operate the process. Accelerated freeze-drying has been very successfully applied to meat, fish—particularly shrimps—fruit and vegetables of various sorts. It has recently been applied successfully on a large scale to egg.

(a) BLANCHING

Fruit and vegetables are blanched, as for quick-freezing, in order to inhibit enzymes that could cause deterioration.

(b) FREEZING

The food is placed in the freeze-dryer in moderately large portions. The plates of the freeze-dryer are arranged so that pressure can be exerted on the food and at the same time a very high vacuum capable of producing an atmosphere of about 1 mm. of mercury is applied. Raw meat subjected simultaneously to a light applied plate pressure and a high vacuum has been successfully frozen by the loss of heat produced by the high rate of evaporation of moisture.

(c) HEATING

When it is clear that the food has been brought into the frozen state, the plates of the freeze-dryer pressing upon it are then heated by the circulation of hot water inside them or by electrical heating. This causes the ice to *sublime,* that is to say, it is converted directly to vapour in the high vacuum of the freeze-drying cabinet. Fish undergoing freeze-drying can be submitted to plates heated to 90°C (194°F) for about one hour; temperatures up to 150°C (300°F) have been used by other operators with promising results.

(d) PACKING

Freeze-dried foods are extremely hygroscopic, and when the vacuum is broken and they are removed from the freeze-dryer their moisture content may rise to more than 3% in 30 minutes. It is, therefore, the practice to introduce nitrogen into the cabinet when the vacuum is released and to pack the food immediately in an impervious wrapper in a room in which the atmosphere is maintained at a controlled low level of humidity.

D. DEHYDRATION

The modern process of dehydration consists of the removal of moisture from foods by the application of heat usually in the presence of a controlled flow of air. The commonest type of dryer is a chamber in which the food to be dried is placed on perforated trays and through which a current of air, heated to an appropriate temperature, is blown by means of a system of fans. A simpler form of this is a kiln in which the warm air passes from below up through the food being dried. Liquid foods may be dried by being run on to a revolving, heated, horizontal drum. Alternatively, they may be sprayed downwards into an inverted cone up which a current of heated air is blown. This process of 'spray-drying' was described for milk in Chapter 5.

CANNING. 90: Filled cans awaiting heat treatment under pressure in the vertical retorts seen in the background. 91: Machine for filling cans with golden syrup. Because of the high sugar concentration these cans do not have to be sterilized.

FREEZING. 92: Retortable pouches filled with cooked potatoes being loaded automatically onto a conveyor by a suction mechanism. 93: A trolley containing trays of retortable pouches ready to enter a horizontal retort to be sterilized.

FREEZING. 94: Peas being frozen on a fluidized bed freezer.

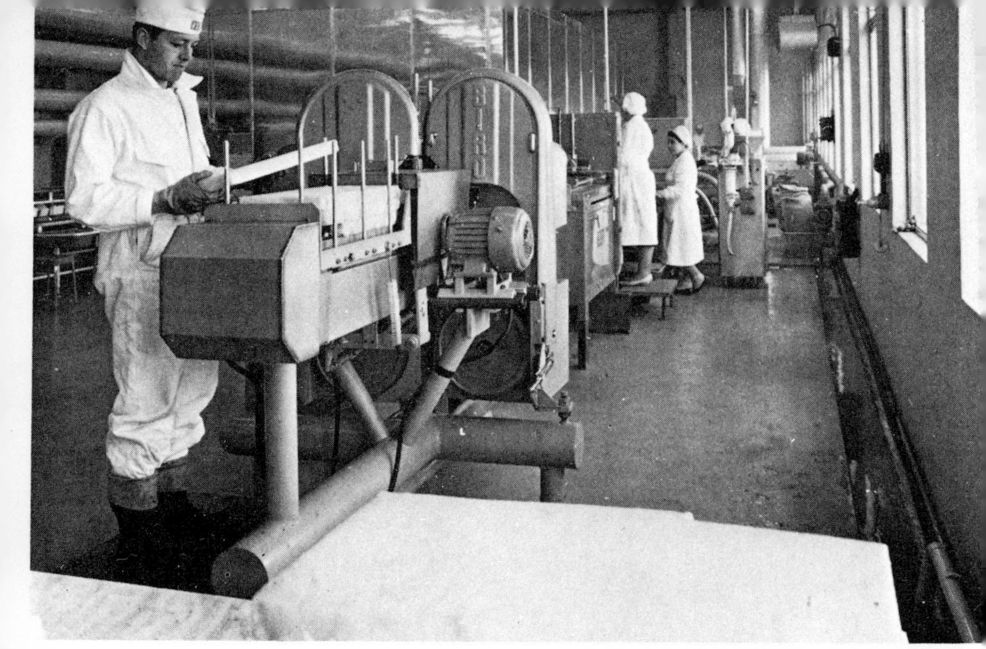

FISH FINGERS. 95: Blocks of frozen fish being cut into 'sticks'. 96–7: Fish fingers being coated with batter and fried before being frozen.

1. Cabbage and other green vegetables

(a) BLANCHING

Green vegetables, after the necessary washing and shredding, must be blanched, in the way that has already been described for canning and accelerated freeze-drying. As before, this is to prevent enzyme action which would destroy the vitamin C content and also affect the colour and flavour during the drying process. In commercial practice, 0·125% of *sodium sulphite* is added to the scalding water used for blanching. This is found to protect the colour and vitamin C content of vegetables and fruit.

(b) COOLING

Vegetables should be cooled in a current of cold air before drying in order to prevent their becoming soft and mushy due to 'over-blanching'.

(c) DRYING

During the early stages of drying, the evaporation of moisture prevents the temperature of the vegetables rising unduly. A current of air at 90–95°C (194–203°F) can, at first, safely be used. As the drying proceeds the temperature must be reduced to 55°C (130°F) to avoid producing a scorched flavour. If possible, the moisture content should be reduced to a final value of less than 5% within about five hours.

2. Potatoes

Potatoes can be dehydrated to produce a useful and attractive material. They may either be peeled or cut into strips, blanched and dried very much as described above for green vegetables. On the other hand, a particularly palatable product can be produced by boiling the peeled potatoes and pressing them through a machine similar to a domestic potato masher. Subsequent drying is improved if 0·05% of calcium chloride is mixed in at this stage.

(a) CONDITIONING

The mashed potato is first partially dried until its moisture content falls to 50%. It is then allowed to cool for about two hours. This 'conditioning' process enables a finer powder to be produced subsequently when the material is fully dried.

(b) SIEVING AND DRYING

The cooled, partially dried potato is sieved to a fine powder and then dried fully to less than 5% moisture on trays in a cabinet or tunnel.

(c) RECONSTITUTION

The dried mashed potato can be readily reconstituted if three and a half to four parts by weight of water, containing 0·5% of salt and at a temperature of 95°C (203°F), are stirred into one part of the powder. The water should not be boiling or the mashed potato will have a pasty consistency.

(d) NUTRITIONAL VALUE

The nutritional value of reconstituted dried mashed potato is approximately the same as that of fresh potato cooked and mashed. About 50 to 55% of the original vitamin C in the raw peeled potatoes reaches the plates of people eating the dried material. This is not very different from that surviving the domestic process of cooking and thorough mashing. The addition of up to 150 p.p.m. of sodium sulphite to the mashed potato before drying has been found to improve the colour of the final product, delay the development of browning on storage, and assist the retention of vitamin C.

3. Meat

(a) COOKING

Meat gives the best quality dried product if, before it is dried, it is first cooked. A convenient process is to cut it into pieces and steam it at 100°C (212°F) for 40 minutes.

(b) COOLING AND MINCING

It is then cooled and minced through a screen containing apertures of about 5/16 in. If the liquid that runs out during the cooking process is separated from fat, concentrated to small volume and returned to the minced meat before it is dried, the flavour of the final product is improved. Meat dries more rapidly and gives a more satisfactory dried product if its fat content is below 35%.

(c) DRYING

A suitable type of drier for meat is one in which the minced meat is in trays over which a current of warm air is passed. During the initial stages of drying, the temperature of the meat remains low due to the evaporation of moisture regardless of the temperature of the drying air. In the later stages, however, care should be taken to avoid the meat temperature exceeding 70°C (158°F). The best results are obtained if a dry-matter content of 96·8% is achieved within four to five hours.

(d) NUTRITIONAL VALUE

The nutritional value of reconstituted dried meat is practically identical with that of cooked fresh meat. The biological value of the protein is unaffected and the vitamins, niacin and riboflavin, are unharmed. The loss of vitamin B_1 is 55–65% of the amount originally present in the raw meat, compared with a loss of 40–60% in domestic cooking.

4. Fish

Fresh, good-quality, low-fat fish, such as cod, haddock and whiting, can be dehydrated to produce an attractive and readily reconstituted article.

(a) PREPARATION

The fish is washed, skinned, filleted and minced in a machine to give pieces about $^1/_4$—$^3/_4$ in. cube.

(b) COOKING

It should then be spread on perforated trays and cooked in steam at 2 lb. pressure for 30 minutes.

(c) MINCING

After having been cooked, the fish needs to be reduced once more to shreds by being passed through the mincer, this time through holes $^3/_{16}$—$^1/_2$ in. in diameter.

(d) DRYING

As with meat, drying should be completed within about four hours. An initial air temperature of 85°C (185°F) should be reduced to 65–70°C (149–158°F) as the fish approaches its final dry matter of 90%.

5. Dried milk and dried egg

The technological problems of making dried milk and dried egg were discussed in Chapter 5.

6. The storage of dehydrated foods

Dehydrated foods will remain stable for periods of a year or more if they are stored under appropriate conditions. The changes that may occur are due to the following factors:

(a) OXIDATION

Fats are most easily affected by oxygen, which can cause oxidative rancidity. Oxidation may also affect the colour of foods, cause loss of vitamin-A activity and vitamin C and produce changes in the essential oils that contribute to flavour.

(b) TEMPERATURE

Prolonged storage above about 28°C (82°F) causes dehydrated foods to darken due to an intermolecular chemical reaction called non-enzymic browning.

(c) CHANGES DUE TO CONTAMINATION

Dehydrated foods may be contaminated by strong-smelling volatile substances—such as those derived from paint, varnish, paraffin or onions or cheese stored near by. The most dangerous contaminant, however, is moisture. If dehydrated products are allowed to become moist, not only will damaging hydrolytic changes occur but bacterial infection will take place.

These factors clearly indicate the requirements for the proper packaging and storage of dehydrated foods. They should be packed in an impervious container, whether this be made of metal, foil, glass or plastic. The container should be freed from oxygen. Finally, the packaged dehydrated food should be stored at a cool temperature certainly not exceeding 28°C (82°F).

E. EXTRUSION COOKING

The extrusion cooking process is one in which starchy, proteinaceous material is plasticized under conditions of high temperature and pressure. Starches are gelatinized and proteins denatured as the starting material is worked, restructured and expanded in a single controlled operation. The raw material feed may be in the form of powdered or granular products, or even whole cereal grains, and the result of the process can vary from light open agglomerates to densely layered structures.

The extruder consists of a barrel with a tightly fitting screen and a cone-shaped end. The outside of the barrel may be heated or cooled. As the material is impelled along the barrel by the action of the screw it is mixed, compressed and heated to temperatures of 100—180°C (212—356°F) for periods of 10—20 seconds before being forced through a restrictive die nozzle. The pressure at the die nozzle normally varies from 20—40 atmospheres (300—400 psi). Extruders come in single- or twin-screw types, and a number of different screw configurations may be used to suit particular applications. A typical single screw extruder is shown in Figure 105.

The attraction of the cooker-extruder to the food processor is its flexibility, low operating costs and efficient use of energy. It now finds application in the manufacture of dry soup mixes, dry baby foods, breakfast cereals, beverage mixes, pre-cooked pasta products, dry and semi-moist pet foods and expanded, puffed snack products. A major use of extrusion cooking is in the preparation of textured vegetable protein (see Chapter 11 for a more detailed discussion). A process for textured soya protein is shown diagrammatically in Figure 107. The main elements are as follows:

(i) Defatted soya flour, together with any minor ingredients that might be added to modify texture, are fed into a high-speed mixer prior to the extruder where they are moistened with water or steam.
(ii) The mixture then enters the extruder. Within the first section it is mixed and worked until a plastic mass or dough is formed.
(iii) The temperature of the dough is then raised to 100–110°C, as it passes along the heated section of the barrel. Enzymes are inactivated, and bitter flavours and various constituents which are nutritionally undesirable are eliminated.
(iv) In the final section the dough is subjected to increased pressure by the cone shaped end with a nozzle of constrictive diameter. The temperature rises rapidly (140—180°C), starches are gelatinized and proteins denatured. The plastic mass is subjected to shearing and stretching forces which produce a woven laminar structure.
(v) The product is expelled through the orifice and cut into

chunks by a spinning knife. It is then dried and cooled, sieved to remove fines and stored for packing.

The result of this process is seen in Figures 106 and 107, photomicrographs of defatted soya flakes before and after extrusion. In 106, the typical appearance of the uncooked protein is seen with individual protein bodies encapsulated in sacs of cellulose. The textured material from ground defatted flakes shows the ruptured individual sacs of protein which have run together in stretchable strands to produce muscle-like structure and chewiness.

F. THE USE OF MICROWAVES

Microwave heating takes place because certain types of molecules are capable of absorbing electromagnetic radiation in the radio-frequency range. Water, the major constituent of most foods, is composed of such molecules. Microwaves are highly penetrative and the absorption of radio-frequency energy within food causes a rapid rise in temperature throughout the material and thus produces a relatively uniform cooking effect. It is lucky that materials such as glass, ceramics, plastics and paper, from which containers and packaging of foodstuffs are commonly made, do not absorb radio-frequency energy so that microwaves pass straight through them without making them hot. On the other hand, metals reflect microwaves and cannot be used in microwave cookers, although recent development in the design of ovens and packaging suggest that aluminium foil, which is a very important packaging material for frozen foods, may soon be able to be accommodated in the technique of microwave processing.

Two wave frequencies are commonly used: for domestic ovens, 2450 MHz is preferred while, in industrial applications, 896 MHz is considered more suitable. The product to be heated is placed in an enclosed oven and microwaves, generated by special oscillator tubes, are guided on to it. The penetrative power of the radiation allows cooking to occur rapidly throughout the product, unlike conventional ovens, where cooking takes place from the outside of the food inwards and rates of heat transfer are relatively slow.

(a) DOMESTIC AND COMMERCIAL CATERING APPLICATIONS

The most useful application of microwave cooking under domestic conditions and for those concerned with food service, has been in heating frozen cooked meals or snacks for consumption. A frozen meal, for example, can be heated to serving temperature in 1½–4 minutes in a microwave oven compared with 20–30 minutes in a conventional oven. Where frozen foods are popular, the use of the microwave oven has grown rapidly. It has been estimated that in the United States, by 1980, 15% of all homes and 50% of all catering establishments had microwave ovens.

The cooking of fresh foods, particularly meats, in microwave ovens suffers from the disadvantage that microwaves cannot brown foods. This has to be done separately under a grill or in an oven and reduces the convenience of using microwaves. Attempts are being made to overcome this by incorporating within ovens a browning element or a special heat sink constructed of absorbing material on which the food may be placed. Beef roasts or poultry may be cooked in 6–7 minutes although this must be followed by a 'resting' period of 15–20 minutes before carving to allow heat to penetrate evenly throughout the mass.

It is expected that the rapid growth in use of microwave ovens will force food manufacturers to develop products especially prepared and packaged for microwave cooking. New opportunities and challenges exist, in particular, for the frozen food industry and the first signs of these being taken up are already evident in the form of frozen pizzas, pancakes and popcorn.

(*b*) INDUSTRIAL APPLICATIONS

The penetrative power of microwaves and their ability to raise temperatures rapidly in frozen foods has led to the widespread use of microwaves to assist thawing of frozen ingredient raw materials in the food industry. Meat, fish and poultry are normally used by the industry in the form of frozen 25–50 kg. blocks. These have to be removed from frozen storage to be tempered at 0°C for several days before use. In contrast, a 20 cm.-thick block of frozen beef weighing 50 kg. can be tempered from −15°C to −4°C in 2 minutes by microwave heating. It is then ready for processing. The commercial advantages of flexibility, energy-saving and the saving of refrigerated and frozen storage space are readily apparent. Frozen ingredients are not thawed completely. Because water absorbs energy more quickly than ice does, the first part of a block to thaw would get hot quickest so that before long water could be boiling at one place adjacent to another place which was still frozen.

Other industrial uses of microwave heating include:

(i) The production of skinless sausages.
(ii) Potato crisp manufacture.
(iii) An aid to freeze-drying and air-drying where case-hardening in the final stages of drying can be avoided.
(iv) Baking of biscuits and cakes.

G. THE USE OF RADIOACTIVITY

Ionizing radiation emitted by radioactive isotopes (for example, gamma rays from cobalt 60) or generated by electrical machines producing electron beams or X-rays are absorbed by all forms of matter. Their energy appears as chemical change and, to a lesser extent, as heat. Living cells are particularly sensitive to these kinds of irradiation which can, therefore, be used to kill micro-organisms, to damage the reproductive mechanism of insects, their eggs and larvae, and to destroy actively growing cells such as those in the sprouts of potatoes or the hearts of onions. Unfortunately, the use of radioactivity to sterilize foodstuffs possesses two awkward drawbacks:

(i) Too large a dose has a harmful effect on quality: butter is bleached; salmon loses its red colour; meat becomes darker; and a burnt off-flavour, which occurring in high-protein foods has been vividly described as 'wet-dog odour', develops.
(ii) It demands a very heavy capital investment if it is to be applied to bulk quantities of food.

The process has, however, possibilities for development in the future and is therefore worth consideration.

The unit of absorbed irradiation is a *rad*, which is equivalent to the absorption of 100 ergs/g. of the absorbing substance.

The following are some of the processes so far explored:

(a) COMPLETE STERILIZATION

To obtain absolute sterility in a foodstuff requires the use of 10 million rads (10 M rad). This damages the quality and flavour so seriously that the food becomes uneatable.

(b) 'COLD STERILIZATION'

3 to 5 M rad will kill most types of harmful bacteria and give a

level of sterility approaching that obtained in normal canning processes. However, even this level causes unacceptable harm to flavour and quality. Some improvement has been achieved by partially cooking the food before it is irradiated or by keeping it well below freezing-point during irradiation.

(c) TREATMENT OF SPICES, ETC.

The use of what are still rather high levels of irradiation, from 1 to 3 M rad, has been applied in the treatment of spices and seeds, which may be quite heavily contaminated with micro-organisms. This level of treatment has also been suggested as a means of reducing the bacterial content of sugar which is to be used for canning.

(d) RADIATION 'PASTEURIZATION'

By irradiating frozen whole egg with from 0·1 to 1·0 M rad, it is possible to destroy certain pathological micro-organisms, and particularly the Salmonellae that cause food poisoning, without having to thaw the egg and pasteurize it by heat. The same treatment can be applied to meat. The process has also been suggested for desiccated coconut which has sometimes been found to be a source of infection. This level of treatment has been found to increase the storage life of such products as sausages and fish. Its main drawback is that it is difficult to avoid the development of 'irradiation flavour'. Radiation 'pasteurization' cannot be used for fruit or vegetables because it appears to damage the cells and, while inhibiting certain bacteria, causes the tissues of the plant to break down.

(e) DISINFESTATION

The irradiation with 0·02 M rad of foodstuffs such as grain or dried fruits while they are being unloaded from ships or handled in bulk stores has been demonstrated to destroy insect eggs and to render the insects themselves incapable of breeding. For the process to be effective, a thin layer of the foodstuff must be exposed to the radioactivity and consequently the capital cost of an installation sufficiently large to deal with materials in bulk is very high.

(f) SPROUT INHIBITION

Of all living cells, those that are actively growing are most susceptible to radiation. It has consequently been found that quite small doses of about 0·01 M rad will destroy the cells which grow into sprouts from the eyes of potatoes without affecting the other cells of the plant.

The use of radioactivity in food technology is still in the stage of development. While certain promising applications have been found, it has yet to be established whether these possess advantages over those of more conventional methods sufficient to justify the cost of the necessary installation. At all the levels of irradiation described above, there is no chance of any harmful degree of radioactivity being transferred to the foods under treatment.

H. CHEMICAL 'ADDITIVES'

Chemical substances have been added to foods for technical reasons long before food technology was developed as an application of science. Salt has been employed as a preservative for many generations, sodium nitrite is traditionally added to the liquor in which bacon is pickled, and hops are used as a preservative in the manufacture of beer. During the present period of the development of food technology, however, a large number of additional substances have been introduced for a variety of purposes. It is therefore important for the technologist to consider whether the action of these compounds in achieving specific technical results is at the same time damaging the food value of the commodities with which he is dealing.

The main categories of food additives are as follows:

(a) Food colours
(b) Flavours
(c) Thickening and gelling agents
(d) Fat 'extenders', emulsifiers and stabilizing agents
(e) Anti-oxidants
(f) Preservatives
(g) Acids, bases and salts
(h) Flour 'improvers'
(i) Nutritional supplements
(j) Adventitious 'additives'

(a) COLOURS

Synthetic organic dyestuffs which belong to the chemical group of *diazo* compounds have been widely used as food colours. Those which are included in 'permitted' lists have been exhaustively tested to ensure their harmlessness. Table 22 shows the current list of food colours officially permitted in the United Kingdom and also shows which of them are permitted by other countries. While some *diazo* compounds have been reported to be carcinogenic when tested on experimental animals, the ones included in various 'permitted' lists have never been shown to be in any way toxic. Nevertheless, there is a tendency for development food technologists to restrict their use and employ, where possible, naturally occurring pigments. Although this may seem to be the most prudent thing to do, there is, of course, no certainty that because a substance is derived from a plant or animal source it is, therefore, necessarily safe.

The most commonly used natural pigments in foods include the yellow carotenoids such as carotene, xanthophyll and bixin (annatto) derived from the green parts of plants, the red-orange anthocyanins from beet, berries and flowers and the green chlorophyll. The major disadvantages of using such pigments and the compelling reason why synthetic dyes will continue to be employed lie in the sensitivity of the former to light and heat, especially in more acid foods. This severely limits their use when foods need to be heated as a preservative measure or during manufacture.

(b) FLAVOURS

(i) *Sweeteners*. Saccharin, the chemical substance ortho-sulpho-benzimide, has been used as a sweetening agent ever since it was discovered by the American chemist Flahbert in 1879 to be 500–600 times as sweet as sugar, weight for weight. Saccharin has long been considered to be entirely inert and harmless when eaten, and excreted from the body unchanged in the urine. Recently the results of tests on laboratory animals in Canada and the USA have suggested that it possesses some toxic properties. Existing legislation in the USA makes a complete ban mandatory on the use of saccharin. However, the pressure of public opinion in the USA, which perceives the benefits of its use to people who must restrict their calorie or sugar intake as greatly outweighing the risks, has effectively prevented such a course of action.

The consequences of a world-wide ban on saccharin are compounded by the earlier ban on *Cyclamate* which had been widely used as a sweetening agent before somewhat controversial evidence of toxicity was reported in 1969. Though many sweetening agents have since been discovered in food science laboratories the very

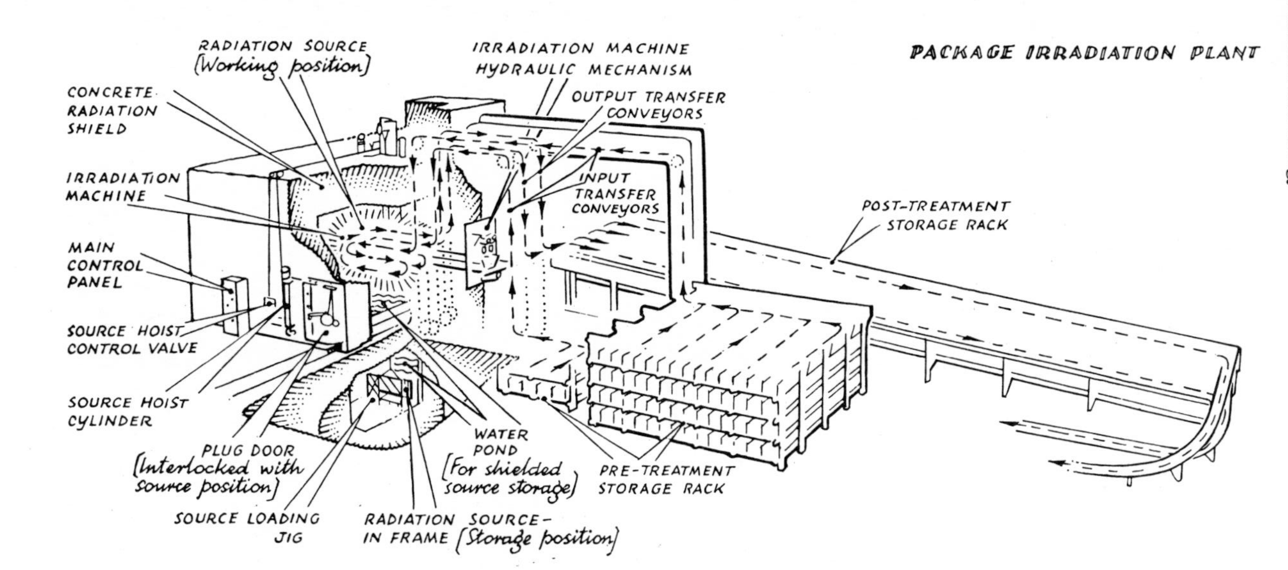

Fig. 26. A simplified flow-diagram of a plant for treating foods with radioactivity.

EXTRUSION. 98: Sheets of pastry, layered with fat, are folded to produce the typical layered dough characteristic of puff pastry. 99: This versatile enrobing machine can continuously produce anything from scotch eggs to sausage rolls by a simple dual-extrusion system.

100: Manually stripped chicken carcasses being loaded into a meat-recovery system. 101: Recovered, cooked chicken meat, showing the coarse fibrous nature of the product, which is free of bone and gristle. 102: Bone residue after the meat has been removed.

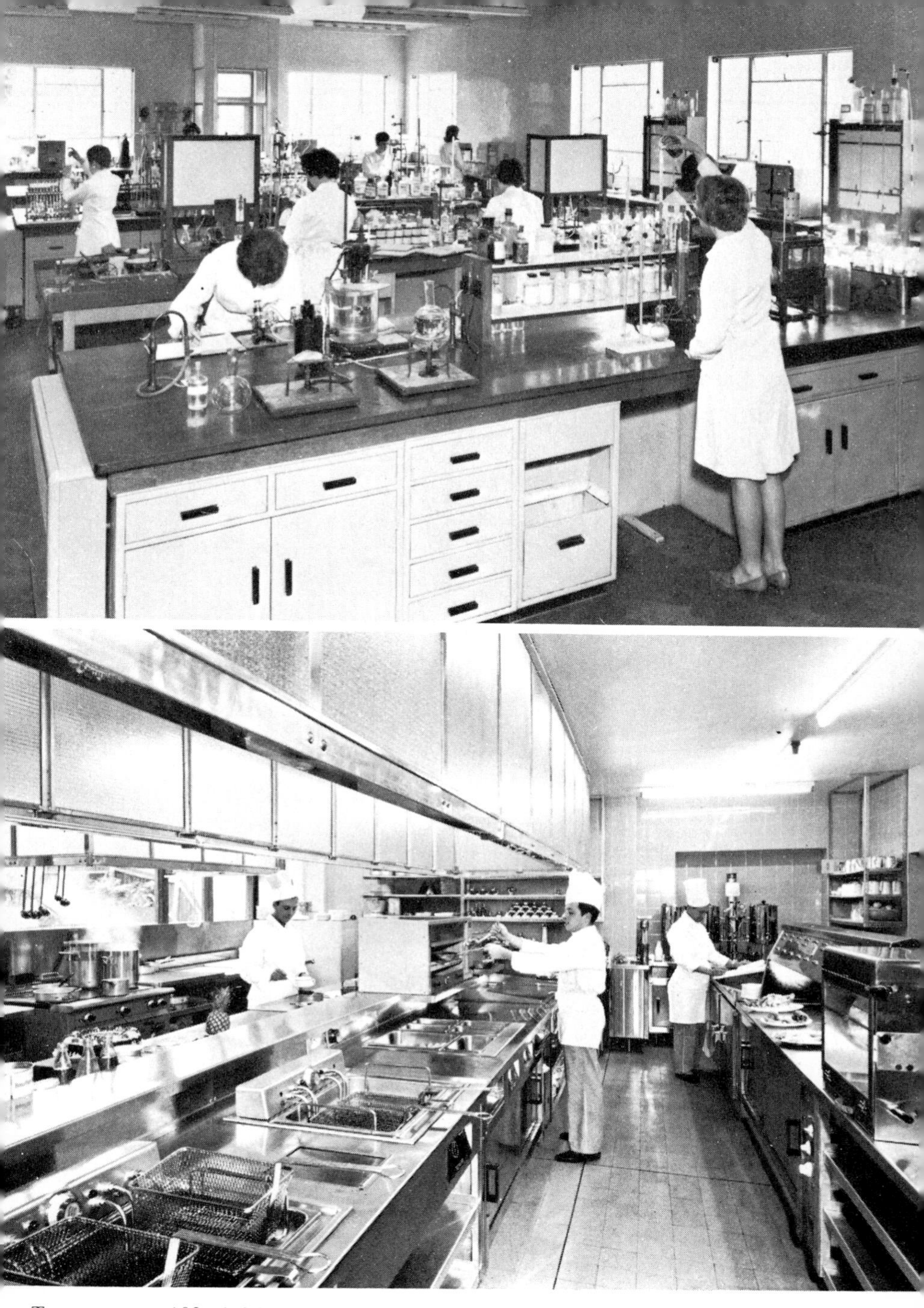

TECHNOLOGY. 103: A laboratory for the testing and analysis of foods. 104: A kitchen – the last stage but one of food technology.

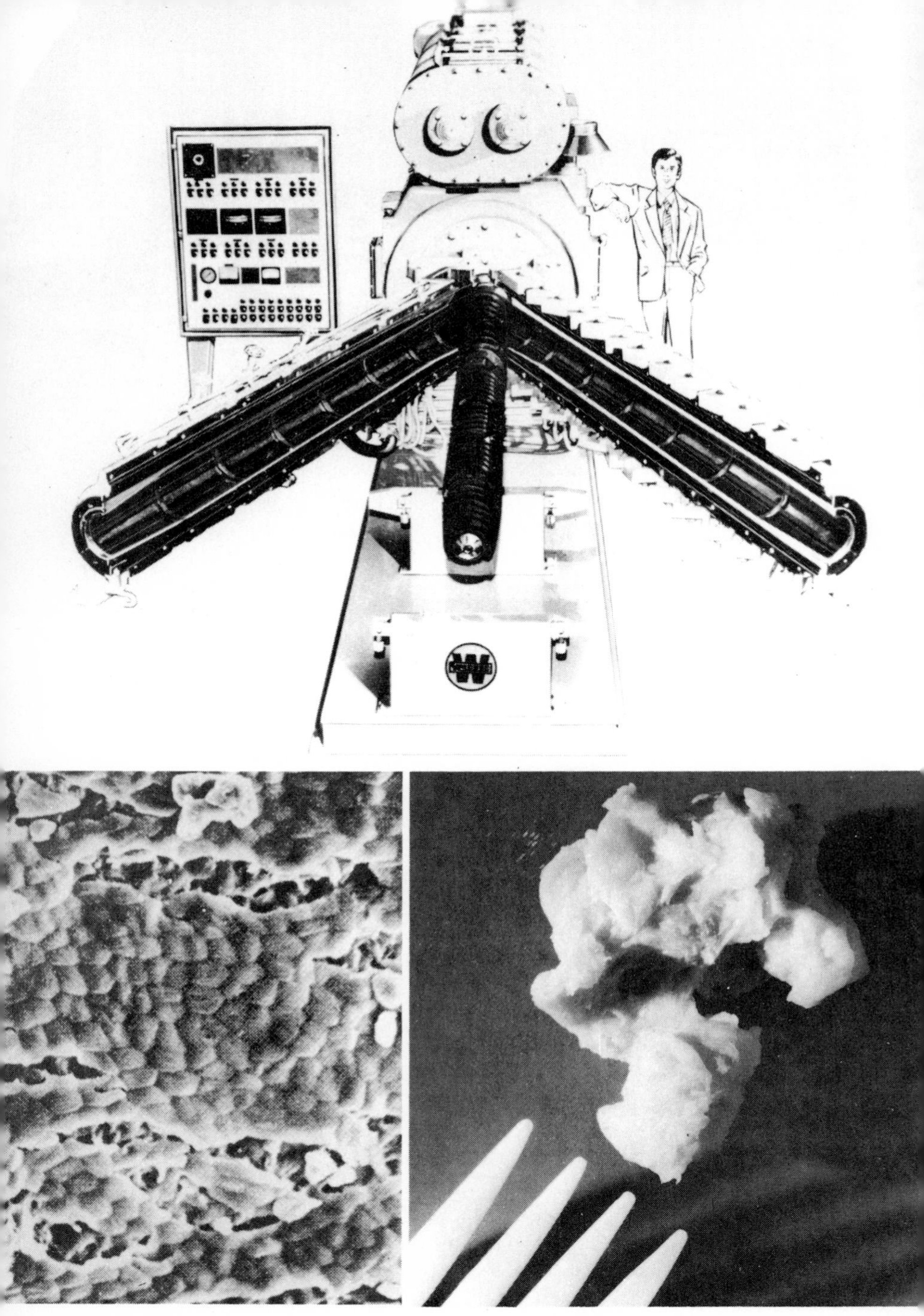

FUTURE TRENDS. 105: Single-screw extruder: the barrel, open for cleaning, reveals the screw configuration. 106: Defatted soya flakes, prior to extrusion cooking. Each protein body is encapsulated individually in a sac of cellulose. 107: Bite-sized piece of textured soya protein, produced from defatted soya flakes.

high costs and uncertainty of completing the extensive toxicity testing to the satisfaction of regulatory authorities has largely inhibited their full development.

(ii) *Flavours.* Flavours are normally minor constituents of foods with insignificant nutritional value. Yet, together with colour, flavour is an important attribute of acceptability. The flavour chemist is concerned with providing the food technologist with substances that enhance, modify or replace the natural flavours of foods and the herbs and spices with which, traditionally, they have been enriched. The diminishing supplies and rising costs of traditional materials; the increasing use of bland or flavourless ingredients such as textured vegetable protein (see Chapter 11); and the increasing demand for processed foods have made the products of the flavour chemist indispensable to the food scientist and stimulated the growth of a large and profitable food flavour industry.

A. *Concentrated natural flavours* are provided as extracts, such as vanilla, or as essential oils distilled from onions, herbs, spices and citrus fruits.

B. *Entirely synthetic flavours* created and produced in the laboratory can be used to enhance or replace costly or less readily available natural flavours. The development of synthetic *vanillin* as a replacement for vanilla is a good example of this approach.

C. *Sodium glutamate (M.S.G.)*, which is the salt of the naturally occurring amino acid, glutamic acid, possesses the capacity to accentuate and enhance meat flavours. It is widely used in meat products, soups and other foods.

D. *5-Ribonucleotides*. At least two substances, *5'-inosinic acid* and *5'-guanilic acid,* prepared from yeast, when used separately, together or in combination with sodium glutamate, enhance the 'meatiness' or 'brothiness' of foods to which they are added.

E. *Hydrolysed vegetable proteins*, produced by the chemical or enzymatic breakdown of carefully selected proteinaceous raw materials, are useful sources of meat flavours and can be used in place of M.S.G.

(c) THICKENING AND GELLING AGENTS

(i) *Starches and modified starches.* Starches are a major source of calories in food and as such play a significant role in nutrition (see p. 20). They also have purely technological uses apart from their food value. Through their thickening and gelling properties they can be employed to modify textural properties and impart stability to foodstuffs, and their availability and low cost make them the most widely used thickeners and stabilizers in the food industry.

Starches are insoluble in cold water but when heated in water above a certain characteristic temperature, which varies with the type of starch, the granules swell and thicken until a stable viscosity is achieved. Natural starches have a number of disadvantages as

Table 22

Permitted Food Colours

Note: These colours are generally premitted. Local regulations may change from time to time and not all foods may be coloured.

Dye		*Other Countries Permitting the Same*										
British List	*EEC No.*	Australia	Canada	EEC Countries	Finland	Japan	Norway*	Spain	Sweden	Switzerland	South Africa	USA
Ponceau 4R	E124	+		+	+	+		+	+	+	+	
Carmoisine	E122	+		+				+		+	+	
Amaranth	E123	+	+	+	+	+		+	+	+		
Erythrosine BS	E127	+	+	+	+	+		+	+	+	+	+
Red 2G	–										+	
Tartrazine	E102	+	+	+	+	+		+	+	+	+	+
Yellow ZG	–	+										
Sunset Yellow FCP	E110	+	+	+	+	+		+	+	+	+	+
Quinoline Yellow	E104			+	+			+	+	+	+	
Green S	E142	+		+					+	+	+	
Indigo Carmine	E132	+	+	+	+	+		+	+	+	+	+
Brilliant Blue FCF	–	+	+	+		+					+	+
Patent Blue V	E131			+				+	+	+	+	
Brown FK	–	+	+								+	
Chocolate Brown	–	+	+								+	
Black PN	E151	+	+	+				+	+	+	+	

* No artificial colours permittted.

Table 23

Some natural gums and thickeners: their sources and uses in manufactured foods

Source	*Material*	*Common uses*
Plant	Gum Arabic Gum Tragacanth	Beverages Salad Dressings, Sauces
Seed Gums	Locust Bean Gum (Carob) Guar Gum	Salad Dressings, Desserts, Sauces Processed Cheese, Ice Cream
Seaweed Extracts	Carrageenans Agar Alginates	Milk Products, Ice Cream Icing, Confectionery Ice Cream, Beer
Microbial	Xanthan Gum	Salad Dressings, Beverages
Polysaccharides	Alginates	Ice Cream, Desserts, Beverages
Plant Extracts	Pectin	Jams, Jelly, Confectionery
Proteins	Casein Gelatine	Sauces, Desserts Confectionery, Table Jelly

thickeners as far as food manufacturers are concerned—the gel is unstable to heat, shear, freezing and acid. In order to overcome these disadvantages starches can be chemically modified to alter their structure and impart more desirable characteristics. Modification treatments include acid hydrolysis, cross-linking of molecules, esterification, etherification and oxidation, alone or in combination. Speciality starches can be produced for use in frozen sauces, highly acid condiments and in foods to be subjected to retort temperatures.

Native starches of importance in the food industry include those derived from maize (corn), potato, wheat and tapioca. A genetic modification of maize, waxy maize, has also become a very important source of food starch.

(ii) *Natural gums*. Many naturally occurring compounds, such as plant exudates, seaweed extracts and gelatine, possess the ability to form gels or highly viscous solutions at low concentrations in foodstuffs containing water. These are widely used in the same way as are the starches to modify and control the structure, texture and shelf stability of manufactured foods. Whereas starches are used at levels of 2–10% in foods, the much higher viscosities that can be achieved with gums allow them to be used effectively at the much lower levels of 0·1 to 1·0%.

A list of gums, their sources and common uses in food products, is shown in Table 23. Many of these materials act synergistically, the combined thickening power of several mixed together exceeding the sum of the thickening effect of individual compounds. Xanthan gum and locust bean gum are good examples of this behaviour which can be usefully and economically exploited by the food technologist. The difficulty and high cost of harvesting naturally occurring vegetable gums has led to a search for replacements, for example, by using modified starches, or alternative means of production. The traditional, increasingly costly and uncertain harvesting of brown seaweed as a source of alginates, for example, is likely to be superseded by its development as a product of microbial fermentation.

(*d*) FAT 'EXTENDERS', EMULSIFIERS AND STABILIZING AGENTS

(i) *Fat extenders.* GMS and POEMS. As was described in Chapter 2, the chemical structure of fats and oils comprises a combination of three fatty acid molecules with one of glycerol. It has been found that in foods such as ice cream or cakes in which the quality is to a large degree dependent on the amount of fat in them, the addition of a proportion of a compound of glycerol and *one* fatty acid molecule, for example, *glyceryl monostearate,* or GMS as it is called, makes a reduced proportion of fat go further. Another compound with similar properties is *poly-oxyethylene-monostearate,* or POEMS.

Glyceryl monostearate can almost be claimed to be a natural food component since it occurs during the breakdown of fats in the body. Some doubts were felt, based on animal tests, as to whether POEMS might possess undesirable physiological action but both have been widely employed by food technologists.

(ii) *Emulsifiers and stabilizing agents.* There are two types of food emulsion: oil-in-water emulsions such as milk and salad dressings and water-in-oil emulsions such as butter. The latter are formed by the dispersion of droplets of water in a continuous oil phase (see p. 147). Conversely, oil-in-water emulsions consist of small oil droplets dispersed in water and is the more common type to be found in manufactured foods. Emulsifying agents are substances which aid in the dispersion of these oil droplets and stabilize them by preventing their coalescence to form larger globules. The progressive coalescence of oil droplets, or 'breaking' of the emulsion, results in the undesirable separation of a fat or oil at the surface of foods. As well as GMS and POEMS emulsifiers in common use include lecithin (as a pure compound or in egg yolk), milk protein, salts of fatty acids and sorbitan or glycerol fatty acid esters.

(e) ANTI-OXIDANTS

Many crude fats and oils contain natural anti-oxidants which prevent the onset of oxidative rancidity. These compounds are removed during the process of refining, so the food technologist has set out to find substances which can safely be added to the refined fats to protect them from becoming rancid.

(i) Acids. *Lactic acid, tartaric acid* and *citric acid* have all been used in amounts of about one part in 15,000 parts of fat. *Phosphoric acid* has also been employed. The effectiveness of these substances, however, is not very great.

(ii) Synthetic compounds. A number of more complex organic substances, among which are *nor-dihydro-guaiaretic acid* (NDGA), *butylated hydroxyanisole* (BHA) and *butylated hydroxytoluene* (BHT), have also been employed.

(iii) Natural substances. It is interesting to note that besides these more esoteric compounds, a number of natural substances have also been studied and found to possess anti-oxidant properties. These include the *tocopherols* (vitamin E), certain *spices* including chillies, turmeric and cinnamon bark and the naturally occurring pigments classified as flavanols.

(f) PRESERVATIVES

A restricted range of chemical compounds of no significant nutritional value are permitted to be added to foods as antimicrobial agents. These preservatives exert their effect by poisoning micro-organisms which would otherwise cause the food to decay or become a public health hazard. In doing this they inevitably tend to have to a lesser degree a toxic effect on the cells of the body of the consumer. The circumstances in which preservatives may legitimately be employed are restricted by statute to those in which a clear technological need is demonstrable. This may be related to the safety of a preserved food product or even to the consumer's expectation of quality. It is, however, the clear policy of regulatory authorities throughout the world that preservatives should not be used to cover poor manufacturing practice.

The type of preservative considered appropriate and the level of usage are legislated for according to each specific product application and this may vary from country to country. For example in the United Kingdom:

(i) Sulphur dioxide can be added to fruit juices, fruit pulp and jam.

(ii) Propionic acid may be added to flour to prevent mould growth in bread.

(iii) Benzoic acid can also be safely used in fruit juices, beer and soft drinks.

Antibiotics have been suggested as food preservatives and pimaricin and nisin have been permitted in certain instances; a danger in using them arises from the possibility that the bacteria they are intended to suppress become genetically modified so that they become permanently resistant. This would be of great concern where the antibiotic had clinical applications. An example of unexpected results of the use of antibiotics was the finding that cows treated with penicillin for some bovine infection produced milk which could not be made into cheese because the cheese-forming organisms would not develop properly in it. Preservatives permitted in foods have been the subject of considerable toxicological testing to ensure safety at the levels used. Such testing is continually reviewed and as new information becomes available modifications are made to permitted lists. A good example of this, and one with far reaching implications, is the use of sodium nitrate for the preservation of cured meats. This compound has been in use as a preservative for over 2,000 years but in 1964 a link was found between nitrites and nitrosamines which were known to be capable of inducing cancer in laboratory animals; more recently it has been suggested that nitrite itself may have some degree of carcinogenicity. This has led to great debate as to whether nitrite should continue to be permitted as a food additive. Nitrite is the key ingredient in meat curing, being responsible for the development of flavour and colour as well as preservation. No alternative currently exists and the technological need is clear. A complete ban would deprive the consumer of traditional staple products such as cured hams, meats and bacon, and the existence of a whole industry would be threatened. The regulatory authorities have considered the risks and benefits of the use of nitrite as a food additive and have recommended its continued use at lower levels than previously permitted until such time as the food scientists can develop a satisfactory alternative process or additive.

(*g*) ACIDS, BASES AND SALTS

Acids, bases and salts find many uses in food processes and product formulation. Acids are used to provide flavour or tartness (acetic acid, vinegar) as preservatives (benzoic acid, sorbic acid) and as part of chemical leavening systems (baking powders). Bases are also used to modify flavour, provide buffering capacity, aid in colour retention and as a processing aid (peeling of fruit and vegetables).

Salts such as phosphates, citrates and tartrates are often used in dairy products such as processed cheese or cheese spreads. In these instances the addition of salt in combination with heat produces a smooth uniform texture by modification of protein structure. Phosphates are increasingly important additives to processed meat products where, by a similar mechanism, they help retain water during handling and processing and impart firm textures to comminuted products such as sausages.

(*h*) FLOUR 'IMPROVERS'

Bread that is made from 'strong' flour from Canadian wheat which contains a comparatively large proportion of an appropriate protein will make a large 'bold' loaf. On the other hand, if the flour is derived from English wheat or from wheat grown in other countries with moist climates it will be 'weak' and the bread made from it will form small loaves with what the baker would consider to be an unsatisfactory, close structure. It has been found that many blended flours made from a mixture of different types of wheat will give a superior loaf of bread if an appropriate amount of a chemical 'improver' is added to the flour blend. These 'improvers' are all compounds which exert a powerful effect when they are added in amounts of the order of ten parts in each million parts of flour.

(i) *Bromate* has been used successfully as an 'improver' for a number of years. Plate 10 shows the effect of treating a flour blend with the appropriate amount of an 'improver', and with too much.

(ii) In 1919, a powerful and effective 'improver' came into use and was employed widely and with great technical success until 1946. In that year it was discovered that this substance, *nitrogen trichloride*, known as 'Agene', caused the production of a substance in flour which was toxic to dogs. This substance was subsequently found to be produced by the conversion of an integral part of the flour protein, the amino acid, *methionine*, into the toxic agent, *methionine suphoximine*. The demonstration that Agene produced toxic effects for animals caused it to be withdrawn as a flour additive. It is now commonly replaced by *chlorine dioxide*. The important lesson for the food technologist is that the use of chemical agents to produce a desired technical effect must be adopted only after the most rigorous biological tests. Even then absolute safety cannot be assured.

(i) NUTRITIONAL SUPPLEMENTS

The processes of modern food technology affect the nutritional value of foodstuffs in many ways. Modern milling methods produce a 'high extraction' flour which, while keeping better than wholemeal flour and being lower in indigestible residue, contains less of the B-vitamins. In several countries, it has been recommended that additions of vitamin B_1 (thiamine), niacin, sometimes riboflavin, and sometimes iron and calcium (as calcium carbonate) as well should be made to white flour. Margarine, made from vegetable fats and whale oil and lacking in butter-fat, is eaten as butter but does not naturally contain the amounts of vitamins A and D present in summer butter. These vitamins may be incorporated as pure chemical 'additives'. As was mentioned in Chapter 1, good nutrition is best ensured by the consumption of a judicious variety of different foods. Nevertheless, where the proportion of processed foods in a community's diet is high, or where variety is beyond the reach of a substantial proportion of the population, it is clearly valuable to add vitamins, minerals such as calcium, or possibly a single amino acid such as *lysine,* which is only present in low proportions in cereal protein, to selected processed foodstuffs. Here again the food technologist must exercise caution. Although a dangerous excess of water-soluble vitamins, such as vitamin C or B vitamins, is unlikely, the fat-soluble vitamins A and D may both be consumed in excess if too many foods are injudiciously enriched. It is also important to be careful that the amount of additive suitable for most people is not harmful to some special group. For example, salt levels appropriate for adult foods may be harmful in baby foods.

(j) ADVENTITIOUS 'ADDITIVES'

The possibility that *penicillin* administered to a cow for veterinary reasons may gain access to the milk as an adventitious 'additive' has already been referred to. A similar possibility arises if cattle are treated with *hormones* to accelerate or modify their growth.

Although modern cans are commonly lacquered, there is a possibility that when canned foods are stored for a long period a slow corrosion process will occur and the content of *tin* and *iron* in the food will increase. Both these metals are non-toxic but may cause discoloration of the food. An upper limit for tin is, therefore, accepted as 250 p.p.m. Regulatory agencies responsible for food safety have been pressing for progressively lower levels of *lead* in canned foods, especially those consumed by children or consumed in large quantities. Canned food manufacturers have therefore become increasingly concerned about contamination of their products by lead which is a component of the solder by which the side seam of a can is made. Most lead pick-up comes from small particles of lead spattered on the surface of the can during the soldering process. In plain, unlacquered cans very little contamination occurs as the electrolytic relation between lead and tin is such that, whereas tin migrates into the food, lead tends to be deposited on to the can. However, in cans that are lacquered to prevent reaction between the tin coating and the product the spatters of lead are not so well protected by the tin and give rise to high lead levels in the product. The problem can largely be overcome by the use of pure tin solder, but only at great cost. The most satisfactory long-term solution will lie in a combination of the 'drawn' can and the welded can which are both in advanced stages of development. The former is drawn in one piece in a press, has a rounded shoulder on the base and requires the application of only one end-piece. The latter will depend for its success on the development of a good sidestripe coating to prevent corrosion of the welded seam.

Plastics used as wrappings or containers are not themselves likely to contaminate food. They may have in them however, traces of the basic material from which they were made. Catalysts, which can be *peroxides* or *complex metal salts*, *anti-oxidants*, *stabilizers*, *plasticizers*, *pigments*, *anti-static agents*, *anti-fogging agents* and *adhesives* may be added and may migrate into the food.

Paper and cardboard may sometimes be sources of adventitious additives. Wet-strength paper may cause contamination by formaldehyde. Printing ink or varnish can be a source of smell derived from wrappings.

The difficulty of determining whether a chemical substance, incorporated purposely in food as an 'additive' or gaining access adventitiously, is harmful or not is extremely difficult. For example, an official committee in the United States, the Panel on Food Additives of the President's Science Advisory Committee, has reached the decision that when testing for potential carcinogenic activity, if no cancers develop in 1000 test animals, the corresponding level of the substance under examination can be classified as 'safe'. Yet two statisticians have calculated that even if a substance were sufficiently toxic to produce 100,000 cases of cancer in a population the size of that of the United States, there is a one-in-three chance that the biological test on the 1000 animals would classify it as 'safe'.

PART 3

THE TRAINING AND EMPLOYMENT OF FOOD TECHNOLOGISTS

10

The present scope of food science and technology

A. THE MODERN SCENE

Food science has been defined by Dr E. C. Bate-Smith, sometime Director of the Low Temperature Research Station in Cambridge, as the body of organized knowledge that is concerned with the *understanding* of the composition of food, whereas food technology is *exploitation* of that knowledge in practical terms.

One of the most striking features of the world in modern times has been the way, in one country after another as industrialization grows, that communities gather themselves together in large towns. These centres of population and industry inevitably possess a complex structure. Not only do they need to be provided with food transported into the towns from outside but, increasingly as industrialization grows and people struggle to raise their economic standards, the quality and variety of the foods demanded by these town-dwellers become more and more sophisticated and the distance over which the foods need to be transported becomes longer.

The scope of food science and technology is threefold: first, to make it possible to assemble the great quantities of food required by a crowded population; second to make the food agreeable to the consumers, that is to say, to provide them so far as is possible with the kind and quality of food they demand at all times of the year, doing this partly by carefully controlling the quality and uniformity of the commodities produced and partly by constant efforts to produce something new—a new breakfast food, a new kind of coffee essence or, indeed, a new kind of food altogether—and by these means keeping up with popular demands; and, third, to maintain, and maybe improve, the nutritional value of the total food supply and hence the health of the community eating it. In the previous chapters of this book I have touched on the principal problems confronting the food processor and manufacturer, dealing with each of the main categories of foodstuffs. But besides those people who are directly involved in the food industry, there are a number of others whose activities are also of direct concern to food technology.

1. Packaging

The industries concerned with the supply of all the diverse materials that are used in packaging foods also come within the scope of food technology and those people who work in them must understand the principles involved.

The packaging of foods is not only restricted to protecting them from deteriorations, although this is its most important function. It serves several other purposes which include:

(a) CONVENIENCE

One of the great advantages of the mass-production of uniform articles of food packed in standard packages is their convenience. For the technologist himself, they can be conveniently stored and transported and distributed accurately. The retailer obtains similar benefits and the consumer also knows exactly what he or she is getting and how to handle it.

(b) AVOIDANCE OF LOSS

Before efficient packaging became part of the technology of food, there was a significant wastage, not only due to deterioration of the outer layers of bulk packages or through moisture or contamination, but also during the course of the dispensing of such foodstuffs as tea, sugar and butter. Milk when distributed unpackaged provided an extreme example of contamination and waste which were almost completely avoided when up-to-date methods of bottling were introduced. A further benefit arising from the packaging of foods is the avoidance of dishonest shortweight, which often occurred when the portion for sale was weighed out or measured by hand.

(c) BRAND CONFIDENCE

The technical processes of food manufacture which have been described in the earlier chapters of this book are generally designed to handle large quantities of food. It has been abundantly demonstrated that consumers like to purchase standardized food when it is packaged in a uniform manner and designated by a brand title which is instantly recognizable. A well-packaged carton of breakfast cereal, or margarine, or canned peaches can be readily and economically marketed and is willingly accepted by consumers. It is immaterial whether the branded, packaged foodstuff is a product of a commercial firm or whether it is a can or carton of dried milk distributed by a social welfare organization, the value of good packaging is the same.

(d) MACHINES

Machines available for packaging foods have been elaborated to a remarkable extent. Automatic equipment can be provided for filling bottles, cans and jars with measured quantities of liquids and semi-liquids such as sauces and mayonnaise and for capping the containers; vacuum-operated machines can be purchased for the high-speed packaging of powders such as dried milk or custard powders; machines can automatically put caps, stoppers or lever lids on to containers. Ingenious mechanisms have been invented for sorting and wrapping loose biscuits rapidly yet without breaking them; other machines wrap irregularly-shaped objects such as kippers, cuts of meat, pies or cakes. There are devices for putting bottles into cartons and then wrapping and labelling the cartons, and as well there are other machines which unpack bottles from the cartons in which they are delivered to the food manufacturer from the bottle maker. One of these, capable of unpacking twenty-four cartons a minute, spaces out the incoming cartons, opens out the flap, brings down a 'grab head', gently picks out the bottles with a multiple cluster of nylon 'fingers' and puts them on to a travelling conveyor. Sophisticated equipment is now available to form from reels of flexible laminated materials trays, pots or cups, then fill and seal the containers, code, label and date-stamp them in successive operations on the same machine. The difficulties of transport, storage and handling of pre-formed packaging are largely eliminated.

(e) MATERIALS

The materials available for packaging are as diverse as the machines are complex. There are papers and cardboards of all sorts, some plain, some reinforced. There are sealing tapes and adhesives in great variety. Aluminium foil can be used for wrapping as well as a multitude of 'plastic' films, polythene by itself or as a lamination with other wrappings, poly-vinyl chloride (PVC), polyester films and laminates, polystyrene, rigid PVC and polypropylene. A modern development in flexible films is metalized polyester, where aluminium metal is vaporized and deposited under vacuum on a continuous reel of polyester. Metal layers of 10–20 microns can be achieved with very good barrier properties approaching those of aluminium foil at potentially much lower costs.

(f) PRECAUTIONS

The engineers who design the packaging machines must, besides understanding the principles of engineering needed to produce reliable equipment, also understand the technical properties of the foods for which the machines are intended. Many foods exert a corrosive action even on certain types of stainless steel, others possess particular physical characteristics which must be understood and respected. In just the same way, the packaging experts who produce the metal foils and plastic films, the adhesives and the printing inks must also comprehend the physical and chemical nature of the foods which are to be packed. A foil to be used outside a can or carton may be well suited to its purpose, whereas the same film used to wrap a chicken or a loaf of bread may contaminate it and spoil its flavour. More important still, the manufacturer of packaging material may treat a film with a softening agent to make it more flexible, or more transparent, or stronger; if he does so, it is his business to ensure that the agent will not be absorbed by the food and perhaps prove toxic to the person who subsequently eats it. The rate of advance in the organic chemistry of plastics is so fast that the food chemist himself can hardly hope to keep abreast of every change in the composition of new qualities and grades of new plastics. It is clearly important, therefore, for the plastics expert to appreciate at least the principles of food technology so that he will understand what properties are desirable for a packaging material and what are not.

2. Food transport

Not long ago, meat used to be transported in slow, horsedrawn vehicles, the floors of which were made of wood and were consequently difficult to clean—if, indeed, any attempt was made to clean them. The vertical and horizontal supports became smeared with blood, it was not possible to control the temperature or humidity of the inside atmosphere or to protect the meat from dust and dirt. The application of the principles of food science has led to the development of modern vehicles, the walls and roofs of which are constructed of a double skin to allow for insulation and the interior of which is constructed so that the meat carcasses can be hung without damage on rails which can be satisfactorily sterilized.

It is only a short further step from this type of vehicle to the use of fully insulated trucks equipped either with compressors to operate refrigeration pipes or with bunkers to hold solid carbon dioxide to serve as a refrigerant. With vehicles such as this, perishable foods can be transported with minimum deterioration or quick-frozen foods can be distributed from the factory where they are originally processed to outlying cold stores.

In the same way that road transport for meat has been adapted to conform to the principles of meat technology, which require that the vehicle provide an appropriate atmosphere and a suitable temperature and also conform to the principles of good hygiene, similar conditions have been made available for transporting other foods. In fact, the technological processing of food cannot be considered as being restricted only to the factory in which the principal operations are carried out. We have already noted that in handling milk the food technologist must concern himself with the conditions of transport from the cow to the collecting station and from the collecting station to the factory, where the milk is to be converted into butter, cheese or condensed milk. The whole process is, indeed, one operation. If for the first stage of the journey the milk is in a can or churn, the vessel must be capable of proper sterilization, be made of a non-corrosive material and be so constructed that the milk in it can be cooled. Under modern conditions this is often done by inserting a cooled stainless-steel coil into the churn. This coil is constructed so that it can be revolved in the milk. The food technologist concerned with milk transport will, therefore, provide a simple motor vehicle capable of carrying churns for the first part of the chain of transport, whereas for the later stage—from, say, a collecting depot to the factory—he will have a glass-lined tanker to ensure absolute cleanliness of the cooled and bulked milk supply.

Food technologists have also played an important part in the design of other forms of transport. One of the major successes of applied food science was the design of insulated ships' holds for the transport of chilled meat from Australia and New Zealand to Europe. The cargo spaces were designed not only to maintain an appropriate low temperature but also to allow the recirculation of air so that proper ventilation and the required concentration of carbon dioxide were provided.

A similar application of scientific principles to food transport has been the development of ships specially designed for the transport of bananas. Here, as described in Chapter 8, it was necessary to ensure that the ships' holds were kept at a steady warm temperature and, once again, the maintenance of a standardized level of carbon dioxide was another factor in the successful conveyance of the fruit from the tropical regions in which it is grown to most of the temperate regions of the world.

The most recent advance in the technology of food transportation is a system developed in the USA and referred to as 'hypobaric' transportation or storage. This sophisticated technique economically keeps perishable foodstuffs at controlled temperatures (20–60°F or −7 to 16°C) and humidity (90–95%) by maintaining reduced pressure within a specially designed bulk container. Sealed containers can be transported by land and sea and are equipped to provide their own micro-environment. The process of maintaining a low pressure involves a continual flushing of the container. Oxygen tension is therefore kept low and the risk of aerobic bacterial spoilage is reduced. Ethylene oxide and carbon dioxide produced during the respiration of fruits are also removed and the rate of ripening is slowed down. Additionally, the provision of a high relative humidity prevents wilting in vegetables and shrinkage in meat. It has been demonstrated that with hypobaric storage the fresh life of both meat and vegetable produce can be extended up to six-fold. As well as being useful in smoothing out fluctuations in production, this order of improvement means that highly perishable produce that could previously only be transported over long distance at great cost by air can now be economically placed in wider markets.

3. Commercial catering

Just as those people whose concern is with food transport, whether they are the engineers and designers of vehicles or the operators of transport fleets, must be aware of the principles of food technology, so also must those who are responsible for catering. The caterers, indeed, are a link in the final chain of food transport as well as being responsible for the last stage of processing.

Modern kitchens which serve large numbers of people, either in hotels or in the different institutions ranging from prisons to schools, hospitals and army barracks where big communities of people are given meals together, must apply the principles of food science in the same way that they are applied in the different kinds of processing units that we have already discussed.

The equipment to be found in the kitchen of a large modern catering establishment is similar to that described in the earlier chapters of this book. The store-rooms must provide the varying conditions appropriate to the different types of food commodities; it is not sufficient to install a cold room only capable of the limited degree of cooling found in a domestic refrigerator. Then, for the next stage of the catering procedure, machines for washing vegetables, peeling potatoes, mincing and chopping meat, mixing dough and for many of the operations already discussed must be available. The equipment for cooking on a large scale—the pressure vessels and steamers, the large kettles for soup, the ovens, and the mechanical bread-slicers and butterers—is precisely the kind of machinery to be found in the factories of food manufacturers. Clearly, large-scale catering, if it is to be carried out efficiently under modern conditions, requires a broader understanding of food technology than that needed in a food factory where, as a general rule, one single commodity may be handled.

In the earlier chapters of this book there has only been space to discuss the main foodstuffs and to touch on the broad principles involved in handling them. But for the large-scale caterer, it is essential to have a detailed knowledge of the chemistry and physics of a wide variety of food. As was described in Chapter 3, millers producing bread for large-scale bakeries must understand the relationship between the nitrogen content of flour and the physical structure of flour protein and the behaviour of a particular wheat when milled. The caterer producing cakes and confectionery has to cope in even more detail with flour of the appropriate chemical and physical structure; with egg or egg-substitute made perhaps from milk or fish protein; with sugar and with fats, also of the required chemical nature and melting-point. If the caterer is producing 'chipped' potatoes on a large scale, he must understand the relationship between the carbohydrate and protein content of the potatoes he chooses. He cannot afford merely to purchase 'potatoes' but must lay down a quite detailed specification. It is for these reasons that all up-to-date large-scale caterers employ food technologists with a proper understanding of the physics and chemistry upon which their practical expertise is based.

The problem of hygiene is of particular importance to the caterer. An efficient food manufacturer making, say, sausages or preparing dressed poultry for the market can—and, indeed, must—organize his factory like the operating theatre in a hospital. And he will also arrange for his raw materials to be processed promptly and held under proper conditions before they are despatched. The caterer, on the other hand, needs to prepare foods divided into small lots for individual consumers and the temperature of meals eaten 'hot' is approximately ideal for the growth of micro-organisms. It is not, therefore, surprising that the most serious outbreaks of food 'poisoning', usually traceable to infection by *Salmonella*, are attributable to catering establishments where either a scientific understanding of microbiology—one of the essential parts of food technology—is insufficient, or where its principles have been neglected.

4. Community feeding

The primary duty of those responsible for community feeding—whether the community are children in a school or institution, soldiers in a camp, industrial workers in a factory or mine, patients in a hospital, or prisoners in a gaol—is to provide adequate supplies of calories and of the appropriate protein, fat, vitamins and minerals for nutritional health. This implies that the catering officer in charge of a community should possess a proper understanding of the principles of nutrition which were briefly outlined in Chapter 1. But although this is indubitably so, it must never be forgotten that men and women—and children too—do not 'ingest nutrients', they eat meals. And meals are made up of foods. In order that the community caterer shall succeed in his or her task, the foods provided must not only supply the necessary nutrients and must not only be available in good quality, properly processed, efficiently stored and free from contamination and microbiological infection, they must also be tasty and attractive. Hence it can be seen that the scope of food technology extends inescapably into the field of community feeding.

It is interesting to study the reports of experienced technologists in widely different branches of community feeding. For example, while it may not be surprising to read in the reports of school-feeding experts, after considering questions of the necessary capacity of refrigerators for 1000 dinners for 12-year-olds, of the steam requirements for soup boilers, or the standard protein content of sausages, to find that the most detailed section of the document is that dealing with acceptable menus. Yet equal emphasis on the same point will be found in similar studies of catering in up-to-date prisons. Even in prisoner-of-war camps where, it might be thought, the acquisition of sufficient nutrients to keep alive might be held as the sole criterion of food quality, men attach the greatest importance to the technical quality of what they eat. It was reported by Drs Anne Burgess and R. Dean that during World War II one of the worst punishments in certain prisoner-of-war camps was to take a man's food parcel and pound it into a mash which contained all the food he required but deprived him entirely of pleasure and satisfaction. So strong was the attraction of the qualities introduced by the food technologist—the agreeably shaped biscuits, the familiar texture of 'Spam', the bar of chocolate and the flavour of the canned pineapple chunks—that many men would ask for rigorous imprisonment rather than this particular punishment.

In the last chapter we discussed the topic of food 'additives'—the dyestuffs, the anti-oxidants, the flour 'improvers', the emulsifiers and the synthetic flavours each of which, to a greater or lesser extent, raises the possibility of introducing a toxic hazard and many of which may involve the accusation of deceiving the consumer. It can be argued that the use of all these technical devices is to be deprecated and, indeed, it is undeniable that fresh food of fine quality is to be preferred. But when, as in the modern conditions under which many of the world's population live, the methods of processing which we have discussed are essential to enable a varied food supply to be made available at all, the production of attractive manufactured foods is a contribution of real value justifying a controlled degree of risk.

Food science and technology are of direct importance in very many ways to the administrators who find themselves responsible for organizing the food supplies for a community. Although the nature of the foods suitable for different categories of a community—work camps, children's homes, refugees or the mixed population of a city or of a country district—and of communities in different parts of the world may differ widely, the principles of community feeding are always the same.

(a) NUTRITIONAL REQUIREMENTS

The nutritional needs of human beings are, broadly speaking, the same wherever they may live and to whatever race they may belong. With some comparatively small margin of variation, the total amount of food required expressed in terms of Calories is always dependent on the amount of physical work done, the body size, sex and the decade of age. The proportions of protein, vitamins, minerals, carbohydrate and fat must conform to the principles described in Chapter 1 and the figures shown there. Hence, the first business of the responsible official in charge of the feeding of a community is to calculate the gross requirements of the population he has to feed. With this calculation in his hand he can begin to assess how best to translate Calories, grams of protein, millions or International Units of vitamin A and all the rest into terms of foodstuffs. At the beginning of World War II, Sir Henry French purchased for the feeding of the British population large quantities of sugar, wheat and whale oil. These commodities were basically intended to supply Calories, but the technique of feeding a community demands more than this. People need Calories, to be sure, but they ask for food.

(b) TECHNOLOGICAL QUALITY

A community requires the quality of food to which it is accustomed. The British do not eat whale oil but they do eat margarine, in which whale oil can serve as a useful component provided the necessary equipment and skill in food technology are available. In more recent times, the United States Federal Civil Defence Administration has planned a 'seven-day emergency pantry' for communities cut off in the event of nuclear warfare. It was a sound adherence to the principles of community nutrition that caused the USFCDA to interpret the appropriate nutritional needs of marooned families in terms of such food items as canned orange, grapefruit and tomato juices; mushroom, bean, vegetable and cream-of-chicken soups; canned beef stew, luncheon meat, tuna, chicken, ham and baked beans; together with pickles, catsup and chilli sauce—all of these being products of food technology to which the United States public is accustomed.

It clearly follows that administrators must be able to assess, first of all, nutritional requirements. When these have been met as well as circumstances allow from the bulk foods which can be obtained, the administrator must appreciate what facilities will be required to process the foods. Flour-milling facilities will be needed, yeast factories and bakeries and the fuel to run them. If milk is to be distributed for mothers, infants and young children, the administrator must grasp the need, either for adequate refrigeration to cool and transport the bottled liquid milk, or for the necessary facilities to condense, evaporate or dry it.

The significance of an understanding of food technology is equally as great for administrators in developing countries as it is for those in the more completely industrial areas. In the Philippines, where rice is the staple cereal, the government was faced with a serious public-health problem from the disease, beri-beri. Knowledge that this was due to a deficiency of the vitamin, thiamine, was only a part of what was needed to solve the problem. In order to make good the deficiency and provide the people who lacked it with the thiamine they needed, it was also necessary to possess an understanding of the technology of rice milling as outlined in Chapter 3. Then means could be worked out of applying the thiamine to a proportion of the rice grains at the polishing stage of their processing. These enriched grains were then available for distribution and could be mixed in the appropriate proportion with the bulk of the rice used by the people in the beri-beri-affected areas.

Behind the provision of food of the appropriate quality for the feeding of diverse communities there lies the need to transport and store the bulk foods that are to be processed. And here again the transportation and storage demand a proper knowledge of the principles of food technology. If the administrators are ignorant of these principles, stocks of food will be lost through the attacks of vermin, through decay due to so apparently trivial an oversight as the neglect to adjust the moisture content by a few per cent, through stifling due to neglect of ventilation where, as we have seen in more than one instance, what appears to be an inert commodity is in fact a living, respiring organism.

5. World food problems

The problem of maintaining an adequate supply of food in the world at the present time and during the last decades of the twentieth century is a very difficult one. The world's population as a whole has never been adequately fed throughout history. Three new factors make this matter one of special significance now. First, the rapid advances in the biological sciences—in medicine, biochemistry, pharmacology, bacteriology and in chemistry—have almost completely overcome many of the diseases which in previous ages kept populations in check. Malaria, plague, smallpox, typhoid, tropical infections of all sorts and even the deficiency diseases of beri-beri, pellagra, anaemia and many others have been checked. The result of these advances in knowledge has been a rapid increase in the world's population. Fewer children and adults die prematurely. This means that the world's population will certainly double between the years 1960 and 2000. And in spite of the very great improvements in agricultural science, the world's food supply may not keep pace with the increasing numbers of men and women. But the people seeing the development of technology with its comforts and conveniencies all around them, demand a better and more sophisticated diet just when they may perhaps get a worse one. The third factor affecting the problem of food supplies for the world at the present time is that the globe is now so close-knit, both by rapid transport and communication and by ties of political and humane linkage, that the problems of poor and distant nations are nowadays the concern of the whole modern world and must be dealt with by the means of modern technology.

Dr Binay Ranjan Sen, who was at one time Director-General of the Food and Agriculture Organization of the United Nations, emphasized that as important as the new scientific knowledge applied to agriculture to produce more food was the application of food technology to preserve, process and distribute food. Food and industrial crops, he reported, may be attacked by pests and diseases so that as much as 25% of the original amount is destroyed. The prevention of these losses comes within the scope of the food technologist. He can develop and apply methods to combat the destructive agents and at the same time circumvent their effect by the processes of canning, dehydration, the use of low temperature or of newer methods still being developed, such as exposure to radioactivity. Dr Sen has also pointed out that in many developing countries only traditional methods of food processing—salting, drying, smoking, pickling and fermentation—are used. While these were adequate when small communities had only to consider feeding themselves and preserving supplies for single families, they frequently involved considerable wastage and, as a general rule, were not adequate for the transport over longer distances and the storage for longer periods of time essential when larger groups of people collected together into towns have to be supplied.

But the scope of food technology in the wide sphere of world food problems impinges very forcibly in a further direction. Food by its very nature tends to be perishable and one of the major difficulties facing the food producer has always been that the crops he grows are as a general rule ripe for harvesting during a single short period of the year. In spite of the progress of agricultural science, there is still a tendency to have a flush of milk and eggs in the spring. Peas and tomatoes tend to be plentiful in their season. Fruit ripen on the trees at a set time of the year. Potatoes and other root crops must be harvested when they are ready. The contribution of food technology to the problem is that the specialized food-processing plants can be sited close to the main producing areas. These factories can be planned to deal with the entire crop as it becomes available. And when the food is processed—whether it is canned peas, condensed milk, frozen chickens or dehydrated mashed potato—it can be stored and distributed when it is needed without loss.

There is one further respect in which food technology makes a contribution to the larger problems of feeding the population of the world. Food-processing plants operate most efficiently when they are geared to handle large quantities of the particular commodity with which they deal. For this reason, such plants are for the most part situated in places where the conditions are best suited for the production of the crop in question. Pea canneries are sited in areas where peas grow well; meat canneries can often best be situated close to the ranching areas where the meat is raised; and the same principle holds for tomatoes or pineapples—or fish. The effect of this arrangement is to encourage large-scale production of foodstuffs in those places where they can be grown most efficiently and with the best quality. Without the existence of the processing plants, the area would either be used for crops to which it was less well suited, or part of the favoured crop would become surplus to the needs of the immediate neighbourhood or be more than the transport and storage systems could handle.

B. TEACHING FOOD TECHNOLOGY

(a) TRADITIONAL KNOWLEDGE

Skilled farmers and ranchers and fishermen, as well as the millers and bakers, the dairymen who make cheese and butter, and the men who cure bacon and salt fish—indeed, all those who for generations have processed foods by the traditional methods described in Chapter 2—possess a large store of useful information which it is valuable for the modern food technologist to know. It is, nevertheless, true to say that the great advances that have taken place in the last 40 years, some of which have been described in the previous chapters of this book, have been due to the application of a quite different kind of knowledge: the knowledge of scientific principles and their technological application. It follows, therefore, that the teaching of food technology must be grounded on science.

(b) THE DISTINCTION BETWEEN TECHNICIANS AND TECHNOLOGISTS

Two main kinds of people are needed for the day-to-day running of the modern food-processing industries: technicians and technologists. The former are the men and women who are trained to operate the equipment installed in a factory and to supervise the processes carried on there; the latter are those who are qualified to manage the factory and design the plant, who work out the processes, who understand the scientific principles upon which they are based, and who are capable of collecting new knowledge and devising new processes.

(i) *Technicians*

Technicians are often trained during the course of their work. This type of teaching is, of course, an apprenticeship. Many technicians who have learned their trade in this way become highly skilled. The disadvantages of this process of training are threefold: first, a man who has learned to operate the plant in a bakery, let us say, may not be able easily to apply himself to tasks in a fish cannery should he be required to change his occupation. The second drawback for a technician trained merely to operate a particular process is that he may be at a loss if the process with which he has become familiar is modified or changed. And the third disadvantage is that training in this way has been shown to be slow. Technicians for the modern, rapidly changing world of food technology are best given a systematic course of instruction. This course may often be profitably given during the time they are already in their employment provided that it follows a systematic syllabus.

Although the teaching of technicians working in different kinds of factories will certainly need to be modified in order to emphasize those aspects of food manufacture with which they are most closely concerned, there are certain basic topics which can always usefully be taught:

A. *Elementary principles of microbiology and hygiene.* All technicians in food industries should know how infections are transmitted, on their hands, by non-sterile equipment and by other means. The main principles by which micro-organisms can be destroyed in sterilization should also be taught.

B. *The use of tools and equipment.* There are approved good practices for handling the basic implements with which technicians deal. Coupling pipes; loosening and tightening bolts; the nature of materials of construction of different composition—for example, the relative hardness of mild steel, stainless steel, copper and brass, of wood, rubber and the principal 'plastic' materials in common use—all these need to be systematically learned by a well-trained technician.

C. *The nature of heat, cold, pressure and vacuum.* Although it cannot be expected that technicians should possess academic understanding of physical science, they must be taught the principles that underlie the transfer of heat through a 'heat-exchanger', whether this is used for heating milk to pasteurize it or to cool it for storage. Similarly, the nature of the heat and energy of steam must be understood so that it can be safely handled; and this leads naturally to teaching the principles of refrigeration. The practical implications arising from the principles of high and low pressures encountered by technicians—on the one hand as compressed air, steam under pressure and pressure cooking, and on the other hand as vacuum packing and other uses of reduced pressure—are also of general importance.

D. *Electricity.* Even those technicians who have no intention of training to be electricians as such, need to understand the nature of electricity and how to handle electrical equipment.

E. *Learning food handling.* Although basic scientific principles underlie all the processes used in food technology, for a man to be skilled in a particular industry or in a particular process in that industry it is clearly necessary for him to be trained and practised in his special job. The comparison can be drawn with a man trained to understand the principles of driving and servicing a motor vehicle: his general training will fit him to deal with many types of automobile but the man who aims to handle sports cars efficiently will require specialist training and experience different from those of a man whose business is with heavy commercial vehicles. Similarly, a milling technician must learn the nature of wheat and flour and the management of the machines with which they are processed, whereas a man in a margarine factory must learn to handle fats.

(ii) *Technologists*

A food technologist, if he is to justify that title, must be a scientist. He needs to know how to apply his science to the particular processing operation with which he deals, but he must nevertheless be trained in those sciences upon which they are based.

To obtain a proper grounding, a food technologist must have an adequate general secondary education, after which he will require at least three and probably four years' specialist scientific study. Under modern conditions, the training of food technologists can involve *(a)* the acquisition of a university degree in chemistry, biochemistry, or perhaps microbiology, followed by post-graduate study of subjects more directly related to food processing. Alternatively, *(b)* the training designed for students in a college of advanced technology or in a technical college of university rank may include a degree course specially designed for the sufficient study of basic science combined with subjects chosen as being of more specific application to the food industries. Whichever way the instruction is arranged, the main topics for the training of a food technologist are these:

A. *Chemistry*. Chemistry is the science of the composition of matter and an understanding of it is essential for a grasp of the principles of the changes that occur during the industrial processing of food or, indeed, any other substance. *Inorganic chemistry* covers the reactions of compounds of the elements other than carbon; *organic chemistry* is concerned with the various classes of carbon compounds of which biological materials are composed; *physical chemistry* deals with the mathematical principles by which the physical effects of chemical change can be related to the chemical reactions taking place. Study covering at least two years is needed to allow a student to obtain a grasp of the fundamental principles of these subjects.

B. *Biochemistry* deals with the chemical reactions which occur in living cells. As should be clearly apparent in the preceding chapters, a grasp of biochemical principles is essential for a proper understanding of such practical matters as the chain of changes that occur when starch in bananas—or in potatoes—becomes converted step by step into intermediate compounds and subsequently into sugar as the living cells respond to the environment in which they are placed. Biochemistry can only usefully be taught to students who already have a grasp of the basic principles of chemistry and preferably have also had some instruction in biology. At least a year's training in biochemistry is probably desirable for a food technologist. The principles of *nutrition* should be included as part of the course in biochemistry.

C. *Microbiology*. Training in the science of microbiology must extend to a course of at least a year's duration, so that study of the nature of micro-organisms and the methods by which they can be handled and distinguished may be made. The chemistry of microbiological growth and fermentation is of direct importance in numerous food processes ranging from the brewing of beer to the manufacture of cheese. The microbiological syllabus will, therefore, need to be integrated into the training in food technology after basic instruction in chemistry. The course will obviously need to give special attention to sanitation and to organisms affecting food spoilage.

D. *Engineering and unit operations*. Some formal training in engineering is obviously required by a food technologist as he will need to understand the operation of a diverse variety of mechanical and electrical equipment and to deal with pressure and vacuum, heat transfer, the principles of drying, evaporation and, possibly, distillation. The modern outlook on the sort of processes with which the food technologist deals is that pioneered by chemical engineers: it is to split up what may appear to be quite complex procedures—margarine manufacture, the production of dried egg, or perhaps the preparation of condensed milk—into a number of 'unit operations'. These unit operations include such effects as heat exchange, evaporation and drying, materials handling and grinding.

E. *Food processing*. In the later third or fourth year of training or, alternatively, in the post-graduate year after the completion of a degree course, a food technologist must take a thorough course in food chemistry and food processing, since this is the subject in which he is to become expert. The basic courses in chemistry will now be applied to food analysis and the study of the chemical changes occurring in foods; physical effects of the processes to which foods are submitted must also be learned in detail; the specific micro-organisms related to food processing and the chemical and physical effects they produce will also need to be included in the syllabus.

As was stated above, a food technologist, to be properly trained, must be educated in his profession fully to the standard of a university graduate in science. This implies that besides having a knowledge of the facts of food technology he also understands the principles upon which these facts are based and the way in which they have been discovered. This involves an appreciation of the nature of science as being a body of knowledge based on experiment and observation from which new discoveries have been derived by intuitive thought based on previous understanding. For this to be properly assimilated, the food technologist needs to have undertaken himself a piece of research, even if of a minor character, before his course of training can be considered complete.

F. *Food laws and regulations.* Different countries have their own laws and regulations controlling the use of chemical additives and setting standards for each kind of process and for the labelling and description of the different kinds of manufactured foods; these, too, must be mastered by the would-be food technologist.

11

Food technology and the next twenty years

During the next 20 years we may expect to see food technology develop in two main directions. On the one hand, the rapid progress towards more sophisticated, more convenient, nutritious and attractive foods which has been so striking a feature in industrialized countries during the past few years can be expected to continue and to accelerate. But on the other hand, it seems certain that scientific thinking will lead to the development of technological processes aimed to convert into acceptable foods materials which at the present time we do not use to full advantage. We can also expect that improved means will be found to process foods so that they can be kept in sound condition and transported to those areas of the world which are at present only in the stage of developing the level of industrialization which only a fortunate minority now enjoys.

A. FOODS AND FOOD PROCESSES OF INCREASING SOPHISTICATION

1. The extension of freezing

In the wealthy industrial nations of the world there has in recent years been a great increase in the amount of frozen food manufactured and distributed. As was described in Chapter 8, this allows perishable foods of all sorts—fish, peas, strawberries and even freshly baked loaves of bread—to be processed when they are freshest and at the peak of their quality. To a large extent, freezing arrests the processes of deterioration and decay and allows the foodstuff, pre-packed and prepared for the table, to be distributed to large towns far removed from the food factories and the sources of supply. Freezing also enables seasonable foods to be stored and eaten at any time of the year. But the present process of preparing quick-frozen food has two drawbacks. First, although the flavour and quality of frozen articles are good, they are not *quite* as good as fresh food. There is often the need to blanch food before freezing, as was described earlier, and this detracts, even if only to a small degree, from the original fresh taste. Again, although freezing arrests most of the processes of deterioration, it does not stop them all—for example, some measure of enzyme action may continue—and those it does check, it does not stop completely. It can be confidently anticipated that within the next 20 years the progress of food technology will bring the taste and consistency of frozen foods even nearer to those of freshly harvested or newly prepared items and that means will be found to halt even more completely than is possible at present, the comparatively slow processes of deterioration that do now take place.

The second drawback of frozen foods is that their preparation costs money and, furthermore, to transport and store them requires the expenditure of energy in the form of refrigeration. This energy is at present normally derived from electricity and is limited in quantity, but we can expect in the future that the pervasive increase of electricity installations and supplies will continue and in the next 20 years, besides the coal and petroleum and water power now used as the source of electrical energy, we can confidently expect a more widespread distribution of atomic energy. The development of an efficient means of harvesting solar energy may possibly provide a new energy source of practical value. The way in which plants achieve the conversion of solar energy to chemical energy in photosynthesis could provide us with a model. The generation of hydrogen, a useful and clean fuel, from water by isolated plant cell enzyme systems is already technically feasible. A further 10–15 years' research may make the direct chemical adsorption of solar energy an economic reality.

2. New methods of sterilization

Sterilization by heat is almost the oldest of the modern methods of food technology used for preserving foodstuffs—after all, 'pasteurization', which is the killing of at least those micro-organisms which are pathogenic to man, bears the name of Louis Pasteur, the gifted French chemist who, more than 100 years ago, laid the foundation of our modern understanding of the part played by microbes in food spoilage. There is little doubt that within the next 20 years other methods of achieving the same ends will be developed.

(a) RADIOACTIVITY

Radioactivity has already been examined, as is described in Chapter 9, and although the problems of maintaining good flavour when this means is employed has yet to be fully solved, we may expect to see it employed increasingly when the appropriate circumstances for its use have been worked out.

(b) ULTRASONICS

Ultrasonics is a further new method which is being examined. In principle, it consists of producing vibrations in the structure of the material of the right amplitude to destroy any living cells which may be present. If this could be made effective, ultrasonics as well as radioactivity would allow food to be made stable wrapped in one of the new plastic materials without the need for heating.

(c) ADDITIVES

As we have already discussed, the indiscriminate use of 'additives' and, in particular, the use of chemical preservatives is accompanied by a risk of including in food substances which may possess some degree of toxicity, no matter how little, for the people who subsequently eat it. While the trend towards restricting more and more the use of chemical 'additives' will almost certainly continue, it is very possible that the researches which are now in progress to discover effective substances which shall at the same time be demonstrably innocuous may be successful. It is, therefore, well within the bounds of possibility that before the next few decades pass we may see foods which have been rendered stable in their freshest state by the use of a preservative—perhaps an antibiotic, or a gas, or a temporary source of some kind of radiation—which could be entirely dissipated before the article was eventually consumed.

One promising area of research into the future use of additives involves attempts to link, chemically, compounds with useful functional properties to innocuous polymers, such as cellulose, that are not absorbed during digestion. Such polymer-linked additives would be designed to fulfil their function in the food product during processing and storage then, on consumption, be excreted with the non-absorbable molecule. In this way, chemicals which are presently considered undesirable in foods due to some toxic effect when absorbed could safely be used as additives. Anti-oxidants have already been successfully linked to polymers with no significant loss in activity and we can expect the same of artificial colours and sweeteners within the next decade.

(d) INTERMEDIATE MOISTURE FOODS

Attempts have been made with modest commercial success to manufacture shelf stable foods by manipulation of their moisture content. These are referred to as intermediate moisture or semi-moist foods since one of the major elements contributing to their stability is a reduction in water content to a level between those commonly encountered in fresh and in dehydrated foods. A certain amount of water is necessary to support microbial growth and undesirable chemical reactions in foods. As the water content is reduced, the conditions in which these reactions take place become progressively less favourable. The availability of water in food to support the growth of micro-organisms and spoilage reactions is best described by the thermodynamic expressions 'water activity' or 'equilibrium relative humidity'. This is reduced by partial removal of water. More important is the addition of water-binding chemicals, such as salts, sugars and glycerol, which are collectively known as humectants. Control of water activity alone is not sufficient to preserve intermediate moisture foods. It is customary to add acids to reduce the pH, chemical preservatives to control yeasts and moulds tolerant to low water activity environments, and anti-oxidants to prevent rancidity. This technology can provide ready-to-eat products that are stable without heat sterilization or refrigerated storage.

Traditional examples of intermediate moisture foods preserved by the addition of humectants are jams, preserves, dried fruit, certain fermented sausages, certain mature cheese, pemmican and fruit cake. The development of modern semi-moist products has been held back by the sweet or salty nature of the humectants which are available as additives to human food. However, the introduction of such products as roast beef cubes, bacon bites, stews, casseroles and nutritionally complete food bars in the US Department of Defense and by the US National Aeronautical and Space Administration as part of the diet of astronauts has renewed interest in commercial development. The logistical advantages of lightweight packaging, low water levels, and long shelf life without refrigerated storage, as well as the facility to control nutrient levels were the major attractions for these agencies. Changing food habits and demands on energy resources are likely to enhance the appeal of such features to food manufacturers. The most successful modern intermediate moisture food development has been that of pet food. Semi-moist food for both cats and dogs is now a major segment of the pet food market.

3. Fabricated foods

Increasing commercial pressure for novel product development, for improved utilization of food materials and for reduced waste has provided incentive for the innovative application of advanced scientific and engineering principles to products and processes. This has led to the appearance of a category of foods labelled fabricated or engineered foods. This new technology encompasses the development of techniques to separate food raw materials into separate components and then recombine them into food products with desired properties to varying degrees of sophistication. The convenience, appeal and cost of fabricated foods can be carefully tailored by the food technologist to the specific requirements of the consumer. In addition to these organoleptic considerations, control can be exercised over nutritional demands. Vitamin and protein fortification, as well as calorie control, are relatively simple to achieve, moreover, a wide range of products can be manufactured for those people with special dietary needs. Some examples of successful fabricated foods are discussed below. These represent only a few examples of foodstuffs that will become increasingly familiar over the next 20 years.

(a) FABRICATED DAIRY PRODUCTS

Many traditional dairy products are now available in alternative forms. In most of these the butter fat is replaced by vegetable fats and oils, and emulsifiers. They are referred to as 'filled' dairy products. Filled milk has already been described as has margarine which may claim to be one of the first and most successful of the fabricated foods. Other examples include coffee whiteners, whipped topping and cheese. Within the next decade we may expect rapid increases in the volume of fabricated cheese, including mozzarella, parmesan, blue and cheddar, as technical improvements are made to existing process and the cost of 'natural' dairy-derived cheeses increases.

(b) REFORMED MEATS

The development of reformed meats is a good example of the increasingly close relationship of the food scientist and the engineer. Inexpensive but highly nutritional cuts of meat are restructured to a more acceptable form free from excessive fat, gristle or connective tissue. Meat, usually finely comminuted, is minced with soya or milk protein as binding agents and extruded or pressure-formed into desirable shapes before being set by heat. These are sold as steaks, cutlets and the like or in the form of chunks for inclusion in pies and stews. Bacon is fabricated from meat trimmings and soya protein with the advantages of having a low fat content, reduced shrinkage and cooking losses, and specially shaped to fit a sandwich or some other uniform shape.

Cleverly designed equipment has been developed to provide meat raw material for these and other applications. These include mechanical de-boning systems to remove meat adhering to carcass bones. Meat can be recovered from animal heads, chicken necks, stripped chicken carcasses and oxtails. An example of such equipment is shown in Plates 100—102. The material is compressed by a piston and the meat is squeezed from the bone through a filter plate. The plate is then blocked off and the waste ejected. Up to 85% of the weight of cooked whole chickens or manually pre-stripped chicken carcasses can be recovered as high-quality fibrous cooked meat. This gives an additional 20% yield over and above the normal hand-stripping yield.

(c) SNACKS

Traditional snack items such as roasted peanuts and potato crisps (chips) are being replaced by fabricated alternatives, usually produced on an extruder. Potato flakes or powder, starch, fat and gums can be mixed to form a dough which is then extruded or rolled into sheets, cut and fried to produce acceptable potato crisp analogues. Benefits over the traditional process include less expensive raw materials, less wastage and greater process control. An increasing proportion of the household food budget is spent on snack items in which convenience and quality are perceived by the consumer as being most important. Price or value for money is often not a factor. It is a curious fact and an indication of the growing importance of the convenience food habit that people will complain bitterly about increases in the price of staple foods such as milk and bread but willingly pay disproportionately large sums for snack items.

4. Extension of 'foods of convenience'

The real wealth of industrial nations has been increasing rapidly in step with the advances in science and technology. In these wealthy countries, it has for the last two generations at least been unnecessary for people to hire themselves out as servants. But at the same time as the working people have been able to enjoy a good standard of living for themselves, the need for human servants of those with more money has dwindled as machines have been developed to do their work. Not all these machines are necessarily installed in the houses where the work was done before. For example, the work of slicing bread is nowadays done by a bread-slicing machine installed as part of a mechanized bakery where sliced, wrapped bread is a product of modern food technology. Other examples of this trend are the use of frozen fish-fingers to avoid the need for a housewife or cook to work at preparing, filleting and cooking fish; frozen peas to make it unnecessary to shell and cook peas purchased at the market in their pods; and 'instant' coffee, prepared at a factory and spray-dried, to avoid the work of roasting and grinding coffee-beans and preparing from the ground beans the beverage. A more novel approach is the attempt by manufacturers to develop products specifically for use in equipment commonly found in kitchens. A good example of this is the frozen, partially cooked waffle designed to be popped into the electric toaster. A similar product is the toaster pastry in which a savoury or fruit filling is enrobed in a pastry case of a dimension to fit the kitchen pop-up toaster.

There is little doubt that this trend will continue to extend in the future. The food technologist of 20 years from now will need to understand what conditions are required for the preparation of cooked meat which, when wrapped or otherwise dispensed and frozen, dehydrated or preserved in some other way, will yet possess the same flavour when it is eaten as freshly cooked meat.

The beginning of what may be expected is already seen in the quick frozen snack and complete meals which are already common. These are marketed in metal-foil or oven-board trays and free the housewife from the need to do any work in the kitchen other than to put the meals to heat. In this she now has the assistance of the domestic microwave oven which will defrost and heat such meals in less than ten minutes. With such aids, other than holding a stock of products in her freezer no advance planning is necessary to thaw out the food. An extension of the convenience trend, where the housewife is not required to soil a plate or a cooking utensil, is the concept of cooking with a kettle. Instant soups, beverages and sauces are now familiar items and within the next five years snack meals based on rice or pasta will become commonplace. Specially developed plastics, laminated to foil or paper-board, are available to construct pots or cups to hold such products which will reconstitute, ready to be eaten in one or two minutes merely by the addition of boiling water.

5. Food and biotechnology

Increasing control and manipulation of biological process seems certain to result in novel food ingredients and more efficient processes for the production of materials currently the subject of lengthy and costly methods.

(a) ENZYMES AND FOOD PROCESSING

Enzymes are proteins which function as biochemical catalysts. They occur naturally in all living cells and are capable of speeding up chemical reactions several million-fold compared with non-catalyzed reactions. They are not consumed in the reactions and can be used over and over again. They are active in very small quantities, are non-toxic and highly specific in their activity, taking part in no undesirable side reactions or affecting other constituents. These advantages, together with the fact that they are easily controlled by pH and temperature and readily inactivated when the reaction is complete, make them useful tools in the armoury of the food scientist and technologist.

Their controlled use in food technology began in the last quarter of the 19th century when rennet for the clotting of cheese was isolated from calves' stomachs, but it is only in the last decade that better understanding of fundamental reaction mechanisms has led to an increasing number of practical applications. Today most commercial enzymes are isolated from microbial cells.

Amylases are used for the liquification of starch and for the production of maltose syrups.

Invertase is widely employed in the confectionery industry to produce glucose and fructose (invert sugar) from sucrose.

Lactase converts the milk sugar lactose into glucose and galactose and is used to avoid lactose crystallization in frozen or concentrated dairy products. This enzyme also offers potential nutritional

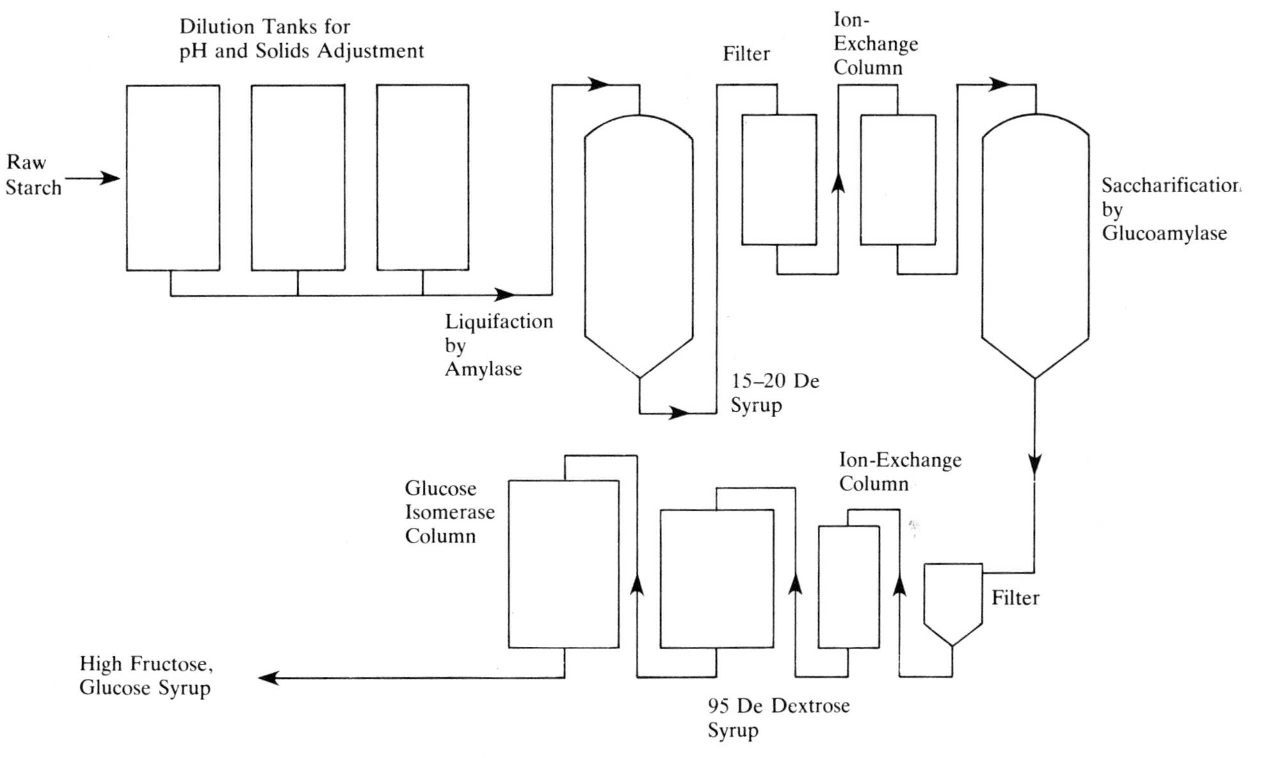

Fig. 27. Simplified flow-diagram of high fructose corn syrup manufacture.

benefits for infants and those adults who suffer from lactose intolerance due to a deficiency in lactose-hydrolyzing enzymes. The ingestion of lactose can result in severe and even fatally acute intestinal disorder in such individuals and the treatment of products with lactase would increase the acceptability of milk and other dairy products and raise the quality of the diet.

The more widespread use of these and other more sophisticated systems in the future is being furthered by the development of immobilized enzymes. In early applications enzyme was added to a batch of product and inactivated but not recovered at the end of the reaction. As one of the features of enzymes is their ability to be used over and over again this was clearly wasteful, especially when very costly pure enzyme preparations were employed. Now more and more enzyme systems are attached by chemical or physical means on to a carrier material such as glass beads or polyacrylamide gels. Product can be passed over or through such materials in tanks, fluidized beds or columns many times before the enzyme has to be replaced. In the next decade increasing numbers of useful enzymes will be successfully adapted thus and made available to the food processor.

High fructose corn syrup (HFCS) is a very good example of how practical use can be made of the sophisticated application of enzyme technology. HFCS is an important sweetener used in soft drinks, canned fruit, jams, preserves and confectionery. It is comparable in sweetness with invert syrup but less expensive.

The process begins with the starch from wet-milled corn which is treated with bacterial amylases to liquify and dextrinize it. The liquified starch is filtered to remove impurities and then passed through a column containing a second enzyme, amyloglucosidase, which converts most of the dextrins to glucose. After a further purification step the glucose syrup is converted to the sweeter fructose syrup by glucose isomerase enzyme in a second immobilized column. This produces syrups containing around 42% fructose which can be purified and concentrated. A number of commercially proven continuous plants are in operation throughout the world producing such high fructose syrup.

Further improvements in immobilization and stabilization will mean an increase in the technological utilization of enzymes in the next two decades. These will clearly include the production of inexpensive flavourings from waste protein material by hydrolytic enzymes and from fats by the fat-splitting enzyme lipase. A major advance will be in the use of enzymes to remove undigestible carbohydrate material such as cellulose and lignin from potentially rich sources of edible vegetable protein in the solid waste from agricultural production. The broken-down carbohydrate will itself be used as a fermentation medium for the production of crude alcohol or 'gasohol' which is likely to become a significant supplement to dwindling reserves of liquid fuel. Other applications of enzyme technology will be found in treating novel sources of food such as leaf protein or yeast (*see below under* New Foods for New Populations) to make them more acceptable as human foods.

These and other applications will increasingly depend for their commercial success on sources of readily available, inexpensive, pure and stable supplies of enzymes. This may be achieved by the food technologist by enlisting the aid of the genetic engineer. There are already indications that certain micro-organisms can, through mutation, be selected to yield large quantities of easily recoverable enzymes. It is likely that the tolerance of such enzymes to heat and acidity could be modified to meet specific food processing needs. Bio-engineering technology, of this nature, and other examples referred to in this chapter are now at a stage to repay the high research investment required through the promise of low energy usage in biological processes and the replacement of the sophisticated, highly capitalized, energy-intensive systems that have been so favoured over the past 20 years.

6. The influence of automation

One of the most striking developments in the industrial countries of the world today is the increasing use of automation. This trend may be said to have started in the first quarter of the century with the introduction of the mass-production methods employed in their most radical form by Henry Ford. This early stage involved the breaking down of the complex process of making a motor-car into a series of simple operations which were capable of mechanization. The modern development of this original idea has taken a further major step forward following the introduction of electronic computers and other types of control instruments which are capable of linking a series of mechanized operations together. The more advanced of these systems are able to correct their own mistakes. Whereas the earlier automatic machine tools mechanized physical work previously done by human operatives, the later instruments of today are tending more and more to mechanize control operations previously calling for human thought and judgement. The result of this trend has been the replacement of men by machines. Put in other terms, this means a great increase in the industrial productivity of each individual worker. The implications of automation are that production previously requiring a week's work by a man can be done in a day. This has meant a reduction in the length of the working week and at the same time an increase in real earnings. We can expect to see this trend accentuated in the next decades.

These developments in industrial methods can be expected to bear on the future of food technology in two ways. On the one hand, food factories will undoubtedly adopt automated processes. These are already being introduced to a quite large extent and although of themselves they may not directly affect the methods and principles that have been described in earlier chapters, their increasing use will mean that the food technologist of the future will need to understand the operation of electronic gear and other types of equipment used in the automated plants.

The main effect of automation on an industrial society seems fairly certain to be a continuous increase in leisure. We have already seen the general introduction of the five-day working week in most advanced countries. Three weeks' paid holiday is also common. If this trend extends as labour-saving automatic devices really do save labour, we can expect that a four-day working week, with adequate pay, will supersede the five-day week, and that holidays will also continue to extend. This increased leisure will accentuate the demands of consumers for 'convenience' manufactured foods.

But at the same time there may be a trend in the opposite direction. A social problem presented by the growth of automation is that arising from the use of the extra leisure that it will bring. Most modern packaged foods claim that they are easy to prepare and that they demand little time, skill or attention. But it may well happen that a woman with an increasing amount of free time at her disposal may find that she wishes voluntarily to do cooking as a hobby. There is not likely to be any desire to return to the drudgery of cleaning, trimming and preparing vegetables or filleting and boning fish. It is, however, reasonable to prophesy that some of the housewives of the future will wish to cook a wider selection of dishes, some of which they have encountered during the course of those more extended holidays abroad that will become increasingly common as the benefits of automation extend. Food technologists may, therefore, need to make available a much wider variety of foods, some fully processed and some only partly prepared, than they do at present.

B. NEW FOODS FOR NEW POPULATIONS

The developments so far discussed in this chapter have been based on the trends occurring in the industrial countries of the world whose standards of real wealth have been steadily rising and may continue to do so. In these countries the nutritional value of the diet is fully adequate for most sections of the population, and although food technology is applied to the basic foodstuffs of the diet and to their distribution, attention is increasingly concentrated on the processing of luxury foods and 'foods of convenience'. For the majority of the world's population, however, in Asia, many parts of Africa, Central and South America and the Caribbean, the situation is different. In these countries, the total amount of food available to the population is inadequate for their needs and the degree of inadequacy has steadily become worse as the twentieth century has continued. For these peoples, although their *liking* for high-quality canned and frozen food, for wrapped and prepared articles and refined sugars and oils may be as strong as those of the wealthy industrialized countries, their *need* is for the application of technology to increase the total amount of food available.

The urgency for every technological process to be applied to preserving and preparing increased amounts of food, in parallel with the similar use of science and technology in agriculture to increase the amounts of food produced is clearly indicated by the graph on p. 276, which shows the increase that has occurred in the world's population since 1900 and the more conservative of the current estimates of what the population will be in the year 2000.

It can also be seen from the graphs that now, when the world's population is about 4000 million people, 1000 million (27%) live in the fortunate wealthy industrial countries and 3000 million (73%) live in the so-called 'developing' countries; yet in 2000 if the present trend has continued unchecked and the population of the world has increased to 6000 million, 1200 million, or 20%, will, if things continue as they are, enjoy the wealth and variety of food of the rich industrial lands, whereas the remaining 80% of the earth's population, which will then comprise 4800 million people, will have insufficient to eat. This is the challenge to food technologists for the future.

1. Leaf protein

The most highly prized types of food are those that provide animal protein. Meat, eggs, milk and fish are foods of this sort that predominate in the diet of peoples whose standards of living are high. On the other hand, they tend to be lacking from the food supplies of countries in developing areas. It is also quite obvious that livestock inevitably consume a larger net amount of nutrients in their own fodder than they give back as edible food for man. Indeed, it can be calculated that only between 5 and 20% of the nutrients fed to livestock are eventually recovered for human consumption in the

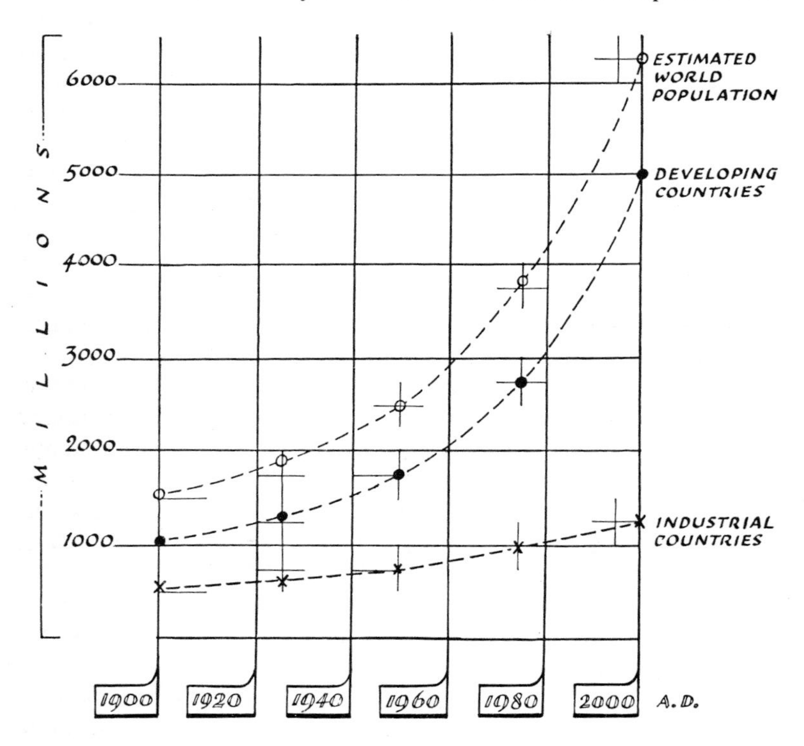

Fig. 28. Change in the population of the world from 1900 to 1960 with an estimate of the numbers to be expected by 1980 and 2000. The upper curve shows the total numbers; the middle curve, the present and forecast population of the developing countries; and the lower curve, the numbers in the industrialized nations.

form of meat or milk. This is so even when account is taken of the fact that certain animals can use the herbage of territories where it would be difficult to grow crops directly edible by human beings. Thus in countries where the economic level and the standard of living is low, it will always be found that the proportion of animal food in the diet will be reduced.

The most efficient organ in plants for synthesizing foodstuffs is the leaves. In terms of the maximum recovery of nutrients it is wasteful to allow the leaves of a wheat plant, say, to synthesize nutrients throughout the summer growing season and then to use only the small fraction eventually stored by the plant in the grain. Even when the grain has been recovered and the straw and husk discarded, we remove a further substantial proportion of the whole grain in the milling process described in Chapter 3. In recent years a great deal of work has been done which shows that it is perfectly feasible to process green leaves so as to extract the protein-containing juice from them, precipitate the protein by heating the juice and separate the protein from the 'whey' for use as human food. Although this material has not so far come into wide use, the technical process which is described below obviously holds considerable promise for the years of mounting population in the future. If the skill of food technologists succeeds, as it seems probable it will, in producing an acceptable food by this means, a way will have been found to circumvent the need to process nutrients through animals in order to concentrate good-quality protein.

So far, a prototype process has been developed capable of handling up to 2 tons of greenstuff an hour. Fresh leaves are passed through a pulper in which a series of beaters set at different angles are revolved in a vertical plane. The leaf juice runs out and the pulp is then re-extracted with the addition of water. The combined liquid is quickly heated to 70–80°C (158–176°F). The protein coagulates and is recovered in a filter press and then washed. At this stage it contains 5–10% of starch mixed with the protein; it can be compressed into blocks and used immediately as a food ingredient or stored under refrigeration. Alternatively, it can be dried and ground. Further research is needed to develop this process to give a more attractive foodstuff, to overcome prejudice against the green colour or to remove the colour altogether. Just as the present milling process is designed to separate as food the more readily edible flour from the less edible husk of grain, so also can this process be thought of as a way to extract the more highly nutritious protein from the inedible fibre of leaf.

2. Algae

A further development of the idea of short-circuiting the need to use animals in producing high-quality food for human consumption is to produce a plant which shall be almost all leaf and which can be eaten entire. By this means, the most efficient plant organ for producing food from carbon dioxide chemically 'reduced' by the energy of the sunlight caught by the green chlorophyll, becomes almost the sole product. There is no root or stalk or husk to be discarded. The plant selected is the minute *Chlorella* which is seen in nature as green scum on ponds or waterways.

Considerable study has been given to the development of technological methods for producing *Chlorella* in quantity in the United States, Great Britain, Israel, Japan and elsewhere. Although some progress has been made, a number of troubles have still to be overcome if this is to be a serious development of food technology for the future. The two most difficult problems are to devise a process capable of being used to produce food economically and, most serious of all, to overcome the unpalatability of the products so far obtained. The diagram on p. 280 shows a system of *Chlorella*-growing developed in Japan. The suspension of *Chlorella* is exposed to sunlight in a trough, which can be covered by a transparent lid, and then circulated through a system where carbon dioxide is introduced into the medium.

3. Yeast as food

(a) A SOURCE OF PROTEIN

Yeast is a unicellular organism which is mainly propagated for use as a leavening agent in bread-making. In order to grow and multiply it must, like every other living creature, be provided with food. The peculiar value of green leaves as a source of human food lies in the fact that they possess the ability to utilize the carbon-dioxide gas from the atmosphere as their main source of food. This ability is due to the property possessed by the chlorophyll in them of trapping the energy from sunlight. Yeast, on the other hand, must obtain some preformed source of nourishment in the form of sugar. It does, however, have the capacity to use inorganic chemical salts as a source of the nitrogen it requires to build up protein. This means that it is possible to convert surplus sugars—for example, the molasses produced by sugar-factories as a by-product of sugar-refining (described in Chapter 2)—into protein.

A number of projects have already been started to propagate yeast specially for food. The seed culture, which may be a strain of bakers' yeast, *Saccharomyces cerevisiae,* or a more strongly growing species, *Torula utilis*, is suspended in water in a large fermenting vessel. A source of phosphate, usually diammonium phosphate, is added and the suspension strongly aerated. Molasses is then added at a gradually increasing rate, in pace with the increase in the amount of growing yeast present, together with an appropriate amount of some inorganic source of nitrogen, usually a mixture of ammonia and ammonium sulphate. The temperature is maintained at about 30°C (86°F) and the pH at between 4·5 and 5·5. The rate of growth is usually regulated so that the original seed-yeast increases five-fold in about 12 hours. When the propagation is finished, the yeast is recovered by centrifuging. It can then be filtered and dried.

The growth of yeast in this way represents a very much more rapid production of protein than is possible by feeding any domestic animal and the conversion of inorganic nitrogen into edible protein is also an achievement which is beyond the powers of any higher animal. The source of carbohydrate may be sugar, in the form of molasses, as has been described, or it may be some otherwise unusable sugar, such as that derived by treating the cellulose from sawdust with a strong acid. Hence, the waste liquor from a paper-works can be used to feed yeast; the liquor from which leaf-protein has been precipitated as described above in the first section of this chapter also contains sugar which can be used for growing yeast.

Although the technological process for propagating yeast in bulk has been worked out in detail, so far it has not to any large degree been able to compete economically with fish meal, *tankage* and other sources of protein for animal feeding, nor has it been possible to make the dried yeast, sufficiently palatable to render it popular as a foodstuff. Clearly, however, it represents a possible source of food for the future. Perhaps in the past research into yeast as a source of food has been too preoccupied with the production of protein, as such, rather than the functional properties of the product. There is some indication that this balance may be redressed. Interference with the cell division cycle of mutant strains of yeast has produced chains of yeast cells which may effectively be used to modify the viscosity and texture of foods in the same way as a number of micromolecular ingredients. Alternatively, cell lysis and recovery of cell wall material (mostly carbohydrate) provides a thickener with the properties of some gums commonly used as food thickeners.

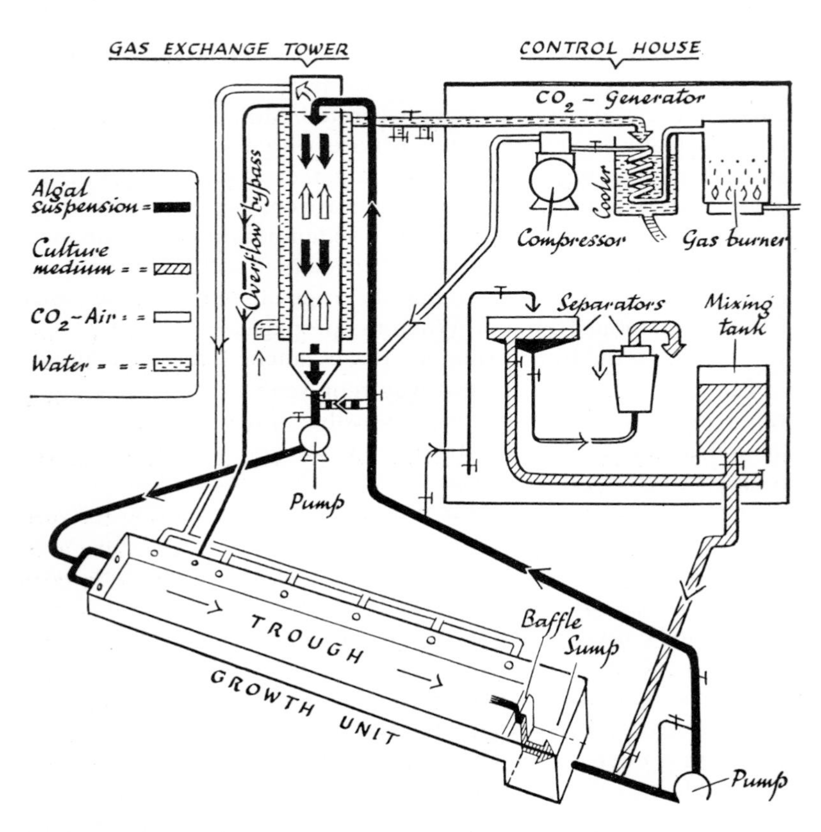

Fig. 29. Simplified flow-diagram of a process for producing algae. The plants grow in a liquid in the trough which has a transparent cover to allow light to pass through. Carbon-dioxide gas is brought in contact with the algal suspension in the gas-exchange tower and it is then recirculated through the trough. Facilities are available for feeding in mineral nutrients and for harvesting a proportion of the algae.

(*b*) A SOURCE OF FAT

The propagation of yeast represents essentially the conversion of carbohydrate into protein. But it is also possible by growing yeast to convert carbohydrate into fat. Yeasts produce fat in their cells when the medium in which they are grown is strongly aerated, the amount of nitrogen provided is restricted and an adequate supply of phosphate is provided. During World War I, German food technologists developed workable processes using chopped straw or sawdust as well as sugar. More recently a yeast-like fungus, *Oospora lactis*, has been found to be a more efficient organism than the yeasts originally employed. Although this is a possible method by which fat could be made by technological means if the increase in the world population caused a serious local shortage, present experience suggests that the technique as so far developed would need to be significantly improved and economic conditions would require to be particularly favourable.

4. The soyabean

The soyabean has a long history as a staple food crop in Asian countries where it is part of the important tradition of mainly fermented vegetable foods. It is the basis of many products, including miso (soyabean paste), soya sauce, tofu (protein curd from soya milk), sofu (soyabean cheese) and tempeh (mould-fermented soyabeans), which are of major nutritional importance in China, Japan and the East Indies.

Recognition of the value of the soyabean in the West at the turn of the century was as an oilseed crop rather than as a source of protein for human food. It is now the largest oilseed crop in both volume and commercial terms. The increasing demand for protein mainly as an animal food concentrate is certain to produce a reversal of roles with the soyabean becoming more important as a source of food protein, previously considered a by-product of oil production. Its potential is highlighted by the F.A.O. statistic that in 1976 twenty-three million tons of soya protein was produced, exceeding the total protein production from all livestock sources and eggs. Only 10% of this was utilized as human food. The world's major producer is currently the USA although South America is expected to become an increasingly major contributor.

Soya protein is available to the food manufacturer in a number of different forms ranging from the whole bean to textured protein (see below). Oil-free meal from the soyabean oil-crushing industry is refined to produce soya flours (40–55% protein), soya concentrates (70% protein) and almost pure protein soya isolates (more than 90% protein) which can be tailor-made to have specific functional properties.

In addition to its nutritional value soya protein has important functional properties which make it a versatile food ingredient. These include swelling and thickening to improve viscosity, gelling to provide texture, water-binding to aid in moisture retention, surfactancy to help form and stabilize fat emulsions, and foam stabilization to entrap air in dessert and cake mixes. It is widely used in infant formula foods, baked goods, pasta, whipped desserts, coffee whitener, salad dressings, soups and sauces where one or more of these properties are required. Soya protein is a valuable ingredient in the processing of meat products where it is employed in comminuted foods such as sausages and hamburgers to reduce shrinkage on cooking and prevent the separation of fat and water. It is a curious fact that the addition of soya protein to such products is looked upon with some suspicion when far less nutritious extenders or fillers such as fat or rusk are readily tolerated. Whole cuts of meat can also be treated with soya protein to improve yield and juiciness. By injection of a suitable solution of soya protein, salt and phosphates, up to 35% added water can be bound into ham, pork and beef joints.

(a) TEXTURED VEGETABLE PROTEIN

The further usefulness of the soyabean was further exemplified when it was found to be a good basis for the manufacture of textured vegetable protein. Although the protein of some cereals, other oilseeds and some of the more novel sources described in this Chapter can and certainly will be textured, the availability, composition and cost of the soyabean has led to it being the preferred raw material and that on which the technology of texturization has been developed.

Textured vegetable protein (TVP) is the generic name given to a range of different products from spun fibres to extruded meat analogues. Texturization involves the conversion of powdered protein into cubes, chunks or granules with the 'mouthfeel' characteristics of meats. Two categories of TVP are recognized, firstly, meat extenders designed to be used to supplement meat and, secondly, meat analogues which can take the place of meat in formulated products. The former have the texture of minced meat while the latter are more sophisticated and attempt to reproduce the mouth-feel and chewing characteristics of cooked muscle tissue.

Texturization has been achieved with commercial success by the three processes:

(i) Wet spinning
(ii) Extrusion cooking
(iii) Steam puffing

Wet spinning is based on the well-known technology used to produce textile fibres. This, however, is a complex and costly process and requires the more expensive soya isolates as a starting material. Its initial attraction lay in its unique ability to produce meat analogues which can command a higher price than extenders. Today this can be done by extrusion, which also has the advantage of being able to use the less expensive soya flours and concentrates as raw material. Indeed, methods have now been developed to allow the use of the whole soyabean as the starting material from which to produce meat analogues. An extrusion process for the manufacture of TVP is described in Chapter 9, p. 221. Although the most widely used commercial method, extrusion has a number of drawbacks. Among these is that of the excessive heat applied to the product during processing. This has a detrimental effect on flavour *per se* and, furthermore, severely limits the use of labile artificial flavours and colours, by the judicious use of which, the acceptability of TVP can be endorsed. Such problems do not apply to the same degree to the steam-puffing process, because shorter more controlled heating times are involved. In this process powdered ingredients are pre-mixed and fed into an elongated pipe or barrel into which superheated steam is simultaneously injected. The ingredients are heated under pressure as they pass along the barrel. As the product is expelled from the 'steam-gun', the superheated moisture flashes off leaving slightly expanded flakes or granules of TVP. The simplicity of the steam-texturizing process which requires neither the high capital investment in equipment or the degree of technology necessary in extrusion cooking or wet spinning could lead to its development to establish TVP industries in developing nations.

Texturization represents a way in which new proteins and more traditional vegetable proteins can be refined for human consumption, and a way in which value can be added by the food manufacturer to inexpensive raw materials. While acceptance of TVP has been slow its full potential will be realized when refining techniques are improved and when methods of satisfactorily flavouring and colouring TVP are devised.

5. Food from petroleum

Almost all the energy we are able to command on earth, whether it is the physical energy of animals or of the muscles of men or industrial power produced by machines, depends on a chemical process, the oxidation of reduced carbon, described in Chapter 1. Burning coal in the boilers of an electricity power station, using diesel oil in a bus or petrol in a car, or eating bread and butter—each of these operations is fundamentally an oxidation of reduced carbon. This reduced carbon from which energy is derived occurs in two different categories of materials. First, there are the substances that can be used as food; these are all made available initially by green plants which restore energy derived from sunlight to the 'spent' carbon present in the atmosphere as carbon dioxide gas. Animal foods are, of course, themselves derived from vegetable foods. The second category of reduced-carbon-containing materials are coal and oil, which are in the main supplies of reduced carbon produced by plants in geological ages long past. Although the energy in coal and oil can be released to run industrial power-plants, it cannot be utilized directly for food.

It has now been shown that it is possible, by the employment of chemical technology, to convert these materials into an edible form. Ten years or so ago large amounts of industrial alcohol were manufactured from molasses by yeast fermentation; nowadays, industrial alcohol is produced by the technical process known as 'cracking' from petroleum. It is feasible to use this alcohol as a food to grow yeast which, as described in Section 3, can itself be used as human food or as a fodder for livestock. An even more direct conversion has been achieved by chemists in Germany and elsewhere who have succeeded in making certain fats from petroleum. There are still a number of technical problems to be overcome before this type of process could be used to produce any substantial amounts of wholesome fats but it is at least a possibility that food technology in the future may enable the deposits of coal and petroleum to be employed as a source of food.

A method for using petroleum for food which has already been shown to be feasible and which may also be proved economic is to use it to supply the main energy source for the growth of yeast which is subsequently dried and used as a protein source for farm livestock.

6. Other protein foods

It is already becoming apparent, even with the world's population passing the 3,000 million mark, that the shortage of nourishing foods in the non-industrial parts of the world is a matter requiring urgent remedy. In a number of places, nutritional experts have carried out studies of the amino-acid composition of available supplies of vegetable protein in order to discover whether it is possible by combining several vegetable proteins, each of which alone would be deficient in one or more of the amino acids necessary for proper growth and health, to make a composite product which would possess a nutritional value equal to that of more expensive meat, milk or eggs. An example of a successful combination is that prepared by the Institute of Nutrition of Central America and Panama (INCAP). This is a mixture of 29% of maize, 29% of sorghum (millet), 38% of cottonseed flour, 3% of dried Torula yeast, 1% of chalk to supply calcium, and a supplement of 4500 International Units of vitamin A per 100 g. The whole is prepared as a powder suitable for making the type of 'soup' which is commonly eaten in Guatemala. The nutritional value of this preparation, which is marketed under the name of '*Incaparina*', is sufficiently high to allow its being fed to young children as a substitute for milk.

Similar preparations employing groundnut meal, chick-pea flour and coconut meal in place of sorghum have been produced in India.

Clearly, the food technologist can play a useful part in the future in preparing formulae such as these in a form acceptable to the populations for which they are intended and packed and marketed so that they can be distributed in satisfactory condition.

To sum up, the present period of history is one of very rapid change. Scientific knowledge is advancing faster than it has ever done before. It is certain, therefore, that major changes will occur in food technology and these changes will follow two main trends.

On the one hand, the production of 'convenience foods'—prewrapped, quick-frozen foods, foods of great technical sophistication including new 'additives' and improvers, coloured with new dyes, stabilized with new preservatives, made elegant with new emulsifiers, sterilized with radioactivity or some other novel physical or chemical treatment—will undoubtedly be developed. But on the other hand, the increase in population and the growing awareness of the less fortunate peoples that this is one world and that, politically, we are all interlinked one with the other will certainly lead increasingly to the application of food technology to the problem of preparing and preserving indigenous foods not so far fully utilized, and to making available as food some of the edible substances which have up till now been neglected.

7. Synthetic food

A further radical development in food technology could have far-reaching effects on the provision of food for the increasing population of the world: the advance of chemical and physical understanding to the point when food could be synthesized in substantial quantities from non-food sources. Vitamins are already being synthesized in bulk; synthetic B-vitamins are added to flour in the West and rice in the East, vitamins A and D are incorporated in margarine, vitamin C is widely used where fresh fruit and vegetables are scarce. Synthetic amino acids, notably lysine, are used to improve the nutritional value of incomplete protein derived from cereals and roots. But new discoveries open up even more remarkable possibilities. Instead of having to synthesize each complex component of protein separately, chemists can now achieve 'pan-synthesis' of groups of amino acids. The possibility is indeed opening that the natural foods derived from the biological processes of plants and animals with which the food technologist has so far been concerned may be supplemented by the new food products of synthetic chemistry in the not too distant future.

APPENDIX *1*

Recommended daily amounts of food energy and some nutrients for population groups in the UK (HMSO, 1980)

Age range(a) years	Occupational category	Energy(b) MJ	Energy(b) Kcal	Protein(d) g	Thiamin mg	Riboflavin mg	Nicotenic acid equivalents mg(f)	Total folate(g) μg	Ascorbic acid mg	Vitamin A retinol equivalents μg(h)	Vitamin D(i) cholecalciferol μg	Calcium mg	Iron mg
Boys													
under 1		(c)	(c)	(e)	0.3	0.4	5	50	20	450	7.5	600	6
1		5.0	1200	30	0.5	0.6	7	100	20	300	10	600	7
2		5.75	1400	35	0.6	0.7	8	100	20	300	10	600	7
3–4		6.5	1560	39	0.6	0.8	9	100	20	300	10	600	8
5–6		7.25	1740	43	0.7	0.9	10	200	20	300	(i)	600	10
7–8		8.25	1980	49	0.8	1.0	11	200	20	400	(i)	600	10
9–11		9.5	2280	57	0.9	1.2	14	200	25	575	(i)	700	12
12–14		11.0	2640	66	1.1	1.4	16	300	25	725	(i)	700	12
15–17		12.0	2880	72	1.2	1.7	19	300	30	750	(i)	600	12
Girls													
under 1		(c)	(c)	(e)	0.3	0.4	5	50	20	450	7.5	600	6
1		4.5	1100	27	0.4	0.6	7	100	20	300	10	600	7
2		5.5	1300	32	0.5	0.7	8	100	20	300	10	600	7
3–4		6.25	1500	37	0.6	0.8	9	100	20	300	10	600	8
5–6		7.0	1680	42	0.7	0.9	10	200	20	300	(i)	600	10
7–8		8.0	1900	47	0.8	1.0	11	200	20	400	(i)	600	10
9–11		8.5	2050	51	0.8	1.2	14	300	25	575	(i)	700	12(k)
12–14		9.0	2150	53	0.9	1.4	16	300	25	725	(i)	700	12(k)
15–17		9.0	2150	53	0.9	1.7	19	300	30	750	(i)	600	12(k)
Men													
18–34	Sedentary	10.5	2510	63	1.0	1.6	18	300	30	750	(i)	500	10
	Moderately active	12.0	2900	72	1.2	1.6	18	300	30	750	(i)	500	10
	Very active	14.0	3350	84	1.3	1.6	18	300	30	750	(i)	500	10
35–64	Sedentary	10.0	2400	60	1.0	1.6	18	300	30	750	(i)	500	10
	Moderately active	11.5	2750	69	1.1	1.6	18	300	30	750	(i)	500	10
	Very active	14.0	3350	84	1.3	1.6	18	300	30	750	(i)	500	10
65–74 }	Assuming a	10.0	2400	60	1.0	1.6	18	300	30	750	(i)	500	10
75+ }	sedentary life	9.0	2150	54	0.9	1.6	18	300	30	750	(i)	500	10
Women													
18–54	Most occupations	9.0	2150	54	0.9	1.3	15	300	30	750	(i)	500	12(k)
	Very active	10.5	2500	62	1.0	1.3	15	300	30	750		500	12(k)
55–74 }	Assuming a	8.0	1900	47	0.8	1.3	15	300	30	750	(i)	500	10
75+ }	sedentary life	7.0	1680	42	0.7	1.3	15	300	30	750	(i)	500	10
Pregnancy		10.0	2400	60	1.0	1.6	18	500	60	750	10	1200(j)	13
Lactation		11.5	2750	69	1.1	1.8	21	400	60	1200	10	1200	15

Notes to Appendix 1

(a) Since the recommendations are average amounts, the figures for each age range represent the amounts recommended at the middle of the range. Within each age range, younger children will need less, and older children more, than the amount recommended.

(b) Megajoules (10^6 joules). Calculated from the relation 1 kilocalorie = 4.184 kilojoules, that is to say, 1 megajoule = 240 kilocalories.

(c) See Appendix 2.

(d) Recommended amounts have been calculated as 10% of the recommendations for energy (paragraph 44).

(e) See Appendix 2.

(f) 1 nicotinic acid equivalent = 1 mg available nicotinic acid or 60 mg tryptophan.

(g) No information is available about requirements of children for folate. Graded amounts are recommended between the figure shown for infants under 1 year, which is based upon the average folate content of mature human milk, and the 300μg daily which is suggested for adults.

(h) 1 retinol equivalent = 1μg retinol of 6μgβ-carotene or 12μg other biologically active carotenoids.

(i) No dietary sources may be necessary for children and adults who are sufficiently exposed to sunlight, but during the winter children and adolescents should receive 10μg (400 i.u.) daily by supplementation. Adults with inadequate exposure to sunlight, for example those who are housebound, may also need a supplement of 10μg daily.

(j) For the third trimester only.

(k) This intake may not be sufficient for 10% of girls and women with large menstrual losses.

APPENDIX 2

The Nutritive Composition of Representative Samples of Various Foods
(composition per oz. of edible portion)

	Waste	*Calories*	*Protein*	*Fat*	*Carbo-hydrate*	*Calcium*	*Iron*	*Vitamin A*	*Vitamin B_1*	*Ribo-flavin*	*Nia-cin*	*Vitamin C*	*Vitamin D*
	%		g.	g.	g.	mg.	mg.	I.U.	mg.	mg.	mg.	mg.	I.U.
1. *Cereal foods*													
Barley, pearl, uncooked	0	97	2·2	0·5	20·8	3	0·2	0	0·03	0·01	0·7	0	0
Biscuits, water	0	107	3·4	0·9	21·3	23	0·6	0	0·04	0·03	0·3	0	0
Biscuits, 'digestive'	0	130	2·7	5·8	16·8	12	0·4	0	0·04	0·03	0·3	0	0
Bread, white (70% extraction)	0	73	2·3	0·2	15·6	30*	0·2	0	0·01	0·01	0·2	0	0
Bread, wholemeal (92% extraction)	0	65	3·1	0·6	11·2	7	0·7	0	0·09	0·05	0·6	0	0
Cornflakes	0	106	2·1	0·1	24·3	3	0·8	0	0	0·02	0·3	0	0
Cornflower, custard powder	0	99	0·2	0·1	24·4	11	0·1	0	0·01	0·02	0·3	0	0
Flour, white (70% extraction)	0	98	2·3	0·3	21·6	40**	0·4	0	0·02	0·01	0·3	0	0
Flour, wholemeal (92% extraction)	0	95	4·3	0·9	17·4	10	1·0	0	0·17	0·06	0·8	0	0
Macaroni, spaghett, un-cooked	0	96	3·0	0·6	19·7	7	0·4	0	0·02	0·02	0·3	0	0
Oatmeal, uncooked	0	111	3·4	2·5	18·6	16	1·2	0	0·17	0·04	0·3	0	0

* Of this 26 mg. is in the U.K. added as calcium carbonate.

** Of this 35 mg. is in the U.K. added as calcium carbonate.

	Waste	*Calories*	*Protein*	*Fat*	*Carbo-hydrate*	*Calcium*	*Iron*	*Vitamin A*	*Vitamin B_1*	*Ribo-flavin*	*Nia-cin*	*Vitamin C*	*Vitamin D*
1. *Cereal Foods, contd*	%		g.	g.	g.	mg.	mg.	I.U.	mg.	mg.	mg.	mg.	I.U.
Rice, white, uncooked	0	99	1·8	0·3	22·2	1	0·1	0	0·02	0·02	0·3	0	0
Sago, uncooked	0	97	0·1	0·1	24·0	3	0·3	0	0	0	0	0	0
Semolina, uncooked	0	96	3·0	0·5	19·8	5	0·3	0	0·03	0·01	0·3	0	0
Tapioca, uncooked	0	98	0·1	0	24·3	2	0·1	0	0	0	0	0	0
2. *Dairy products*													
Butter	0	211	0·1	23·4	0	4	0	1200†	0	0	0	0	17†
Cheese, Cheddar type	5	117	7·1	9·8	0	230	0·2	400	0·01	0·14	0·1	0	10
Eggs	12	45	3·5	3·3	0·3	17	0·8	300	0·04	0·11	0·1	0	17
Milk, fresh	0	17	0·9	1·0	1·2	34	0	30	0·01	0·04	0	0·3	0·3
Milk, evaporated unsweetened	0	46	2·4	2·6	3·3	83	0·1	100	0·02	0·10	0·1	0	1
Milk, condensed, sweetened	0	89	2·3	2·6	14·1	82	0·1	100	0·03	0·10	0·1	1	1
Milk, dried, full cream	0	138	7·3	7·6	10·1	250	0·2	300	0·08	0·33	0·2	0	3
Milk, dried, skimmed	0	97	10·2	0·2	13·6	350	0·3	10	0·11	0·45	0·3	0	0

The Nutritive Composition of Representative Samples of Various Foods—continued

3. *Fats*													
Cooking fat	0	253	0	28·1	0	0	0	0	0	0	0	0	0
Dripping	0	253	0	28·1	0	0	0	30	0	0	0	0	8
Margarine	0	218	0	24·1	0	1	0·1	600††	0	0	0	0	60††
4. *Fish*													
Cod, white fish, uncooked	45	21	4·5	0·3	0	7	0·3	0	0·02	0·04	0·6	0	0
Cod, fried in batter	35	57	5·3	3·4	1·4	24	0·3	0	0·01	0·03	0·4	0	0
Haddock, smoked	45	22	5·1	0·2	0	8	0·3	0	0·02	0·04	0·6	0	0
Herring	30	47	4·5	3·3	0	28	0·4	40	0	0·08	1·0	0	250
Kipper	40	62	5·4	4·5	0	34	0·6	50	0	0·09	1·2	0	250
Salmon, canned	0	48	5·7	2·8	0	85	0·4	70	0·01	0·06	1·8	0	170
Sardine, canned in oil	0	84	5·7	6·8	0	114	1·1	80	0·01	0·08	1·3	0	280
Shellfish, crab, lobster	60	34	5·7	1·1	0·3	13	0·3	0	0·03	0·07	2·5	0	0
5. *Meat*													
Bacon	12	128	3·1	12·8	0	3	0·3	0	0·17	0·06	0·3	0	0
Beef, corned	0	69	7·1	4·5	0	3	3·1	0	0	0·04	0·5	0	0
Beef, average quality	17	89	4·2	8·0	0	3	1·1	14	0·02	0·07	1·3	0	0
Beef, stewing	25	60	4·8	4·5	0	3	1·1	14	0·02	0·07	1·3	0	0
Chicken	30	38	5·1	2·0	0	3	1·0	0	0·04	0·03	2·3	0	0

† The vitamin content varies with the season and the way the cow is fed.

†† Margarines may be fortified to different degrees; for the bakery trade margarine is not fortified at all.

	Waste	Calories	Protein	Fat	Carbo-hydrate	Calcium	Iron	Vitamin A	Vitamin B_1	Ribo-flavin	Nia-cin	Vitamin C	Vitamin D
5. *Meat—continued*	%		g.	g.	g.	mg.	mg.	I.U.	mg.	mg.	mg.	mg.	I.U.
Kidney	0	36	4·5	2·0	0	3	3·8	300	0·07	0·37	3·8	0	0
Liver, ox	0	40	4·8	1·7	1·4	3	3·9	4000	0·11	0·85	3·8	0	0
Mutton, lamb, average quality	17	94	3·7	8·8	0	3	0·6	14	0·04	0·05	1·2	0	0
Pork	15	116	3·4	11·4	0	3	0·3	0	0·20	0·06	1·7	0	0
Rabbit	17	38	5·7	1·6	0	3	0·6	0	0·01	0·14	1·8	0	0
Sausages, beef	0	61	3·3	3·7	3·7	9	0·6	0	0·04	0·02	0·5	0	0
Sausages, pork	0	73	3·0	5·1	3·7	9	0·3	0	0·04	0·02	0·5	0	0
Sweetbreads	40	68	6·2	4·5	0	18	0·4	10	0·09	0·03	1·0	0	0
Tongue, canned	0	73	5·4	5·7	0	3	0·9	0	0·08	0·03	3·6	0	0
Tripe	45	17	3·3	0·3	0	20	0·2	10	0·05	0·03	1·0	0	0
Veal	27	36	5·1	1·7	0	3	0·6	15	0·02	0·04	2·0	0	0
6. *Vegetables*													
Beans, broad	75	20	2·0	0·1	2·7	8	0·3	0	0·05	0·04	0·3	8	0
Beans, French	5	4	0·3	0	0·7	9	0·2	60	0·02	0·03	0·1	3	0
Beans, baked, canned	0	25	1·7	0	4·5	16	0·7	0	0·02	0·01	0·2	0	0
Beans, haricot, uncooked	0	71	6·1	0	11·6	51	1·9	0	0·13	0·08	0·6	0	0
Beetroot, boiled	0	12	0·5	0	2·5	8	0·2	0	0·01	0·02	0·1	2	0
Brussels sprouts	25	10	1·2	0	1·1	8	0·3	40	0·03	0·02	0·1	28	0
Cabbage	30	7	0·4	0	1·4	18	0·3	90	0·02	0·02	0·1	20	0
Carrot	5–20	6	0·2	0	1·4	14	0·2	1700	0·02	0·01	0·2	3	0
Cauliflower	30	6	0·7	0	0·8	14	0·2	0	0·03	0·02	0·2	20	0

The Nutritive Composition of Representative Samples of Various Foods—continued

Leeks	50	7	0·7	0	1·1	14	0·4	70	0·03	0·02	0·2	6	0
Lentils	0	82	6·8	0	13·6	11	2·2	0	0·13	0·02	0·9	0	0
Lettuce	20	3	0·3	0	0·5	7	0·2	400	0·02	0·02	0·1	4	0
Onion	5	6	0·3	0	1·3	9	0·1	0	0·01	0·01	0·1	3	0
Peas, green	60	17	1·6	0	2·7	14	0·5	50	0·12	0·03	0·2	8	0
Peas, dried	0	85	7·0	0	14·2	7	1·3	20	0·13	0·08	0·6	0	0
Potatoes	7–25	21	0·6	0	4·6	2	0·2	0	0·03	0·02	0·3	2–8 §	0
Spinach	25	6	0·8	0	0·7	20	0·9	1200	0·03	0·06	0·1	18	0
Tomato	15	4	0·3	0	0·7	4	0·1	300	0·02	0·01	0·1	7	0
Turnip	35	5	0·2	0	1·0	17	0·1	0	0·01	0·01	0·3	7	0
Watercress	15	4	0·8	0	0·2	63	0·4	500	0·03	0·02	0·5	17	0
7. *Fruit*													
Apple	20	12	0·1	0	3·0	1	0·1	0	0·01	0·01	0·1	1	0
Apricot, dried	0	50	1·4	0	11·1	26	1·2	500	0	0·12	0·6	0	0
Banana	40	21	0·3	0	4·9	2	0·1	10	0·01	0·01	0·2	3	0
Blackberry	0	8	0·4	0	1·6	18	0·3	30	0·01	0·01	0·1	6	0
Blackcurrant	0	8	0·3	0	1·7	17	0·4	10	0·01	0·01	0·1	60	0
Dates	14	68	0·6	0	16·3	19	0·4	10	0	0·01	0·1	0	0
Figs, dried	0	58	1·0	0	13·5	81	1·2	10	0	0·08	0·5	0	0
Goosberries	0	10	0·2	0	2·4	5	0·2	20	0·01	0·01	0·1	11	0
Grapes	10	17	0·2	0	4·1	5	0·1	5	0·01	0·01	0·1	1	0
Grapefruit	50	6	0·2	0	1·4	5	0·1	0	0·02	0·01	0·1	14	0
Lemon	30	5	0·2	0	0·8	20	0·1	0	0·01	0·01	0·1	12	0
Orange	25	10	0·2	0	2·2	12	0·1	30	0·02	0·01	0·1	16	0
Pineapple, canned	0	20	0·1	0	4·9	3	0·2	5	0·01	0·01	0·1	3	0
Plums	6	7	0·2	0	1·6	4	0·1	40	0·02	0·01	0·2	1	0
Prunes, dried	17	44	0·7	0	10·3	11	0·8	250	0	0·04	0·6	0	0
Raisins, dried	8	67	0·3	0	16·5	17	0·5	5	0	0·01	0·1	0	0
Raspberries	0	7	0·3	0	1·4	12	0·3	10	0·01	0·01	0·2	9	0
Rhubarb	25	2	0·2	0	0·3	29	0·1	0	0	0	0	3	0
Strawberries	3	7	0·2	0	1·6	6	0·2	0	0	0·01	0·1	17	0

§ The vitamin C content falls steadily during the months of storage.

	Waste	Calories	Protein	Fat	Carbo-hydrate	Calcium	Iron	Vitamin A	Vitamin B_1	Ribo-flavin	Nia-cin	Vitamin C	Vitamin D
8. *Nuts*	%		g.	g.	g.	mg.	mg.	I.U.	mg.	mg.	mg.	mg.	I.U.
Almonds	65	164	5·8	15·2	1·1	70	1·2	0	0·07	0·05	0·4	0	0
Brazil nuts	55	177	3·9	17·5	1·0	50	0·8	0	0·30	0·05	0·4	0	0
Chestnuts	20	47	0·6	0·8	9·3	13	0·3	0	0·06	0·05	0·4	0	0
Peanuts	30	166	8·0	13·9	2·2	17	0·7	0	0·25	0·08	0·6	0	0
Walnuts	40	151	3·5	14·6	1·3	17	0·7	0	0·08	0·05	0·4	0	0
9. *Sugar, sweets and preserves*													
Chocolate, plain	0	148	1·3	9·2	15·0	7	0·9	0	0·03	0·07	0·3	0	0
Honey	0	78	0·1	0	19·5	1	0·1	0	0	0·02	0·1	0	0
Jam	0	71	0·1	0	17·6	3	0·3	0	0	0	0	3	0
Sugar	0	108	0	0	27·0	0	0	0	0	0	0	0	0
Syrup, golden	0	81	0·1	0	20·2	7	0·4	0	0	0	0	0	0
Treacle, black	0	70	0·3	0	17·2	70	2·6	0	0	0·02	1·1	0	0
10. *Beverages*													
Beer, bitter	0	16	0·1	0	(2·6)	1	0	0	0	0·02	0·4	0	0
Beer, mild	0	10	0·1	0	(1·5)	3	0	0	0	0·01	0·4	0	0
Cocoa, beverage as drunk	0	6	0·2	0·2	0·9	3	0	3	0	0	0	0	0
Cocoa, powder	0	125	5·8	7·3	8·9	14	41	15	0·03	0·08	0·3	0	0
Tea, beverage as drunk	0	5	0·1	0·1	0·8	3	0	4	0	0	0	0	0
Whisky	0	70	0	0	(9·9)	0	0	0	0	0	0	0	0

Index